FLASHING SABERS

FLASHING SABERS

Bert Chole

To order additional copies of this book, contact:
Xlibris Corporation
1-888-795-4274
www.Xlibris.com
Orders@Xlibris.com
24558

CONTENTS

ACKNOWLEDGEMENTS

I need to say thank you to the many people who supported me during the preparation of this manuscript. First my lovely wife Eileen who encouraged me and prodded me to get it finished. She suffered through several years as I played around with this and finally got serious about it. Thank you sweetie. Jim Stimpson who took the time to read and offer some great suggestions on how to present the material. This is a much better story because of his efforts and advice.

Thank you to the guys from Bravo Troop 1st Squadron 9th (Air) Cavalry who shared their photographs and their support—Joe Rawl, Jim Pratt, Larry Brown, and Terry Young.

To all of the Heroes who made this Troop the most outstanding group of men I have had the honor and privilege of knowing—the maintenance and supply guys who made it possible for this Troop to accomplish all we did, the Operations personnel who managed our records and arranged for all of our support, the cooks who kept us fed, the Blues who always came to our rescue, our First Sergeant who somehow kept it all organized and managed our security, and last but not least, all those Cavalrymen—Pilots, Door Gunners and Crew Chiefs who flew those missions, thank you for enriching my life and teaching me what brotherhood is all about.

Together we accomplished our mission in the truest, most spectacular Cavalry style.

CHAPTER ONE
PRELUDE TO WAR

Struggling to reach a level of consciousness that would comprehend what I was hearing, I slowly pushed the fog of sleep, fatigue, and alcohol from my mind as I heard the announcement again. "Please bring your seat to an upright position and fasten your seat belt. We are about to land at Tan San Nhut airfield," the stewardess announced. As I slowly came fully awake, the captain had his own announcement to make. "To limit the time we can be shot at, this will be the steepest approach you will ever have on a commercial airliner. Hang on!" With that, the nose of the aircraft was pushed downward, and the chartered 727 Tiger Airlines flight began its descent to Tan San Nhut Air Force Base in the Republic of Vietnam. The captain lived up to his word, and I breathed a sigh of relief as we taxied down the runway.

A portable ramp was pushed to the aircraft after we rolled to a stop. A sergeant at the foot of the stairs directed us to an open shed where we would receive our baggage. Although it was 0300 hours, it was still ninety degrees, and I was sweating. I was dressed in a Class B uniform of khakis with no tie and was still hurting from the going-away party I had given myself in San Francisco. I smiled to myself, remembering some of the details; but at the moment, all I wanted to do was get my duffel bag, my B4 bag, take a shower, shave, and get some sleep.

While we waited for the bags to be unloaded, I looked around and noticed we were near a perimeter of some sort. I didn't know if it was the perimeter of the arrival area or of the air base. In any case, there was little visible security, and that made me a bit apprehensive. I looked at the rest of the men standing around, waiting for their bags, and it was apparent that I was the oldest guy there. I was a captain who would turn thirty-one in two days. I had ten years' enlisted service in the infantry, had gone to Officer Candidate School (OCS), received my commission in armor branch, attended Jump School at Fort Benning, and had been assigned to the 101st Airborne Division at Fort Campbell, Kentucky, following graduation from OCS.

By the time I arrived in Vietnam, I had already served thirteen years in the army, was twice married with six children, had never experienced combat, and was a brand-new pilot with a grand total of two hundred hours of flight-school experience. My second marriage had been in trouble for several years and would remain in trouble until it was ended by divorce in 1982. Standing there, waiting for the bags to be unloaded, I reached into my breast pocket and pulled out a pack of cigarettes. Fishing a Lucky Strike from the pack, I absently noticed that the pack was already getting damp. I lit the cigarette and took a deep drag. The humidity was stifling and sweat trickled down my neck as I found a post to lean against while the baggage was being unloaded. As I waited, my mind replayed the last year I had spent in flight school, and I again reviewed the life-altering events that had brought me to Vietnam as a helicopter pilot.

The first of these events occurred while I was the adjutant of the Second Squadron, Seventeenth (Airborne) Cavalry, 101st Airborne Division at Fort Campbell, Kentucky. The adjutant of a cavalry squadron serves as the squadron commander's chief administrative officer. Normally, this was a captain's position; however, Lieutenant Colonel John T. Hodes, the squadron commander, had appointed me his adjutant while I was still a second lieutenant, his rationale being that I had plenty of experience as a noncommissioned officer (NCO), that I knew my way around the army, and what I needed was some administrative experience. While I was not happy with the prospect of being behind a desk and objected as forcefully as a second lieutenant can object to a lieutenant colonel, in retrospect, it was exactly the type of experience

I needed. I have often commented on what a wonderful opportunity that assignment gave me. To be able to observe, listen, and participate in the day-to-day decisions made by a cavalry squadron commander, as a second lieutenant, did more to prepare me for future command than any subsequent assignment.

The arrival of our sister squadron—the Third Squadron, Seventeenth (Air) Cavalry from Fort Benning, Georgia—was about to change my life. The Third Squadron, Seventeenth (Air) Cavalry was the first air cavalry squadron in the army and was part of the experimental Eleventh Air Assault Division stationed at Fort Benning. The squadron had already earned a reputation as a unit filled with mavericks, and their commander, Lieutenant Colonel Stockton, appeared to cultivate that reputation. He was about five feet ten inches tall, had a handlebar moustache, and was as colorful a cavalry officer as ever graced the ranks of the United States Army. He was also the officer who reintroduced the cavalry Stetson to the "modern army." Ironically, it was this cavalry Stetson and his stubborn insistence that his soldiers wear it that soon earned this obscure lieutenant colonel a notoriety that was rare for any officer. He was well known throughout the U.S. Army due to the stories, published and unpublished, about the wearing of the Stetson by these air cavalry soldiers and the controversy this "unauthorized headgear" was creating in the upper echelons of the army.

The division commander and assistant division commander were not happy with the notoriety this unit was earning as a result of wearing these Stetsons. Colonel Stockton received a telephone call one Sunday afternoon at his quarters at Fort Benning from the vice chief of staff of the United States Army. The vice chief of staff is a four-star general not prone to calling battalion commanders in the field. He lectured him not to wear the Stetson outside of the squadron area, and when worn, it could only be worn for special functions. That call got his attention for about two minutes.

When it was learned that the 3-17 was going to train at Fort Campbell, the chief of staff of the 101st Airborne Division called our squadron commander and told him that we were to host this squadron when they arrived. He also had a message from the division commander, MG Beverly E. Powell, that he wanted passed on to Lieutenant Colonel Stockton: "Do not, under any circumstances, fly over the division headquarters!"

Several weeks later, I heard the unmistakable rumble and felt the unimaginable vibration of a large number of helicopters flying very low. I was in my office, and as I got to my feet to go to a window, the phone rang. A livid chief of staff was on the phone, wanting to speak to Colonel Hodes. The approaching choppers had just flown over division headquarters and were now flying down the street that contained all the subordinate headquarters for the 101st Airborne Division. After I transferred the call to Colonel Hodes, I put on my hat and went outside to see this spectacle.

Looking up, I saw the first helicopter overhead. In trail behind him were about fifty-five other helicopters in a staggered column formation at approximately one hundred feet in altitude. The noise of the rotor blades beating the air, traveling at about one hundred knots just above my head, was something I shall never forget. It overpowered the senses and left me staring in awe.

I didn't meet Colonel Stockton until the following morning at our squadron headquarters. He wasn't the person I had imagined in my mind's eye. After hearing so many tales of the man and this unit, I had pictured a very large man in stature, similar to John Wayne. While his physical size was not as tall as I had imagined, he very definitely had command presence and projected self-assurance, which made him appear at least six feet five inches tall. Traveling with him was a small dog named Susie. This dog went everywhere with him. Colonel Stockton needed a ride to the drop zone where his helicopters were parked, and Colonel Hodes instructed me to take him to his aircraft. Colonel Stockton got in the front seat next to the driver; the dog and I got in the back. We drove to the drop zone (DZ) where the helicopters were parked. When we arrived at the DZ, Colonel Stockton's pilot was already strapped into the left seat, and the crew chief was standing by the right front door of the helicopter. Colonel Stockton shook my hand, said thanks; we exchanged salutes, and he moved to his helicopter. As the colonel approached, the crew chief came to attention, saluted him, and stood by to help him get strapped in. Colonel Stockton picked up the dog and placed him in the back of the helicopter, handed the crew chief his cavalry (cav) hat, boarded the helicopter, and strapped himself in. The crew chief grabbed a fire extinguisher and stood near the engine compartment, waiting for the aircraft to start. I saw the rotating beacon on top of the helicopter come on and, at the same time, heard fifty helicopters start. I thought to myself, "*They may be a bunch of mavericks, but they're disciplined mavericks.*"

It was an awesome display of raw power as those helicopters took off, one after another, beating the air into submission.

The second event occurred approximately six months later when I received a letter from Mike Cherup who had just left the squadron to go to Vietnam. Mike and I had gone to OCS together and had been assigned to this same squadron upon our graduation from OCS. We were both staff sergeants when we went to OCS, he an armor NCO and I an infantry NCO. He was one of the guys who convinced me to apply for a branch transfer to armor with the rationale "why walk when you can ride?" I had been a "grunt" long enough, and memories of humping the *yammas* (hills) in Korea were very fresh in my mind when I applied for a branch transfer to armor branch.

Mike's letter began,

Dear Bert,

"I am standing in water up to my armpits in the middle of a rice paddy as I write this letter. I am an advisor to a Vietnamese rifle battalion and I want to tell you, this is not a job for an armor officer."

Coincidentally, with the arrival of his letter was another Department of the Army Personnel memo, encouraging people to apply for flight training. I thought, "*Why ride when you can fly?*"

and submitted my application for flight school. My application was approved, and in August of 1966, I moved the family to Ozark, Alabama, on the outskirts of Fort Rucker. When they were settled, I reported to Fort Wolters, Texas, on 6 September 1966 and began the primary phase of instruction in what was to lead to my certification as a rotary-wing pilot.

CHAPTER TWO
FORT WOLTERS, TEXAS

Fort Wolters was running two separate aviation programs. One was for enlisted personnel who were undergoing training to become warrant-officer pilots, called warrant-officer candidates (WOCs). These classes consisted mostly of young men seventeen to twenty years of age.

The other program in operation was the aviation program for commissioned officers and direct-commission warrant officers. The latter were mostly men who had a lot of civilian-flying experience, so the army brought them in as warrant officers. Most of the officers were lieutenants, but it was not unusual to encounter captains or an occasional major. The officer classes were filled with a group of men mostly between the ages of twenty-one to twenty-five, but there were a few older guys such as myself, at thirty, and Warrant Officer Bud Green who was thirty-two years old.

The date of our graduation determined our class number; and we were scheduled to graduate in late May or early June of 1967, so our class number was 67-6. To distinguish the various classes, each class was assigned a different color baseball cap. Our class was the Green Hat class.

On our first day of instruction, we attended classes in the morning on how to preflight an OH-23 helicopter. In the afternoon, we met our instructor pilots for the first time. Although I can't remember his name, I shall never forget his grizzled and weathered face. He was a contract pilot working for Ross Aviation, a retired warrant officer with the patience of Job. That's not to say that he didn't give firm, and often very vocal, criticism of his student's obvious lack of coordination. He often wondered out loud where the army was dredging up such a collection of uncoordinated, uncooperative, unthinking imbeciles. His was a dangerous job, a job in which many of the instructor pilots lost their lives. To turn out good helicopter pilots required an ability to know when to sit on your hands and when to snatch the controls away from a student who was about to kill himself and you.

After a short conversation at the table in the briefing room, giving him an opportunity to size us up, we went to the flight line where there appeared to be hundreds of helicopters lined up on the apron. We moved to an OH-23 where he showed us how to preflight the aircraft.

There were two students per instructor pilot (IP), and we rotated flying with him. This meant that we would get approximately one and half to two hours of personalized flight instruction per day. Our first day was designed to familiarize us with the aircraft and get our hands on the controls. He explained how to start the aircraft, how to contact the tower, and what to say to the tower. The student sat in the left seat of this two-passenger helicopter with the IP in the right seat. I was selected to ride with him first. After starting the helicopter and making his radio calls to the tower, he brought us to a hover, taxied to the takeoff point, flew to a large field nearby, and came to a hover. We were just a few inches off the ground, and he turned to me and said, "See that big tree at the end of the field?" I replied that I did. "All I want you to do is keep the aircraft pointed at that tree. Now, place your feet on the pedals. Pushing the left pedal brings the aircraft nose to the left, and pushing the right pedal brings the nose to the right. I'm going to keep my feet on the pedals for a moment longer, and you go ahead and point the nose left and right." After I had accomplished what he wanted, he said, "I am taking my feet off the pedals. You have the pedals."

He had instructed us in the classroom earlier that transferring controls between pilots was very important. To make sure someone did not let go of the controls believing the other guy had them, when they didn't, we would always follow this procedure: The pilot who was flying would tell the other pilot, "Take the controls." The pilot who was taking the controls would get on the controls and announce, "I have the aircraft." The pilot relinquishing the controls would then say, "You have the aircraft" and then take his hands and feet off the controls. Remembering that discussion, I said, "I have the pedals."

My IP answered, "You have the pedals," taking his feet off the pedals. And there we sat, pointed at the tree. I thought to myself, *"Shit, this is a piece of cake. No problem!"*

My IP said, "Okay, turn ninety degrees to the left." I noticed that the movement wasn't as smooth as I thought it would be. After I completed the movement, he told me to move back to the tree. As I started to move back toward the tree, he said, "Stop your movement when you are lined up with the tree." I tried to do that but went just a little bit past where he wanted me to stop the movement. "Lieutenant, you're doing fine; just relax and do a ninety-degree turn to the right." I did that, and he said, "Okay, let's do a couple more of those turns."

I practiced that for a few more minutes and said to myself, *"Bert, you've got this nailed!"*

"Okay," he said, "it looks like you have a feel for the pedals; let's work on the cyclic next. The cyclic is that stick coming out of the floor that I have my right hand on. Moving it forward makes the aircraft move forward, and moving the cyclic to the rear makes the aircraft move to the rear." He then demonstrated what he meant and went on to say, "Moving the cyclic to the right makes the aircraft move to the right, and moving the cyclic to the left makes it move left." After demonstrating this explanation too, I heard, "Lieutenant, you take the cyclic."

Full of confidence, I grabbed the cyclic with my right hand and said, "I have the cyclic." "You have the cyclic," he replied, and he took his hand off the cyclic. We remained stationary for all of about one second, and then the nose dipped ever so slightly, and the aircraft started to move forward. He said, "Don't let it drift on you; bring the cyclic back toward you." Well, when I moved the cyclic back toward me about two inches, the nose came up, the tail dipped, and we started hauling ass backward! I panicked and shoved the cyclic forward, and the nose dipped, and we started really moving forward. I started to sweat. Pretty soon, we were in a rapid back-and-forth motion that was getting more rapid with each movement. He put his hand on the cyclic and said, "Your corrections are too large. Small movements. Just *think* about making the correction. Don't overcorrect." With his hand on the cyclic, he prevented me from overcorrecting, and the rapid back-and-forth movement stopped. He next said, "Okay, move it to your left." Rather than moving the cyclic ninety degrees to the left, I kind of pushed it to the left front, and we moved off at an oblique angle. I immediately knew that that was wrong and overcorrected to the right rear. In the middle of all these gyrations, he said, "You're not oriented on the tree."

I thought, "*You've got to be kidding!*" After what seemed about ten minutes of this, I finally settled down and was generally orientated toward the tree.

"Okay, it looks like you have a handle on the cyclic; let's talk about the collective. The collective is next to your left leg and is the control I have my left hand on. At the end of the collective is the throttle. You have to maintain 3,200 rpm to operate safely." He pointed to the tachometer. "Notice the green arc they have painted on the face of the tachometer. There are two needles there: the long one represents the engine speed, and the short one represents the rotor speed. Right now, they are joined, and that is how you will usually see them. When we practice autorotations, we'll talk more about the needles. For now, just keep them in the green arc." He went on, "To increase the rpm, rotate the throttle toward the outside of the aircraft, and to decrease the rpm, roll the throttle toward you. That's just one function of the collective. The other is to move the aircraft up and down. If you want the aircraft higher, just raise the collective. If you want it lower, just lower the collective. One other thing. When you raise the collective, you are actually increasing the pitch on the rotors, which requires more power; so remember when you raise the collective to roll on more throttle, and of course, when you lower the collective, you have to roll off on the throttle. Oh yeah, the more power you apply to the rotors, the more centrifugal force you create, which means you have to increase the antitorque pitch on the tail rotor, which, in turn, means you have to increase the pressure on your left pedal.

When you reduce power, you must decrease your antitorque setting by pressing your right pedal."

"*What did he say?*" I thought to myself.

"Do you understand?"

I said, "Go over that one more time."

"Look," he said, "let me phrase it this way: If you want to go up, pull up on the collective, roll on more throttle, and push in your left pedal. To go down, push down on the collective, roll off the throttle, and press your right pedal. Nothing to it."

"*Right!*" I thought.

"Do you understand?"

"Yes, sir!"

"Okay," he said, "you have the aircraft." I was concentrating and did not respond. Louder the second time, he said, "You have the aircraft!"

I replied, "I have the aircraft," and *that* was the biggest lie I told in flight school.

Within two seconds, we were oscillating back and forth, up and down, and side to side. He kept shouting, "Rpm! Rpm!" At one point, I glanced out of the aircraft and saw a WOC at the side of the field who was laughing so hard tears were running down his cheeks, and he was grabbing his sides. I didn't think it was one damned bit funny, and anyway, I was having trouble seeing because sweat was pouring off my face, running into my eyes, and dripping off my nose. Trying to control that damned thing was like trying to ride a tornado! We had started out in the middle of a clear ten-acre field, and now I was wondering, "*Why did he select such a small place to practice?*"

He let me damn near kill us both several times before he got back on the controls and said, "I have the aircraft."

With a sense of immense relief and a sigh of gratitude, I said, "You have the aircraft." As soon as I let go of the controls, the helicopter was as steady as a rock.

"Lieutenant, you remind me of a butcher trying to chop his way through a side of beef. A light touch is what is needed here. Just THINK about making a correction. Don't consciously make it. This aircraft is like a tender woman who wants to be caressed and gently led toward the bedroom. Shit, you were wiping out the cockpit, and I damn near got a hernia just watching you!

"Let me show you something," he said as he started to move across the field. "See that stake?" he asked as we approached a stake about two feet high stuck in the ground.

"Yes," I replied as we came to a hover next to it.

"I'm going to put the toe of the left skid on top of it, rotate 360 degrees around it, and not take the toe off of it." He was on the right side of the aircraft and couldn't even see the toe on the left skid. I watched as he placed the toe of the skid on top of the stake and then rotated 360 degrees around the stake. During the entire time, the toe of the skid never left the top of the stake. The aircraft felt as if the entire maneuver was done on a tabletop!

While he was doing this demonstration, he was talking to me. "You have to feel the aircraft and watch for the visual clues that the aircraft is moving in a direction you don't want it to move. Watch the cyclic as I do this, and you will see that a quarter will cover the movement area I use with the cyclic." As I watched the top of the cyclic, I noticed imperceptible movement, and he was right. A quarter would have covered the area that the cyclic moved in. "You will learn to feel and anticipate what the aircraft will do when you are downwind, crosswind, or upwind. But most importantly, relax and THINK about making the aircraft move in the direction you want it to move."

As I watched this demonstration, I thought, *"In your dreams! I'll never be as smooth as that!"* We flew back to the heliport, landed, shut down the aircraft, performed a postflight walk around inspection, and filled out the maintenance logbook. We had a short discussion on filling out his logbook correctly and then returned to the briefing room.

I was drenched with sweat and felt like I had just been through a wringer. As we walked into the briefing room, we both stopped at the Coke machine and got a Coke and then walked to our table.

I put my flight bag (which contained my flight helmet) on the floor, pulled out a chair, and sat down. His other student was waiting for us, and it was obvious he had been studying the manuals that were strewn on the tabletop. My IP reached into his flight-helmet bag, pulled out a notepad that consisted of preprinted forms, and laid it on the table. He then unzipped the pocket on the left sleeve of his flight suit, pulled out a pack of cigarettes, shook a cigarette free, lit it up, took a deep drag, and reached for his Coke. He leaned back in his chair and looked at both of us.

"After each ride, I will critique your performance. I will use this form and grade you on everything that is on this form." As he said that, he pulled two forms off the pad and handed one to each of us. He went on to say, "A copy of this critique sheet will be placed in your folder at the end of each day. A white grade slip is a satisfactory ride, and a pink grade slip is an unsatisfactory ride. If you get too many pink slips, you will receive an evaluation ride by another IP to determine if you should continue in the program. Any questions about this?"

"I have a question," I said. "How many pink slips are you allowed before you have to take an evaluation ride?"

"Three." He then proceeded to critique my performance on this first flight. "This is a free ride today; we don't give pink slips on the first day." He raised the Coke bottle to his lips, and I watched his Adam's apple move as the Coke slid down his throat. My heightened sense of awareness reminded me of my first parachute jump when I actually felt the rubber bands, which held the static line, pop as the static line was pulled from the parachute backpack as I plummeted toward the ground. "Lieutenant," he said as he looked at me, "you aren't the worst student I've had on a first-day flight, but you need to relax. I will expect some improvement in that area on tomorrow's flight." With that, he turned toward the lieutenant who was going to be his next student and asked him what he had been reading while we were flying.

I pulled my pack of Luckys from the zippered pocket on my flight suit, shook out a cigarette, lit it up, and allowed myself to lean back in the chair. *"Man, what the hell did you get yourself into?"* I thought as he continued talking to the other student.

CHAPTER THREE
PRIMARY FLIGHT TRAINING

Flight school was different from any other type of educational experience I had encountered up to that point in my life. What made the biggest impression was the emphasis placed on individual performance. Daily, you were graded on your ability to perform not only on your understanding of the concepts involved but also on your individual skill in performing those tasks. In most academic situations, you have time to consider your response and work out an acceptable solution to a given problem. Only infrequently are you called upon to do it on a daily basis, and when called upon to demonstrate your knowledge, you are usually graded in degrees of correctness. Seldom are we held to a standard that is either correct or not correct (pass or fail). In flight school, either you could do it or you couldn't, and daily, there was the instructor with pen poised, recording what you couldn't do. In many respects, this was the apprentice system at its best. Men who were masters of their trade taught us, and they were the ones who established the standards we strove to attain.

The officer's class was organized into two sections. One section would receive classroom instruction in the morning while the other section would be out, actually flying. In the afternoon, the sections would reverse the order. It was scheduled so that one week, your section would fly in the morning, and the next week, you would fly in the afternoon. We rotated like that throughout our time in flight school. The classroom sessions started with maintenance and how to inspect the helicopter for excessive wearing and/or damage. What was interesting was that the classroom instructor would explain the tolerances that were acceptable on the various "push-pull linkages," such as the tail rotor, and say something like, "The maximum wear allowable on the push-pull linkage is 1/32 of an inch." Since we had no calipers, determining what was acceptable and what might cause us to crash was, I thought, a little iffy. I would sit there and think, *"Right, now how the hell would I know if it was 1/32 or 1/8?"* There was no way for a pilot to measure that type of wear. Well, you actually learned what was acceptable, and what wasn't, from your IP. When the student performed the preflight inspection, the IP would follow behind and do his own preflight. If he found something that was not safe, he would say, for example, "Feel the wear in this push-pull linkage. That's too much movement; we're turning down this aircraft." He would then have us grab the linkage and move it back and forth to give us an idea of what excessive wear felt like. It was that way with all of our subjects.

We progressed from initial maintenance and inspections to theory of flight; theory of helicopter flight, takeoff, landing; landing and takeoff from a slope, pinnacle, confined area; emergency procedures, etc. During our flight periods, the IP would demonstrate what we had learned in the classroom, and then we would practice until we could demonstrate our understanding of the principle and our ability to perform it.

Our initial flight training was conducted at stage fields. A stage field was a remote area that had two paved runways with a tower, helicopter parking area, and some bleachers. These stage fields were scattered throughout the area on the Fort Wolters reservation. During the first part of our training, our IP flew with us the entire period. After we had soloed, there were days when the IP would not fly with us at all and other times when he would fly a partial period with us. Before you could solo, you had to demonstrate that you knew how to take off, land, enter, and exit a traffic pattern; how to use the radios; and how to make an emergency landing with no power. (We had no simulators then, so things considered too dangerous to do now were a routine part of training at that time.) Most of our early training was devoted to learning and practicing the items that were required before we could solo, and most of those things were taught in the traffic pattern at the stage field. I spent a *lot* of time in the traffic pattern.

Learning how to autorotate was the most difficult part of this early training for me. We were taught to execute an autorotation whenever we lost power, i.e., the engine quit. The first day my IP demonstrated an autorotation, he gave me the following explanation while we were in the traffic pattern.

"The next maneuver I'll show you is what to do if your engine quits, or you have a partial power failure. The first thing you do is immediately push your collective to the floor. You want to take all the pitch out of the main rotor. We call that flat pitch. At the same time, push in on your right pedal to remove the antitorque setting on the tail rotor. You want to stay lined up with the runway. Once you have stabilized your descent, make your Mayday call on the radio. As you are descending, keep your eye on the tachometer and make sure that the rotor stays in the green. When you get about one hundred feet from the ground, do a slight flare with the cyclic and then level the aircraft. At about twenty-five feet, pop the collective, hold what you have, and as the aircraft settles, smoothly pull the collective all the way up to the stop." By this time, we had turned on course to the final approach, only this time we were at five hundred feet and not descending. He said, "You have to pick your entry point to make sure you land on the runway." With that said, he cut the power (rolled off the throttle). I felt for a moment as if I were weightless, my heart jumped to my throat, I was pushed up into my seat belt, and we fell like a stone toward the earth.

As we were plummeting from the sky, he was calling off the things he was doing, "Collective down. Aircraft is in trim." (He was referring to keeping the ball centered in the turn-and-bank indicator by pushing in on the right pedal.) "Rotor in the green. I've got my landing spot." He pushed the intercom switch on his cyclic and said, "Mayday, Mayday, Mayday! One hundred feet flare. Level, pop the collective, and hold what I have. Ease the collective up to the stop, touchdown. Lower collective and stop forward movement." We were on the ground in less time than it takes to tell about it.

As we skidded to a screeching stop on the runway, he brought the engine back up to operating rpm. My heart was pounding; I forced my muscles to relax, and it felt as if my heart were still in my throat. I thought, "*That was like riding the biggest roller coaster in the world. What if we had hit something on the runway? We would have tipped over. Can I do what he just did? Will I have to do this?*" knowing the answer was yes.

He gave me the aircraft, and as we were on the downwind leg of the traffic pattern, he commented, "If you have an engine failure, look down through the bottom half of the bubble and pick a place to land. This aircraft has the worst autorotation capabilities of any aircraft we have in the fleet. You're going to land somewhere within twenty to thirty degrees of where the engine stops." He went on, "Autorotations in this aircraft are just like riding a stone to the ground: you just don't have any ability to glide."

Unspoken was the implied knowledge that if anyone screwed this up, there was a high probability he wouldn't live to talk about it. We had several students in our class who landed too hard during practice autorotations. When the main rotor flexed, it actually chopped off the tail boom, which was better than what happened to Cobra (gunship) pilots in similar circumstances. In a Cobra, hard landings often resulted in the main rotor flexing downward, coming through the cockpit, and decapitating the front-seat pilot.

Thereafter, during every flight period, he would give me a forced landing by suddenly rolling off the throttle. If we were over a stage field, we did autorotations to the ground. If we were en route somewhere else, we went through standard autorotation procedure and then rolled on the throttle to full power at about one hundred feet and recovered to powered flight and a hover, about ten feet off the ground.

The second most difficult maneuver for me to learn was landing on a slope. You would shoot an approach to a designated spot and terminate your approach about one foot off the ground, then slide your upslope skid over to touch the side of the hill. That skid would come in contact with the side of the hill, and you had to keep the aircraft level, which meant the other skid was one to three feet off the ground. If the slope was too steep, there was the danger of getting into what was referred to as "mast bumping." This meant that the hub of the rotor blades might accidentally touch the mast, which could cause the mast to shear off at that point, sending the rotor blades off into orbit and the rest of the aircraft crashing to the ground. This was also a dangerous maneuver for the troops we carried. Slope landings meant that the troops had to dismount on the upslope side, which meant the main rotor was one to three feet lower than they were used to. More than one soldier was decapitated on slope landings. Not only would it ruin *his* day there was a high probability *your* day would be ruined also.

As I write these words, I still use the euphemism of "ruining your day" to mean getting killed. It was during flight school that we started the black humor that only intensified when we got into combat. This was another similarity between the airborne soldiers and helicopter pilots. One of the favorite songs in the airborne is entitled "Blood upon the Risers." Part of one verse and chorus to this song, sung to the tune of the "Battle Hymn of the Republic," goes as follows:

> *There was blood upon the risers, there were brains upon his chute.*
> *His intestines were a dangling from his paratrooper boots.*
> *He jumped into the icy blast, his static line unhooked*
> *And he ain't gonna jump no more!*
> *Gory, gory, what a hell of a way to die.*
> *Gory, gory, what a hell of a way to die.*
> *Gory, gory, what a hell of a way to die.*
> *And he ain't gonna jump no more!*

There was a student in a class ahead of us who crashed and burned to death while on a solo-training flight. I used to think some people laughed at death. Then there were some pilots who were so confident of their skills that they felt there was nothing they couldn't overcome. It was rumored that this pilot decided to change seats while in the air. If true, we all agreed that that was the dumbest thing we ever heard of. And thus began our acceptance of the possibility of death as a part of flying.

After several weeks of practice, some of the guys in the class were allowed to solo. This was a *big* deal. It meant that the student had progressed far enough that his IP had confidence he could make it around the pattern at the stage field on his own. Whenever a student soloed, we would stop by the Holiday Inn on the way back from the stage field and wet down his wings by tossing him in the swimming pool. Of course, on Friday night, we would expect those students that had soloed the past week to buy drinks for everyone and really wet down his achievement. The owner of the Holiday Inn allowed the flight program to use his pool for this purpose because he was very supportive of the army's presence at Fort Wolters in general and the pilots in particular.

My solo flight was unexpected because I didn't believe I was ready to solo. That particular morning, we had practiced a couple of approaches and a couple of autorotations at the stage field. After our last autorotation, my IP said, "Move it off the lane and set down in front of the tower." I expected we were going to discuss my shortcomings as a pilot in more detail. Instead, when we were parked in front of the tower, he unbuckled his seat belt, looked at me, and shouted over the engine noise, "Take this hummer around the pattern twice. When you're done, park behind the tower, and I'll see you when you're on the ground." I couldn't believe it; he expected me to fly this thing all by myself! As I was considering this development, he was buckling up his seat belts. When they were secure, he looked up at me, grinned, gave me a thumbs-up, and walked toward the tower. Well, I made it around the pattern the required two times and hovered over to the parking lot behind the tower. I saw a parking spot near the tower and turned to hover to that spot. As I did, the nose of the aircraft dropped, the tail came up, and I started hauling ass toward the tower. I was caught downwind and totally unprepared for the speed at which I was moving. I pulled back on the cyclic, but it didn't slow my forward movement.

The tower operator was looking out the window, and the next thing I heard on the radio is "Helicopter in the parking lot, don't come too near the tower." I thought, "*Man, if I could get this thing stopped, I would!*" I pulled the cyclic back farther but was still moving toward the tower too fast for parking. The tower operator was watching me and moved out to the stairs. He was getting ready to un-ass the tower. I pulled back farther on the cyclic, and all I could think of was that if I pulled it back much farther, I could get into "mast bumping," and I didn't want that to happen. Eventually, I got the aircraft stopped, and the tower operator went back inside his tower. After I had it parked and shut down, my enthusiasm over my solo flight was tempered by the realization that I *still* had a long way to go.

CHAPTER FOUR
THE LIGHT SIDE

We aren't no thin red 'eroes, nor we aren't no blackguards too,
But single men in barricks, most remarkable like you;
An' if sometimes our conduck isn't all your fancy paints:
Why, single men in barricks don't grow into plaster saints.

—Rudyard Kipling, "Tommy"

For the warrant-officer candidates, there wasn't much time to play since off the flight line, they were working hard, learning how to become warrant officers. This phase of their training was very similar to Officer Candidate School and was very demanding. They just didn't have the free time the commissioned officers had.

As background to those times, I should point out that the army of the fifties and early sixties was hard drinking, hard charging, full of rituals and customs that we expected to find in every unit as we moved from one assignment to another. Virtually, every branch of the army had their "dining in," which was a very formal affair before and during dinner. It reflected that particular branch and unit's history and traditions. After dinner, the evening became considerably more relaxed and informal.

The airborne had another tradition called a "prop blast," an initiation rite into the elite airborne ranks. You really weren't accepted as a "real" airborne soldier until you had made your "cherry blast" (first jump with the unit after jump school), and you had gone through the prop-blast ceremony. Essentially, this was a series of events you had to perform properly. Prior to beginning of these events, you filled your canteen with the prop-blast concoction.

This consisted of bourbon, gin, vodka, beer, and whatever else was handy. If you screwed up (in the eyes and mind of the jump master in control of your group) as you went through these events, you were required to drink from your canteen while your fellow "blastees" counted aloud, "One thousand and one, one thousand and two, one thousand and three, one thousand and four." The liquid was to pour down your throat during this countdown, and if you paused during the countdown, you were rewarded with another opportunity to demonstrate your ability to drink properly. Needless to say, within a few hours, everyone was falling down drunk. But you had been prop blasted!

While assigned to the Second Squadron, Seventeenth Cavalry at Fort Campbell, Kentucky, we had an informal gathering every Friday night we were in garrison. This gathering was called "fiddler's green." The legend has it that every true cavalryman, when he dies, is going to spend eternity in hell. On the way to hell, he stops off at this tavern called Fiddler's Green to have one last drink with his comrades. It turns out that he has such a good time he never leaves Fiddler's Green.

To organize this gathering, we would put tables end to end until we had one long table. At the head of the table sat the "head fiddler," normally the squadron commander. At the other end sat the "tail fiddler," always the junior officer present. The objective was to have a good time, poke fun at one another, and build the comradeship within the unit. To accomplish the latter, everyone had the opportunity to nominate some officer for the biggest goof of the week. The officer who had pulled the biggest goof and got the most votes was awarded the Goof Croup, which he had to carry everywhere with him the following week. The Goof Croup was nothing more than a leather riding croup, but everyone in the squadron knew what it symbolized. The head fiddler opened the gathering and awarded the Goof Croup. The tail fiddler accepted nominations from the floor, ruled on parliamentary procedure, kept a tally of the votes and, most important of all, made sure there was never an empty pitcher of beer on the table.

The head fiddler opened the gathering by proposing a toast to the United States of America. Everyone stood and repeated, "To the United States of America," drained their glasses, and sat down. The senior troop commander would stand and propose a toast to the president of the United States. Everyone stood and repeated, "To the commander in chief," drained their glasses, and sat down. Each subsequent troop commander made a toast to the 101st Airborne Division, to armor branch, to the cavalry, and the tail fiddler always made the toast "to the ladies." In the space of five minutes, we had all chugged six glasses of beer and were starting to get a little loose.

At that point, the tail fiddler announced that nominations were open for the recipient of the Goof Croup, and he took charge of the proceedings. His rulings were absolute, and he could rule you "out of order" any time he chose, which he did sometimes for no discernible reason. The officer ruled out of order had to stand and chug a glass of beer. Of course, while he was on his feet, he could propose a toast (to West Point, to OCS, to Alpha Troop, etc.), and all those to whom the toast applied would stand and drink with him.

We eventually closed the nominations about an hour later, and the tail fiddler had to read off the nominations, assuming he could still read at this point. After all the nominations had been read, he called for a vote. Every appendage that was above the table was counted as one vote. If we had a particularly good nominee when it came time to take the vote, both hands would be held up, and quite frequently, both feet would be on top of the table. This often resulted in a chair sliding out from beneath someone. By the end of the evening, we had a new recipient of the Goof Croup; everyone was thoroughly bombed out of his mind, and the husbands in the group knew they were in deep shit.

Two of us from this squadron went to flight school at the same time. Charlie Rayl had been the squadron communications officer while I had been the squadron adjutant and a troop commander. While at Fort Wolters, he and I and another lieutenant, Jim Cully, would go to the Officer's Club on Friday nights. After a couple of weeks (about the same time people started to solo), we started holding our own version of fiddler's green. Our Goof Croup was a toilet plunger wrapped with plastic flowers. It was really funny to see the looks that the recipient received as he walked around the flight line, stage field, and on post with that stupid plunger. We all got a lot of laughs out of it. Our usual routine after fiddler's green was to load up in Corvettes or Mustangs and head for Dallas. Big D was quite a town, and nothing was too good for the boys going to Vietnam. Wine, women, song, and party hardy were the objective. Hell, in six months, we might all be dead.

On the way to or from Big D, we frequently stopped at a Shakey's pizza parlor in Fort Worth, ate a pizza or two, drank a couple of beers, and started singing along with the piano player. We were a little loud; but generally, the staff and the patrons soon joined in, and we would start another party.

We usually went to this piano bar in Dallas where we soon became part of the Friday-night crowd and the favorites of the waitresses. After the bar closed, we would continue the party at someone's house or apartment and, frequently, would not return to Fort Wolters until late Saturday or Sunday. One Saturday afternoon, a couple of the waitresses returned to Fort Wolters with us. We were going water skiing. As we were driving down the freeway, one of the girls took off her sweater and perched herself on the rear deck of the convertible and nearly caused three wrecks before she got back in the car and put her sweater on. This was, after all, the middle of the sixties.

I guess it was the knowledge in the back of our minds that we were going to Vietnam as soon as we graduated from flight school that contributed somewhat to our devil-may-care attitude. The rest of that attitude mostly just came from being a pilot and challenging fate every time we left the ground. I had learned quite a few things about flying, and the truest thing I learned was that old adage, "There are old pilots, there are bold pilots—but there are no old bold pilots!" In December, we finished our primary training, said our farewells to all of our friends in Texas, packed our bags, and headed for Fort Rucker, Alabama, where we would get our advanced helicopter training.

CHAPTER FIVE
FORT RUCKER, ALABAMA

At Fort Rucker, we received contact and tactical training on the Huey helicopter and basic instrument training using the OH-13 helicopter. We were issued another load of manuals and met our new IPs. The IPs for the contact and tactical training were all active-duty warrant officers and commissioned officers. My IP for instrument training was another contract pilot from Ross Aviation and also a retired warrant officer.

The initial training on the Huey was designed to get us checked out on the aircraft. This meant a lot of time studying the various systems, knowing what the various circuit breakers had an affect upon, learning how to conduct a thorough preflight inspection, and, of course, a lot of time just flying the aircraft. During this period, we spent most of our classroom time on theory of flight, maintenance, safety precautions, and a great deal of time on emergency procedures. I often thought that the amount of time spent on emergency procedures was excessive. We learned so much about what could go wrong with a helicopter that I started feeling apprehensive every time I got in one. It was during this period of time that I heard an IP say, "There are just too damn many moving parts on this aircraft!"

We learned that control input had a slight delay because it acted upon the retreating blade. We learned that the two rotor blades acted in unison but independent of each other: the advancing blade was moving through clean air, and the retreating blade was moving through disturbed air. We learned about such terms as "retreating blade stall," "settling with power," "compressor blade stall," "hunting and flapping," "density altitude," etc. What I ended up remembering from theory classes were those items that had impact on me, as a pilot, and those items that the pilot had to understand in an emergency situation. The maintenance classes, on the other hand, were very practical. Virtually, all the students were mechanically inclined. We were raised during a period of time when an individual could still work on his own automobile, and I would venture to say that most pilots were able to repair their own cars. Certainly, we all understood the necessity of having clean air filters and maintaining proper fluid levels and understood why certain components required safety wire or cotter pins. We understood how the horizontal thrust of the engine was converted to vertical thrust through the use of the transmission, the importance of hanger bearings on the tail-rotor drive shaft being mounted securely and being well lubricated, the importance of maintaining proper fluid levels to prevent moving parts from seizing up, and we understood what the critical parts were that could cause catastrophic failure if not maintained properly. The rotor systems (main rotor and tail rotor) and, of course, the engine were the two systems that were critical to getting and remaining airborne. They received the majority of my inspection efforts.

You could always count on a pilot's macabre sense of humor. Whoever named the nut that holds the main rotor to the main mast the "Jesus nut" was absolutely correct. If that nut came off in flight, you were certainly going to meet Jesus up close and personal. When we inspected the main rotor system, that was one item that was inspected *very* closely.

Our flight training started with a lot of traffic-pattern work until we learned to land, takeoff, and perform both hovering autorotations and autorotations from altitude. We now started practicing how to do 180-degree autorotations. The reason for doing a 180-degree autorotation was to ensure that you landed into the wind. That meant that you always had to know the direction the wind was blowing from. Our daily flight briefing included wind direction and speed, but that didn't mean that over any particular spot on the ground that was the direction it would be blowing from. The IPs taught us to constantly look for indicators that told us the true direction of the wind. Ponds were very good indicators; so were smoke and vegetation. They would often cut the power when they knew we were downwind just to see if we had been paying attention as we were flying. You soon learned that you *had* to know the wind direction. If we were away from a stage field and were given a forced landing, we terminated the autorotation at a hover, over the spot we told the IP we were going to land. If we were at a stage field, we did them to the ground.

During this phase of our training, we practiced fixed-pitch tail-rotor failures. Those always made me sweat. These were hairy rides; if you touched the runway while you were still flying sideways, the aircraft could flip over and definitely ruin your day. As you slid down the runway, there was the screech of metal, sparks were flying, and the only way you could control the direction you were sliding was the use of the throttle. If the nose of the aircraft started to swing right, you rolled off throttle, and if it started to swing left, you rolled on throttle.

Then there were the "hydraulics off" landings. If you lost your hydraulic system on the A-, B-, or D-model Hueys, there was a chance you could get it landed. If you were flying a C-model Huey and lost hydraulics, well, bend over and kiss your ass goodbye because it was unlikely you would be able to land it. To land these aircraft without hydraulics required brute strength. These were always running landings with a very shallow approach. You learned that all of your maneuvers required lead time. The less you had to maneuver the aircraft, the better. Frequently, it would require both the pilot and the copilot pushing or pulling on the controls to get them to move.

On my first try at a hydraulics-off landing, I was trying to lower the collective, but it didn't appear to be moving. I hit my intercom button and said to the IP, "Give me a hand!" He looked at me, grinned, and started to applaud. "No, damn it," I yelled. "Push down on the collective." He replied, "You're a big boy; push it down." I pushed as hard as I could, partially lifting myself out of the seat. The collective moved ever so slightly, and we started to lose altitude and, eventually, got it safely on the ground.

We also had the regular contact work to master, slope landings, pinnacle landings, maximum-performance takeoffs, confined-area approaches, and autorotations. At Fort Wolters, my IP always had his hands and feet on the controls when we practiced autorotations. I don't believe I did a single one at Fort Wolters without him making some minor adjustment on the way down. At Fort Rucker, the IP stayed on the controls for the first couple; but thereafter, I was on my own, and both of our lives were in my hands. I always admired those IPs. I never had a desire to become an IP; I could never have made myself stay off the controls during some of the more dangerous maneuvers we performed.

After we were checked out on the Huey, we started instrument training and tactical training. The instrument training we received was the minimum required to save our lives if we were caught in weather. We received classroom instruction on instrument techniques and practical application using the OH-13 helicopter. These flight periods were always flown with an IP, and as a result, we were not checked out on the OH-13. This aircraft, at Fort Rucker, was only used to teach basic instrument flying. At this time, there were no flight simulators for helicopters. The only other training device we had to teach instrument flying was the old blue box that was used in World War II to teach fixed-wing pilots how to fly on instruments.

Although we learned about flight information publications, navigation charts, instrument landing systems, holding patterns, clearances, Federal Aviation Administration rules and regulations, etc., we were not being prepared to take an examination for a regular instrument ticket. If we didn't crash the trainer and we could get the aircraft on the ground safely, we would receive a tactical-instrument card. That meant that if we were caught in weather, we might be able to shoot an approach to a tactical nondirectional beacon, presuming, of course, we remembered enough of the procedures. My most memorable experience of this training was going under the "hood" the first time.

The OH-13 helicopter was a two-seat aircraft, had a reciprocating engine, and burned aviation gas. It had a large Plexiglas bubble that enclosed the pilot and his passenger and a tail boom that looked like it was made from an erector set and was used extensively during the Korean War. If you've ever watched the TV series M*A*S*H, you are familiar with the OH-13. The bottom half of the bubble on the side where the student was seated was painted opaque so that you couldn't see through it. The "hood" was made of four pieces of metal. The base of the hood had a hook that you attached to your flight helmet. Once it was attached, you flipped the other three pieces down, one on each side and one to the front. You now could see only what was in front of you: the instrument panel.

On our first instrument takeoff from the ground, my IP went through an explanation of the "before takeoff checklist." We made sure that all of our radios were set to the proper frequencies and worked and that all the other instruments worked properly. He had me make a simulated call to the tower and gave me a simulated instrument flight rules (IFR) clearance that I had to copy down. When that was completed, he took the controls and taxied to the active runway where he set it down. He then talked me through making an instrument takeoff as he performed the takeoff. Once we were clear of the airfield and at altitude, he gave the aircraft to me. All this time, I was under the "hood" and could see nothing but the instrument panel.

I performed some standard-rate turns to the right and left. We climbed and descended straight ahead, and then we practiced some climbing turns and some descending turns. During our classroom instruction, we had discussed what caused vertigo and how it felt, but no amount of discussion had prepared me for the actual experience.

After about fifteen minutes of performing these basic maneuvers, he took the aircraft, and I sat back and listened as he talked about various aspects of instrument flying. He stressed the importance of cross-checking all your instruments, developing a pattern for your cross-check, understanding what you were seeing displayed on the instruments, and not relying on your senses to tell you what was happening with the aircraft. After about five minutes of this, he instructed me to lean forward and lower my head as close to my knees as I could. As I was doing this, he turned the aircraft left and right and then told me to take the controls.

As I straightened up, I *felt* that the aircraft was in a climbing turn to the left. I glanced at the artificial horizon, and I *thought* I saw the nose of the aircraft in the white part of the ball. That confirmed it: we were in a climbing left turn. (Actually, we were in a standard-rate turn to the right, neither climbing nor descending.) He said, "Okay, let's get to straight-and-level flight."

I was trying to make the instruments confirm what I *felt*, and it felt as if we were in a climbing left turn. I pushed forward on the cyclic and moved the cyclic farther to the right. (This increased my rate of turn to the right, and we started to descend.)

"Cross-check," said my IP. Then he asked, "Are you climbing or descending?"

"Climbing," I replied. If I had looked, my vertical speed indicator (VSI) was showing a rate of descent of about three hundred feet per minute.

Again, my IP said, "Cross-check." I looked at all my instruments, but I still felt I was in a climbing left turn and made no correction. Then I heard, "I have the aircraft, and I am holding what you had. Take off the hood."

As I removed the hood, I immediately saw we were in a descending right-hand turn, and as soon as my brain received the visual input, my senses started to feel the truth that we were in a descending right turn. "Captain," said my IP, "that's what we call a graveyard spiral. Damn it, you have got to believe what the instruments are telling you! When you get in the clouds and have lost reference to the ground, you cannot trust your senses! Put on your hood and let's try it again." That was the only time I experienced vertigo while flying, and it certainly made a believer out of me.

Our tactical training concentrated on formation flying, cross-country navigation, sling loads, gunnery training, combat-assault training, and night landings to a flashlight with landing lights on and off. There were other items covered during this phase of our training, but those are the ones that stand out in my mind. The formation flying made the biggest impression, with the cross-country navigation causing me to become the recipient of the Goof Croup for a week.

Formation flying required you to concentrate on the lead aircraft to the exclusion of everything else. You used visual clues to maintain the proper distance and altitude. If you were in a V or echelon formation, the crossbars of the lead aircraft's skids should be positioned so they appeared to form an X, and the rotor disc of the lead aircraft should be on the horizon. If you were in a trail formation, the rotor disc of the lead aircraft should be on the horizon, and you had to estimate two rotor discs between you and the aircraft in front of you. Many of us had to overcome our fear of flying too close to the aircraft in front of us. We were required to maintain two rotor-discs separation between the aircraft. Little did I know that I wouldn't really find out about close-formation flying until I got to Vietnam. We practiced formation flying at altitude and landing and taking off in formation. We all learned how important it was to have a lead-aircraft pilot who knew what he was doing. If the lead slowed too fast, took off too fast, or turned too steeply, everyone else in the formation had to jockey for position, often calling for some wild maneuvers.

The gunnery training was accomplished in a C-model gunship. You practiced in different configurations of the C model. Some had four nineteen-round rocket pods, some had machine guns on the outboard-wing stores with two nineteen-round rocket pods inboard, some just had rockets and a forty-millimeter grenade launcher on the nose (referred to as a chunker), and some had rockets and a minigun (Gatling gun) in the nose. There was a real thrill in rolling in on a gun run, punching off those rockets as you dove on the target. They had a sight that hung in front of the pilot that was used to aim the rockets. I shall never forget one of my IPs who was having difficulty hitting the target say, "Shit!" Pulling a grease pencil from the sleeve of his flight suit, he reached up and drew a cross on the windscreen, saying, "This is the way we do it in the cav [First Cavalry Division]." He then executed a return-to-target maneuver and blew the target away. I couldn't believe he was using a grease-pencil mark as his aiming point.

Cross-country navigation was an art you learned with practice. Using 1:50,000 tactical maps meant that you covered a lot of ground quickly, and it took some time to get accustomed to how fast you could fly across the ground. In Alabama, virtually every town has a water tower with the name of the town painted on it. You could always tell when students were lost: they were circling some water tower, trying to read the name on it. When you were required to use your instruments to fly, you followed the instrument flight rules (IFR). If a person flew into weather, he was said to have "gone IFR." In this phase of our training, IFR took on another meaning: I Follow Roads.

Our last week of tactical training was conducted from field sites. We spent the week applying all the skills we had learned to that point. We practiced combat assaults, single-ship resupply (with and without sling loads), a little gunnery, and relied a lot on our skill in cross-country navigation. With this type of navigation, you flew a heading for a certain amount of time (time and distance) and started looking for where you were supposed to be. Hopefully, you ended up at the right place.

On the night cross-country portion of our training, I was teamed up with another student. We took off on a course that only had four turning points on the entire course, and we got so lost it was unbelievable! As we passed the time in which we were supposed to have completed the course, we both knew we were lost. We contacted the tower back at Fort Rucker and asked for a direction-finding steer. They asked us to identify ourselves with our transponder, which we did. They indicated they had us, gave us a heading, and we moved out on that heading. We flew on that heading for about ten minutes with no further instructions. After ten or fifteen minutes, I called them again, and they indicated they had lost us and asked us to identify ourselves again. We did, but we did not appear on their scope.

Now we were really lost, but in the distance, we saw a water tower and flew to it. We tried to read the name on it, but it was too dark. As we were circling the tower, a caution light flashed on, and my heart jumped to my throat. It turned out to be the twenty-minute fuel light. Now we knew there was no hope of salvaging our pride or reputation; we didn't have a clue where we were, and we were running out of fuel. Near the edge of town, I saw some runway lights. We overflew the field and tried to contact the tower. There was no response, so we thought this was a dirt strip that probably belonged to some farmer. We landed, hovered off the runway, and shut down the aircraft. I found a telephone box halfway down the runway, picked up the receiver, and when the operator answered, I asked her, "What town is this?"

In her charming Southern accent, she said, "Pardon me, sir?"

"Ma'am, I'm a helicopter pilot from Fort Rucker, and I'm lost. I landed at this airstrip, found this phone, picked it up, and you answered. What I'm trying to find out is where am I?"

There was this short sniggering on the phone, and this charming lady, controlling her laughter, said, "Well, sir, Ah don't know where you are, but Ah'm in Camilla, Georgia."

"*Shit!*" I thought, "*We're not even in the right state!*"

I called Fort Rucker and told them where I thought we were. They told me to stay with the aircraft, get some sleep, and they would be out in the morning. In the morning, one of the IPs, "out gathering the flock" as he put it, brought some fuel, and we followed him back to the tactical site. The razzing I took from that little incident was monumental, but then, what could you expect when the section leader was the only one from the section to get lost?

Our last flight at Fort Rucker occurred when we flew back from our week of tactical training. Both the officer and warrant-officer candidates from the Green Hat class combined our flights to fly back en masse. We formed up in Vs of three in a trail formation. It felt great to fly in that formation, and I believe all of us swelled up with the sense of accomplishment we felt at successfully completing this training.

By this time, we had all received our orders. Everyone was going to Vietnam. Some would delay their departure to attend maintenance, safety, or some other course en route, but ultimately, all of us were headed to Vietnam.

The night before our graduation ceremony, we had a class party at the Fort Rucker Officer's Club. Since I was one of the section leaders, I was called upon to offer some remarks for the class. I had previously been called forward to receive a small gift, as had other leaders of the class, but *my* gift was wrapped in a road map of Georgia and Alabama! There were two circles drawn on the map. One circle was drawn around Fort Rucker and was labeled, "Where you were supposed to land," and the other circle was drawn around Camilla, Georgia, and labeled, "Where you actually landed." Another notation on the map said, "Good luck in Vietnam." We all had a big laugh, and during my speech, I mentioned this incident again.

I concluded my remarks by saying, "We've made mistakes, and we've learned a lot. As we leave here, we will not dwell on our mistakes; rather, we will concentrate on what we know we can do. As a class, I would say our motto has been NEVER A BACKWARD GLANCE OR A MOMENT'S HESITATION. DRIVE ON!" That phrase remained a part of my outlook since that night when I first uttered it and became an operational phrase for every unit I subsequently commanded.

The next day, we received our wings, congratulated one another, and as we slowly broke up to go our separate ways, we all realized that school was over. For most of us, the next time we flew would be in Vietnam.

CHAPTER SIX
WELCOME TO VIETNAM

The arrival of the baggage trucks brought me back to reality. "*Tan San Nhut is getting busy*," I thought as I field stripped my cigarette. A pair of fighters was screaming down the runway, and a couple of C-130 Hercules were taxiing toward the runway as I watched a couple of deuce-and-a-half trucks (2 1/2-ton trucks) back toward the shed.

We had been waiting around a large open shed that had a wooden platform that ran the length of it. The shed was open on all sides, and when the arriving trucks backed up to the platform, a couple of soldiers from our plane jumped onto the bed of each truck as it arrived and started hefting the bags from the truck to the platform. After we finally sorted it all out, we boarded buses and left for some unknown destination.

As we drove, it became apparent that we were still on the air base. In a few minutes, we passed through a gate and were off the base. There were five buses escorted by an military police (MP) gun jeep at the head of the column and another at the rear. The sun was starting its climb over the horizon, giving me my first opportunity to look at this land called Vietnam.

All the windows on the bus were open, and each window was covered with a metal mesh with the obvious purpose of preventing grenades or bombs from being thrown into the bus. None of us were armed. The thought crossed my mind. "*What the hell do we do if we're ambushed?*" The only answer was to pray.

We were in a town, and the street was filling with people. The people were small in stature, and most were wearing loose-fitting clothes of very thin cloth that looked like pajamas. There were sandals on their feet and conical straw hats on their heads, and I couldn't help but reflect on the TV images and the battles these people (North Vietnamese) were waging against us. "*Well,*" I thought, "*a gun in your hand is a mighty strong equalizer.*"

Very shortly, we turned off this street and passed through a perimeter that I thought was another part of the air base but was actually the Bien Hoa inprocessing center. This gate was manned by MPs and guarded with sandbagged machine-gun emplacements. In another ten minutes, we arrived at the replacement detachment and unloaded the buses. The officers were sent to one barrack and the enlisted men to another. We were told where the mess hall and showers were located and that we had two hours until we were to start our in processing.

I claimed a bunk, stripped off my shirt, and took off my shoes. Rummaging through my B4 bag, I retrieved my shaving kit, a set of underwear, and a set of fatigues, my boots, socks, shower shoes, and towel; and headed for the shower. I noticed on my return from the shower that a detail was pulling half of a fifty-five-gallon drum from the latrine. They moved it about ten feet from the latrine, poured some diesel fuel into the barrel, and set it on fire. This was a morning ritual at every installation throughout Vietnam. A very effective way to dispose of human waste, but it created a stench that you endured every morning you served in Vietnam.

The in processing was completed the next day, and the following morning, at o' dark thirty, a group of us boarded buses and were taken to the flight line. At the Departure Area Control Group (DACG), we were manifested and boarded an Army Caribou. There was one stop en route to An Khe where about half of the soldiers off-loaded, and then we were airborne again. By the time we arrived at An Khe, the sun was up, and as the pilot initiated a very steep approach to the airstrip, the loadmaster was yelling for everyone going to the First Cavalry Division to get ready to unload. As the Caribou rolled to a stop, the loadmaster dropped the ramp, and six of us left the aircraft. The last of us barely cleared the ramp when the engines were turned up to takeoff power, the ramp raised, and the Caribou took off for parts unknown.

We were standing on the airstrip, and as the noise and dust swirling around us settled to the ground, I noticed that we were alone. There was no one there to meet us, and it was obvious that this airstrip was not on a military installation.

Since I was the ranking person, I told everyone to pick up their gear and move to a clump of trees near the airstrip. Moving toward the trees, I thought, *"Isn't this great! No weapons, I haven't a clue where we are, no radio, and no way to defend ourselves! I hope to hell they dropped us at the right place!"*

We made it to the edge of some trees and moved into the shade offered by them. It was getting hot, and all of us were sweating by the time we were in the tree line. I pulled a damp cigarette out of the pack and lit up. A sergeant first class came to where I was standing. "Sir," he said, "do you want me to put out some security?" Looking across the landing strip and in either direction, I replied, "Sergeant, no one here has a weapon, we don't know where we're at, and I don't know how long we will be here. But yes, have a couple of guys posted over there and down there" as I gestured toward the areas that appeared to give the best observation. "At least, they can give us a head start if any viet cong (VC) shows up," I said.

After the sergeant posted the two men, the rest of us sat down, and I positioned my B4 bag to lean against it. I field stripped the cigarette and pulled another one from the pack. *"Ain't this a hell of a note,"* I thought as I lit up the next cigarette. *"I hope to hell that someone is coming to get us—soon!"* I forced our precarious situation from my mind as I looked around the area. There were hills all around us—tall trees—and it was apparent that someone had removed the heavy underbrush around the airstrip. I knew that the First Cavalry Division headquarters was located near An Khe, in the central highlands, and I presumed we were somewhere near there. It was quiet with none of the other guys talking, each of us lost in our own thoughts.

My mind went back to my departure from Seattle and how my wife lost her temper just hours before I departed. For the last couple of years, our relationship had gotten worse and worse. I never knew what to expect when I walked in the door. Would I be met by Ms. Jekyll or Ms. Hyde? *"It's tough on the kids,"* I thought.

We had spent a few days with my folks in Bremerton prior to my departure for Vietnam. My children from my first marriage, Lance and Valerie, lived there with their mother and new dad. I had made a tough decision six years earlier when their new dad wanted to adopt them. I was a professional soldier, constantly moving from one place to another, and had previously been told by an attorney that there was no chance I would have custody of them as long as I was a soldier. I made the decision, when asked, to allow their new dad to adopt them. Now, as I sat on the ground in Vietnam, I questioned that decision and the other decision I had made years earlier not to disrupt their lives by dropping in and out their lives. I had made no effort to contact them while in Bremerton and wondered if that was the right decision.

I had adopted two children, Lucille and Julie, from my second wife's previous marriage and loved them as my own. We had two children, Bert and April, who were still so young they didn't realize what it meant that Daddy was going to Vietnam. As I said goodbye to my children in the Sea-Tac airport, Lucille and Julie, both beautiful young teenage girls, held on to their emotions and bravely gave me a hug and kiss, knowing full well what it meant for me to go to Vietnam. Young Bert thought this was just another of many separations, and April, the youngest, cried as I picked her up and kissed her goodbye.

"A truck is coming," yelled one of the sentries as a deuce-and-a-half truck came bumping down the road to pick us up. I got in the front seat with the driver, and as we drove toward the division headquarters, I asked him, "We don't have an escort. Is it that safe around here?"

"Shit, sir," he replied, "we've pacified this place. The gooks know not to fuck with the cav."

"Welcome to cav country!" I thought.

Within a few minutes, we were driving through Sin City, a collection of brothels located across the street from the main gate at An Khe. This was the only time I saw this infamous place during my tour. The number of GIs that were walking around the town at this time of the morning surprised me. Soon, we arrived at the replacement detachment, had breakfast, and started our inprocessing to the division. I went to the Officer Assignment section at the adjutant general's (AG) office. A clerk reviewed my records, making sure they reflected correct data, and then said, "Well, sir, you're an armor officer and will probably go to the 1-9, the division cavalry squadron. We do have vacancies in the 227th and the 229th. If you'd like, I could ask the assignment officer to assign you there."

I remembered the conversations I had listened to at Fort Rucker. The IPs who had already served in Vietnam had two very different opinions about the 1-9. The first was emphatic. "Do everything possible to avoid getting assigned to this unit!" The other was "If you want to be in on the action, this is the unit to get assigned to. You may not live long, but you will definitely learn what helicopter warfare is about!" A veteran of the 1-9 always spoke the latter opinion.

I told the clerk to assign me to the 1-9. He said, "Yes, sir" and went to cut my assignment orders. When he returned, he told me that he had called squadron headquarters, and they wanted me assigned to Bravo Troop. He went on to say that he had already called the troop, and they were sending a jeep over to pick me up. Having completed the record review and the assignment process, I stood up to leave. The clerk looked up at me and said, "Good luck, sir. That unit has a high casualty rate and a large turnover. I hope you make it."

Stepping outside, I fished a Lucky from my pocket, lit up, and moved to some shade next to the building. Squatting down on my haunches, I wiped the sweat from my brow and waited for the jeep to arrive. Sitting there, it suddenly occurred to me that today was the sixteenth of June—my thirty-first birthday. "*Happy Birthday, Bert,*" I thought as I stood up, watching a jeep coming my way with "1-9" stenciled on its bumper.

I grabbed my gear and threw it in the back of the jeep before the driver had an opportunity to get out. While we drove back to

the 1-9 area, I chatted with him. He was a "short timer" and was
down to counting the hours before he left. He informed me that
most of the soldiers in the rear area (An Khe was definitely a rear
area as far as he was concerned) had served their year and were
waiting for their DEROS (date of expected return from overseas)
to arrive. He slowed the jeep, downshifted, and turned off the
main road, announcing that this was the beginning of the cav
area.

We were on a narrow dirt road that was lined on either side by
wood-framed buildings covered with the width of one sheet of
plywood on the bottom half of the sides and a GP (general purpose)
tent draped across the ridge pole and extending down on the sides
to meet the plywood. It was around 1100 hours, and the
temperature was already in the nineties. The sides of the tents
were rolled up to allow any stray breeze to circulate through.
Noticing that some of the buildings were entirely covered with
plywood, I asked the driver what was in them. He replied, "Those
are supply rooms and mess halls."

The road was getting steeper and was not visible beyond the
crest of the hill in front of us. On the side of the hill were numerous
shacks. Turning to the driver, I asked, "What'n hell are all those
shacks doing there on the side of the hill?"

Grinning, he said, "Those are living quarters made out of ammo
boxes that a lot of the guys built when the cav first got here. Most
of them are vacant now since we operate from forward operational
bases."

The 11th Air Assault (Test) Division had been redesignated
the First Cavalry (Airmobile) Division on 1 July 1965 and deployed
to Vietnam in August 1965. The Third Squadron 17th Cavalry
had also been redesignated the First Squadron (Air) Ninth Cavalry
at the same time. When the squadron deployed, they loaded their
helicopters onto ships and sailed from Jacksonville, Florida and
Mobile, Alabama to Vietnam on those same ships. Since then that
group of soldiers have been referred to as the "boat people."

We pulled off the road into a makeshift parking spot in front
of a building. The driver killed the engine. "Here we are, sir. Bravo

Troop." With that, he dismounted and walked to the orderly room screen door and held it, inviting me in.

I walked in and looked around. A clerk typist was hunting and pecking on the typewriter. A nonrated (not a pilot) infantry first lieutenant got up from a desk and came toward me. I noticed that he had a boot on one foot and a shower shoe on the other. After greeting me and introducing himself, he said, "The troop commander told me that the next captain that came in was going to be the new scout platoon leader. He'll be happy to hear you've arrived."

That hadn't been my plan, so I responded, "I'd rather fly gunships than be in the scout platoon."

He smiled. "Well, we've lost thirteen scout platoon leaders in the last ten months, and you're going to be number fourteen." Whoa! His choice of words may not have been intentional, but if he wanted to get my attention, he certainly succeeded.

I looked at him and said, "I would really rather fly guns." He indicated that he would pass that on to the major but was pretty sure that I was going to be the next scout platoon leader.

We stepped outside the orderly room, and he began pointing out the various places whose locations I would need to know: the mess hall, the supply room, the flight line, etc. Then we got back in the jeep and drove to the top of the hill and unloaded my baggage into the building where I would stay while back at An Khe. He pointed out that we were on the edge of the "Green Line," which was the perimeter around An Khe. He pointed to another building about twenty feet from where I was going to stay and told me that this was the Officer's Club for the cav. He said, "They have steak and beer every night, and you should try it out." With that, we drove back to the orderly room and had lunch in the mess hall.

After lunch, I went to the supply room and received the equipment I would need: .38 pistol with shoulder holster and three boxes of ammunition, a new flight helmet, and armored chest plate (referred to as a chicken plate), jungle boots, five pair of OD (olive drab) shorts and T-shirts, and a handful of First Cavalry

Division patches. While I was signing for this equipment, a warrant officer walked in and introduced himself. He went on to tell me how lucky I was that he was leaving because now I would be able to buy his "hooch."

"What do you mean buy your hooch?"

"Come here," he said as he stepped outside the supply room. When I walked out, he was pointing at one of the shacks I had noticed on the side of the hill when I arrived. "That one," he said. "I'll let you have it for five hundred dollars."

Looking at him, I started to laugh. "Let me get this straight. You want me to buy that shack for five hundred dollars. Why would I want to do that?"

"Well," he said reasonably, "you have to leave some of your stuff here when you go forward, and it gives you some place to rack out when you get back here."

I stared at him and thought, *"Maybe these guys are crazy!"* Slapping him on the shoulder and laughing still harder, I told him that I wasn't interested. I would leave the stuff I didn't need in the supply room, and I'd make out all right when I returned from the fire-support base. He immediately dropped the price to two hundred fifty dollars and told me that I was getting a bargain.

"Well," I thought, *"now I've heard it all. I can't believe this guy is actually trying to sell me a place to stay in the middle of An Khe."*

Laughing harder still, I turned to go back inside the supply room, and then he gave me his final argument, "Hell, I paid six hundred dollars for it when I got here!"

I damned near convulsed when he said that but managed to get out a "no thanks" as I stepped back inside the supply room.

That evening, I went to the Officers Club, called the Shenandoah, and had a steak and a couple of beers. There were pictures of former cav officers sitting in poses that reminded me of Brady's civil-war photos on the walls. There was one of Colonel Stockton and his troop commanders that really reminded me of one of those photos. They were posed with their arms crossed in front of them, handlebar mustaches in full glory, cigars clamped securely in their mouths, and their cavalry hats perched solidly on their heads. If it weren't for the uniforms they were wearing, you would swear you were looking at a photo from the 1860s.

There were about five short timers sitting at a makeshift bar, getting bombed out of their minds. I went to the bar and ordered a steak and a beer. I sat there, listening to the conversation that was going on between them. One of them said, "Did you hear about the squadron surgeon buying it today? He was out flying with one of the gunships, and a single round hit him right between the eyes. He didn't know he was dead!" The talk centered on all the action that had occurred within the last week. Soon I was included in their conversation when they learned I was going to be the new Saber White (Bravo Troop's radio call sign was Saber, and the scout platoon leader's call sign was White). Every one of them offered a heartfelt wish of good luck, and they hoped I would make it through the tour.

One of the officers had been a scout pilot in one of the other troops, and he started telling me, "Scouts are where it's at!" He went on to say, "I killed over one hundred of them fucking gooks." He turned to address the rest of the group and started recounting some of his brushes with death. During this, he casually said, "Yeah, my torque [this, I learned, was slang for the scout observer who flew with the pilot] always made sure they were dead. He would carve his initials in their chests with his sixty [an M-60 machine gun]." The pilot started to laugh, "Man, he really made sure they were dead!"

That brought forth more stories from the other pilots, all of them dealing with the more unusual kills they had made. They started talking of this one gunship pilot who had fired all his rockets and machine-gun ammunition and saw this one gook trying to run away. He dropped down from altitude and chased him down, pulled out his pistol, and "shot the bastard in the balls before he put one through his head." This brought forth a round of laughter, and another pilot started another story of how he had cheated death.

I finished my steak and last beer, excused myself, and returned to my hooch, thinking, *"Some things never change. I'm the new guy, and they were going to impress me with all these stories. I wonder how much of it was true."* Sitting on the edge of my bunk, I cleaned my pistol, loaded it, and placed it on the floor next to my bunk as I lay down to sleep.

I awoke to the sound of a mortar round leaving the tube. I had been a mortar squad leader as an enlisted man, and I knew that sound. I rolled out of the bunk, grabbed my pistol, and hugged the floor. Within a minute, I heard the round impact on the other side of the Green Line. I quickly got dressed and went outside. Crouching near the building, I heard fire commands being issued, and within seconds, I heard more rounds leaving the tubes. The firing position was about ten meters from my hooch, and understanding dawned on me. *"Hell, those are our mortars firing H&I* [harassing and interdiction] *fires!"* Feeling foolish, I returned to the hooch, thinking, *"Shit! They could have told me they had a mortar position next to the hooch."*

At breakfast the next morning, the lieutenant who was in charge of the rear area informed me that he had spoken to Major Beasley (the troop commander) the night before, and he was adamant; I was going to be the next scout platoon leader. I was to get started on the OH-13 checkout today. Having taken my instrument training in the OH-13, I realized I would be flying an old aircraft that dated back to the Korean War. *"Damn, a manual throttle again!"* I thought as he told me this. As we finished breakfast, I learned that the lieutenant had been the infantry platoon leader, was getting short, and, on top of that, had jungle rot on his foot. In World Wars I and II, it was called trench foot and later immersion foot, but they all meant the same thing. Your feet stayed wet for too long and started to rot.

I met Chief Warrant Officer Joseph Rawl at the orderly room later in the morning. He was the IP for the OH-13 and a member of the Bravo Troop scout platoon. We started our transition training into the H-13 that afternoon. The next day, there was an administrative flight going to Duc Pho, and I was to go along with them so I could meet the troop commander and the members of the scout platoon. The aircraft that flew up to Duc Pho was a D-model Huey, and I couldn't help but bemoan the fact that I would not be able to fly this latest version of the Huey.

When we arrived at Duc Pho and stepped out of the aircraft, I noticed that my feet were sticking to the substance that was covering the flight line. I was informed they had just laid another layer of PermaPrime, a mixture of oil and tar, which was used for dust control. Dust is a major problem for helicopters, and this material was used throughout Vietnam in temporary areas where helicopters landed and took off. It became one of those things you were aware of but stopped thinking about it because it was everywhere.

We spent several hours at Duc Pho, and I had the opportunity to meet quite a few of the men in the troop. It was here that I learned that the troop had picked up the nickname of "Beasley's Barbarians." Who knows how people or, in this case, a unit picks up a nickname? My observation and subsequent reflection on the matter led me to believe that at this particular time and place, with this particular group of men, we had warriors assembled who practiced the art of war in its most basic form. Wherever we went, we brought death and destruction to the enemy. There was nothing subtle about it. It was pure warfare with no hesitation in the application of our power.

The most memorable conversation was with Warrant Officer Jere Anderson. We were standing beside his aircraft when the artillery battery located about fifty meters from us fired a salvo. He jumped, then ducked, and nearly fell to the ground, seeking shelter. He was one of my scout pilots who had been flying scouts about five months, and it was obvious his nerves were strung taunt.

We returned to An Khe, and I continued my checkout in the H-13. At the end of the week, I took my check ride with Chief Warrant Officer Rawl. When we finished, he said, "Sir, let me offer a recommendation to you. One of the reasons we lose so many scout pilots is the fact that they all want to go low level as soon as possible. What every scout pilot should do is get about one hundred hours in this bird before they are cleared for low-level flight. That way, they will know what it will do but, more importantly, what it won't do. As it is, when they run into trouble, they run out of airspeed, altitude, and ideas all at the same time! That is simply from a lack of experience in flying the aircraft."

As he was offering his comments, I was thinking of the characteristics of the H-13. This was a two-place helicopter, with the pilot sitting on the left side and the observer on the right. As I recall, the maximum cabin load was around four hundred pounds. I weighed around 190 pounds, and if I had an observer that weighed the same as I, we were at the maximum load. On top of that, the observer had an M-60 machine gun and approximately 1,200 rounds of ammunition that was in a box at his feet. We also had a box of grenades sitting between us on the seat, and we had about eight smoke grenades hanging from a wire on the instrument console.

The pilot and observer sat on a bench seat that we covered with a sheet of armor plating that weighed about fifty pounds, and we flew with the doors removed. The aircraft was powered with a supercharged, piston-driven, reciprocating engine that burned aviation gas. I had already noticed that it was woefully underpowered and, on two occasions, had run out of power when I needed it. There is nothing as disconcerting as attempting to roll on more throttle and discovering you are already at full throttle. Joe Rawl had already cautioned me about flying in the mountains. "Make sure you fly with the mountain on your side of the aircraft. That way, if you run out of power, push right pedal, turn to the right, and fall down the mountainside until you regain power." Turning toward the left required more power, and if you were already out of power, there was nothing left to enable you to turn left. We flew so overloaded and were so underpowered I thought, *"How the hell does this thing stay in the air?"*

I finished my transition into the H-13 and was ready to leave An Khe and join my platoon. The week at An Khe had enabled me to get all the patches and name tags sewn on my uniforms and to order my cavalry Stetson. I sorted my gear, and everything I didn't need with me I packed in my B4 bag and stored it in the supply room. Everything else was packed in my duffel bag. The next morning, I received instructions on how to locate Landing Zone (LZ) Two Bits. The troop was located at Two Bits South. I was given a heading, the approximate time it would take me, and the radio frequencies of the tower and flight following. Taking off from An Khe and the golf course (the flight line was called the golf course), I didn't realize this would be the last time I would see this place until I went on R&R leave.

Departing northeast toward LZ Two Bits, I took one last look at the tarp hanging on the side of the mountain overlooking the golf course. The tarp was about fifty feet long, and painted on it was the First Cavalry Division patch in bright yellow and black. A blatant, in-your-face, arrogant statement that this was "cav country."

I climbed to altitude (about four thousand feet) and remained there until I arrived at Two Bits. En route, I flew over "Happy Valley," the site of previous heavy fighting for the cav. It was a beautiful morning with clear skies, and you could see forever. I had my duffel bag strapped into the right seat, and as I flew north, I kept pushing the thought, *"What if the engine quits and I go down in this area? I'm by myself, I have no compass, I only have a puny .38 revolver, one canteen of water, but no halogen tablets, and if I go down, who knows if they would ever find me?"* out of my mind.

The flight was uneventful, and soon, I was on final approach to Two Bits South. After I landed, the tower gave me instructions on where to hover to get to the Bravo Troop flight line. I didn't have the frequency for troop operations, but as I turned onto the flight line, I saw where the H-13s were parked and hovered toward them. One of the crew chiefs saw me hovering in and stopped what he was doing and acted as my ground guide to a parking spot.

The parking spot was inside of what was called a revetment. It consisted of two rows of fifty-five-gallon drums filled with sand. You had about a foot clearance on either side of the aircraft when it was parked inside the revetment. Turning the nose into the revetment, I felt the tail go up, and I knew the wind was blowing from my rear. As I set the aircraft down, I wondered, *"Does the wind always blow from the southeast?"* If it did, it would be interesting backing out of the revetment since there was a hill directly in front of the parking spot.

After shutting down the aircraft, doing the postflight inspection, and making the entries in the logbook, I asked the crew chief where troop operations was located. He told me it was up the hill, pointing in the direction of the tents I had noticed as I came in. He then commented that he was glad to see this bird back. "We had a hell of a firefight yesterday, and two of the birds are still down. Having another scout bird here will help," he said.

He offered to help me as I unstrapped the duffel bag, but I waved him away and said, "I can handle this. You have plenty of work to do, but thanks for the offer." I slung the duffel bag on my right shoulder, grabbed my flight-helmet bag with my left hand, and started trudging up the hill. *"Well, Bert, here you are. I wonder what it's going to be like."*

CHAPTER SEVEN
THE NEW GUY

Approaching the top of the little hill, I noticed we had a "company street." All the tents on the top of the hill were GP medium. There were about five tents on the left and five on the right. They were "dress right dress," and in between them was the company street. Off to the left, near the base of the hill, was the mess-hall tent. The sides were rolled up on all the tents, and I noticed that the tent on the right had a bunch of folding chairs set up in front of a map board. The map board split the tent in half, and to the rear of the map board, I could hear the tactical radios. This was the operations tent.

I entered the tent, deposited my duffel bag on the dirt floor, and placed my flight-helmet bag next to it. I took my hat off and, using my finger, scraped the sweat from my brow. The smell of treated canvas was heavy in the air. The chatter on the radios and the muted conversations from behind the map board were all very familiar to me. I took a Lucky Strike from a soggy cigarette pack, thinking, *"I've been in hundreds of operation tents just like this all over the world—Korea, Germany, Fort Polk, Fort Carson, Fort Riley— it feels like home."*

All the tents had the long axis oriented east, west. Sunlight was streaming across the dirt floor on the south side of the tent. Near the north side, out of the sunlight, sat two warrant officers. As I entered the tent, I noticed that one of them was reading a pocketbook, and the other was reading the *Stars and Stripes* newspaper. They both looked at me, and I said, "I'm Captain Chole, the new scout platoon leader. Is the troop commander around?" They got up, stuck their hands out, and introduced themselves.

Captain Hasselgrove, the operations officer, appeared from behind the map board and introduced himself. He said, "The old man is in the AO [area of operations] right now and should be back in about an hour." He had me sit down and offered me a cup of coffee. As he hit the spigot on the coffee urn, he told one of the operations clerks to get Captain Williams up to the operations tent. Immediately, I heard a loudspeaker announce, "Captain Williams, report to operations."

Just as Captain Hasselgrove and I started our conversation, Captain Williams entered the tent. We looked at each other, and he said, "I'll be a son of a bitch! Don't tell me you're the new scout platoon leader?"

I put my coffee cup on the floor, stood up, and walked toward him. Grabbing his hand, I said, "You're damn right I am! Man, isn't this a small world!" This was the same Captain Williams that had given me my flight-orientation ride at Fort Campbell over a year ago. We sat down and brought each other up-to-date.

Leaving the operations tent, we moved down the company street and entered the third tent on the left. He told me that this was the scout platoon officer's tent. He pointed to some empty ammunition boxes laid out on the floor next to the entrance and said, "There's your bunk." I dropped my duffel bag, and he introduced me to the men who were in the tent. As I recall, there were only Lieutenant Porrazzo, Mr. Anderson, Mr. Andrews, and one more warrant officer in the tent. After a brief exchange, Captain Williams informed me that he had to go to operations for a briefing and that I should go ahead and get settled in.

I retrieved my air mattress and sleeping bag from the duffel bag. I blew up the air mattress, laid it on top of the ammo boxes, and laid my sleeping bag on top of that. Mr. Anderson appeared with two T-bars and a mosquito net. I drove one T-bar into the ground at the head of my improvised bunk and the other at the foot. I draped the mosquito net over either T-bar, stood back, and announced, "Well, I'm settled in." Mr. Anderson, watching with a critical eye, suggested that I better tuck the mosquito net under my air mattress unless, of course, I didn't mind having all the mosquitoes in the area inside the mosquito net when I went to sleep that night. I tucked in the mosquito net.

Lieutenant Porrazzo showed me around the troop area, pointing out where the enlisted men for the scout platoon slept; what platoons were in the other tents; where the mess hall, showers, and supply tent were located; and where the troop commander's tent was, etc. During this tour, Major Beasley had returned from his mission, and I went to operations to meet him.

Major Beasley was a very intense person. He was focused on his job and allowed few distractions. He was not unfriendly, and he had a sense of humor, but he was focused on the troop performing its job correctly. We went to his tent where I gave him a short review of my previous assignments in the army, and then he gave me a fast review of the troop and what my job was going to be.

He started by explaining the troop organization. "We have three platoons. The scout platoon is called the 'White' platoon, the weapons platoon called the 'Red' platoon, and the infantry platoon called the 'Blue' platoon. The infantry platoon has its own helicopters, and we call them 'Blue Lift.' Under troop headquarters, we have a maintenance section, mess section, supply section, and an operations section. We also have a Direct Support Maintenance Detachment attached to the troop."

He went on, "Our job is to locate the enemy, and that is the primary job of the scouts and the infantry platoon. When we find them, we either kill them, or if they are too large a force for us to kill, we try to hold them in place until we can get a larger force in to kill them." He paused and took a sip of iced tea. "We put the Blues on the ground for two reasons: the first is to conduct ground reconnaissance when your scouts can't determine from the air what is going on in the jungle and the second is to secure any aircraft that are shot down."

I noticed that he was phrasing his thoughts very carefully, and he was intense. I also noticed that the scout platoon was my platoon.

"I make the decision on where and when the Blues are inserted. I will take recommendations, but I make the decision. When the

Blues are on the ground, either you, Captain Hughes, the weapons platoon leader, or I will be on station over them. One of us will be over them at all times. They are not equipped to spend a long period of time on the ground. We load them up with ammunition and water, and their mission is ground reconnaissance. If they make contact with the enemy, they fight an intense battle. If the enemy force is smaller or the same size, they usually win."

Again, he paused as if deciding how much detail to go into. "One of the reasons I monitor their actions so closely is that they are usually put on the ground out of the range of supporting artillery. The division AO [area of operations] is split into three smaller brigade AOs. We normally operate in the Third Brigade AO. Before we put the Blues on the ground, we coordinate with the brigade S3 and get permission to put them on the ground. The brigade will designate the nearest rifle company as the Ready Reaction Force (RRF). When a rifle company is designated the RRF, they, in turn, designate one of their platoons as the Quick Reaction Force (QRF). The QRF moves to the nearest pickup zone (PZ), places out security, and waits. If the Blues get in a firefight with an unknown-size enemy force, or if we can tell it is a larger force, we call for the QRF. Normally, our Blue Lift section will pick them up and insert them into the contact area; as soon as the QRF is inserted, the RRF moves to the nearest PZ and gets ready to *pile on* if these two platoons can't kill the enemy. Once the decision is made to insert the RRF, it becomes the infantry-battalion operation. Until the RRF is called for, I am in charge of the operation. When the RRF is inserted, we move the Blues to a PZ and pull them out and bring them back here. We keep one Pink team on station over the infantry until they tell us they don't need us any longer."

I asked him, "What is a Pink team?"

"A White bird [scout] and a Red bird [weapons aircraft]," he replied.

"How often do we put the Blues on the ground?" I asked.

"Whenever we need to check out something you guys can't make a decision about from the air. Some days they don't go in at all, and other days they go in four or five times. By the way, I want you to go on the ground with them at least once so you can appreciate just how goddamned tough it is moving through that jungle."

He continued by saying, "I also want you to fly a mission with the weapons platoon and the lift section. You need to understand what everyone in the troop does and how they do it. Now, the first thing you need to accomplish is to get familiar with how we operate, and the best way to do that is to watch us do it. We have an artillery forward observer attached to the troop, a Captain Maier. I want him to fly with you until you get a handle on what we're doing. You will fly at altitude and should go out on every mission for the next week or two. This accomplishes two things: you get trained, and Captain Maier can call for artillery fire if we need it."

He looked at his watch and stood up. I stood, and he said, "Get with Captain Hasselgrove, the operations officer, and he'll brief you on some of the more routine procedures we use around here. We have a briefing in the operations tent every evening at 1800 hours; all the officers attend. You've got a big job ahead of you, Captain."

The conversation was finished. I saluted, and from force of habit, he returned my salute and then said, "We don't salute each other in this forward area." With that, he turned to pick up some paperwork, and I left the tent.

I stopped by the operations tent and was issued a signal operating instructions (SOI) pamphlet. It contained all the radio frequencies and call signs of every unit in the division. The operations sergeant told me that the SOI had to be secured to my person at all times. The SOI had a cardboard front and back cover and a hole punched in the upper-left corner through which a cord was tied. I noticed that one of the pilots had his SOI in his breast pocket with the other end of the cord tied to the pocket flap. The operations sergeant explained how to use the SOI and explained that the authentication and shackle code (a code used to transmit friendly troop location over the radio in the clear) was tied to a particular day of the month and that at the end of each month we had to get new inserts for the SOI. He explained that the troop operations section maintained a daily staff journal in which every spot report was recorded. They posted the map with information from the spot reports, sent the reports to squadron headquarters every half hour, did the flight following for the troop, and maintained my flight records.

That evening, I met all the officers at the 1800-hour briefing. Captain Hughes was the weapons platoon leader (Red), Lieutenant Chilcoate was the infantry platoon leader (Blue), and Captain Burnam was the Blue Lift section leader (call sign Three-Five). Captain Williams was the current scout platoon leader (White), and Warrant Officer Kohler was the maintenance officer for the troop. As I looked around the tent, I noticed that about half of the officers were wearing their Cav hats. We faced the map board, all the platoon leaders sitting on the front row. The troop commander's chair was on our right, also facing the map board. While waiting for the briefing to begin, I mentally categorized my first impressions of some of the men I had met:

- Major Beasley was a no-nonsense type of commander. He ran a very tight operation but kept his distance from any type of personal interaction.
- Red Hughes was cocky, arrogant, and, according to him, had done it all. He had a good sense of humor and was a good ole boy from Alabama with a perpetual cigar stuck in his mouth.
- Lieutenant Chilcoate was confident, quiet but assertive—an individual who knew who he was and what he had to do. He had a ready smile and a good sense of humor.
- Captain Burnham was open, friendly and appeared to have a good sense of humor.
- Captain Williams was the happiest man present. He was going back to An Khe in the morning and, from there, home.
- Captain Hasselgrove gave me the impression of being under pressure. He took his job seriously, and he did not want to make any mistakes. He also had a good sense of humor.

We were waiting for the troop commander to arrive. When he did, Captain Hasselgrove announced, "The troop commander." We all stood and stopped talking. When he took his seat, we sat down. The nightly briefing followed the same format every night. Captain Hasselgrove started the briefing by covering that day's operations. He covered every contact in detail. When that was finished, he discussed what we were going to do tomorrow, and he concluded by covering the statistics for our current operation. These included friendly killed in action (KIA) and wounded in action (WIA). Also, how many of the enemy we had killed, wounded, or captured. When he was finished, he sat down to our left on the last chair of the front row. Captain Maier would then announce any changes in artillery support and concentrate on supporting artillery we might use for tomorrow's missions. Mr. Kohler would then give a short briefing on any maintenance problems, and this was followed by each platoon leader (Red, White, Blue, and Blue Lift in turn) giving the status of their men and aircraft. When we had an executive officer, he discussed the status of supplies and administrative matters. He was occasionally followed by the first sergeant who discussed any enlisted concerns. The troop commander finished the briefing by commenting on any problems he had observed during the day, giving attaboy and giving his guidance for the next day's operations. When he was finished, he stood up, and we stood at attention until he exited behind the map board, and then we started talking to one another.

Following the briefing, the Red and White platoon leaders posted the operations chart for the next day and the order their pilots would fly in. This system was simplicity in action. The pilots flew missions in the order in which their names were posted on the chart. First man on the list today dropped to last position for tomorrow, and everyone else moved up one space. It enabled the operations officer to always know who would fly the next mission. It was an equitable way to spread the danger since we had no idea which missions would result in contact.

The first-light mission was flown every day. A Pink team would takeoff before daylight and fly to the fire-support base that was the greatest distance from our location. They would time their takeoff to ensure they were on station as dawn was breaking. The team would check all around the fire-support base to detect any signs of enemy activity. If there were none, they would fly to the next fire-support base, conduct the same type of reconnaissance, and move on to the next until they had performed a reconnaissance around each fire-support base in the Third Brigade AO.

The next few missions during the day were usually in response to a squadron or brigade request to perform reconnaissance in a specific area. If we had no requests, the troop commander selected areas for reconnaissance. Pink teams conducted the reconnaissance missions. The scout flew low level (about one foot above the terrain or trees), looking for the enemy, and the weapons aircraft flew at about 1,500 to 2,000 feet—always in position to place fire on anyone who fired on the scout. If the scout had contact with the enemy or thought the enemy was present, the Blues were inserted to conduct ground reconnaissance. If we developed a contact with the enemy, we rotated teams to the contact site so that we had a team constantly over the fight. To accomplish constant coverage meant that a Pink team took off every one and a half hours. If we had heavy contact, a Pink team would take off every half hour. We usually had from six to eight teams flying during the day.

The last-light mission was flown every day and was conducted the same as the first-light mission except it was conducted at dusk.

When the operations chart had been posted, the platoon leaders went to their respective platoons and conducted their own briefing. Captain Williams and I returned to the scout platoon tent and conducted the briefing for the next day's operation. He said his goodbye and introduced me as the new scout platoon leader.

I gave a short talk on my background, what they could expect from me, and what I expected of them. I had given similar talks to units I had assumed command of in the past, but this was a different situation. What lay on the ground between us was the unspoken thought, "*That sounds great, Captain, but can you cut it when the bullets start flying?*"

From a leadership point of view, I knew that these men were withholding judgment until I had proven myself in combat. No one trusted a "new guy" because you never knew how a "new guy" would react under fire. Until I passed my test by fire, I would remain an unknown quantity.

CHAPTER EIGHT
LEARNING THE TRADE

At 0500 hours, the operations radio telephone operator (RTO) shook me awake. I lay there for a second and then acknowledged that I was awake. I heard him wake up the other scout and the sound of the tent flap parting as he left the tent. I had gone to sleep on top of my sleeping bag last night but noticed I was inside of it now. The sound of sleeping men was the prevalent sound, and then I saw a flashlight go on at the other end of the tent. I turned on my flashlight, found my trousers and socks, and slipped into them. Pulling the mosquito net aside, I picked up my boots and banged the heels on the floor and then turned them upside down to get any critters out of them that may have crawled inside overnight.

I smiled as I did that, thinking back to the scorpions that used to crawl into my boots when I was training in the Mojave Desert. "*I wonder if they have scorpions here.*" I thought as I laced up my boots. I stood up; put on my fatigue jacket; straightened out my sleeping bag; tucked in the mosquito net; slipped into my shoulder harness for my .38; grabbed my flight-helmet bag, chicken plate, and map; and walked down to the operations tent. The sides were down, and as I slid the curtain aside, I noticed that the interior of the tent was brightly lit. I deposited my belongings on a chair and, walking over, poured myself a cup of coffee.

Captain Hasselgrove appeared from behind the map board and said, "Good morning, White. Are you ready for today?"

Smiling, I replied, "It's too early to tell."

"Did they tell you that you can go to the mess tent, and they will fix you early breakfast?" he asked.

68

I replied, "Yes, but I think I'll pass on that this morning. All I really need is a couple of cups of coffee to keep me going. You're going to brief the first-light team in a half hour?"

"Yes," he said and then busied himself preparing for the briefing.

What I didn't say was that I was nervous and a little bit scared. This was going to be my first combat mission, and I didn't know how I would react when and if I was fired at. I didn't want to take a chance of screwing up the mission by being late for the briefing. "*No*," I thought, "*I'll pass on breakfast.*" I noticed that I had butterflies in my stomach and tried to recall that saying "*It's all right to have butterflies. Just get them to fly in formation!*" I smiled to myself as that thought passed through my mind.

Finishing my coffee, I reflected on my preparations last night. Captain Williams had given me his map that had all the fire-support bases and boundaries already posted to it. I had gone back to the flight line and preflighted my aircraft and talked to Captain Maier about his flying with me today. He was going to meet me here for the briefing, and we would fly with the first-light team this morning. I had studied the map last night but could not relate it to any terrain features I had noticed as I flew in yesterday. I knew which fire-support bases we were going to check and the order in which that would be done. I had gone through the SOI and made myself familiar with it.

Captain Williams had explained that the scout platoon call signs were all the one series, i.e., one-one, one-two, etc. The weapons platoon call signs were all in the two series, i.e., two-one, two-two, etc. The Blue platoon call signs were somewhat different. The First Infantry squad was three-one, the Second Infantry squad was three-two, the Third Infantry squad was three-three, and the Fourth Infantry squad was three-four. The Blue Lift helicopters started with three-five and went through three-nine. The infantry platoon leader (on the ground) was Blue, and his platoon sergeant was Blue Mike. The Blue Lift flight leader was three-five.

I finished my coffee and, grabbing my gear, walked to the flight line. As I walked down the slight incline, I could see the flashlights of the other scout pilot and one of the weapons pilots giving a final check of the rotor and mast assembly. I plugged in my helmet, put my flight gloves inside the helmet, and hung it on the hook on the firewall. I placed the chicken plate on the seat and did another check of the fluid levels. Although I had checked everything the night before, I climbed up to check the Jesus nut one more time. I opened the logbook and checked for any entries the crew chief may have made. Satisfied that I was ready to go, I switched off my flashlight and returned to the operations tent.

I don't recall with certainty who was flying on this mission, but I believe it was One-One and Two-Three. Captain Hasselgrove indicated that there was little activity last night, and the only thing we should check was a reported movement in the vicinity of one of the fire-support bases. He gave us the forecast weather and asked if we had any questions. I asked what radio frequency the team would be on. Two-Three turned to me and said, "The way we normally work is the White bird gets tower clearance, I call us off to troop operations, and I make all the spot reports back to operations." Turning to the scout pilot, he asked, "What ultra high frequency (UHF) frequency do you want to operate on?" One-One gave him a frequency, and I wrote it down.

As Captain Maier and I walked to the flight line, I was thinking, "*This is the first time I will be flying a real passenger. I wonder if he realizes that.*"

As we approached the aircraft, I noticed that one of the crew chiefs was standing by the revetment. We exchanged "good mornings," and he said he would ground guide us out of the revetment. Captain Maier and I strapped in; I turned on the rotating beacon, hollered "clear," and started the engine. As the engine came up to operating rpm, I checked my gages, turned on the radios, and tuned them to the correct frequencies.

Everything was in the green, and I turned on my landing light. The crew chief was in front of the aircraft and extended his arms horizontally. I got the helicopter light on its skids, checked everything one more time, and lifted up to a hover. The crew chief started to motion me to back up, and I gently brought the cyclic back and thought once again, "*Man, these revetments are tight.*" As

I cleared the revetment, he motioned me to swing my tail left, and when I lined up with the taxiway, I sat it down.

On the radio, I heard, "Two-Three's up. One-One is up." I pushed my radio switch and said, "White's up."

In a minute, I heard One-One announce, "We're clear to hover." One-One was right in front of me, and Two-Three was up the hill to our left. I saw One-One come to a hover followed by Two-Three. I got on the radio and said, "I'll follow Two-Three out."

Two-Three replied, "Roger." We taxied to the runway and held short.

In a minute, One-One announced, "We're clear to take the active, departing to the south on One-Eight." With that, he turned right and flew down the runway. Two-Three followed, and I was right behind him.

When we climbed to altitude, I noticed that it was getting lighter on the horizon. We climbed to two thousand feet and leveled off in a loose-trail formation. This was the first time I had flown this early in the morning since I had arrived in Vietnam, and it was cold with no doors on the aircraft. As we cleared the perimeter, I heard Two-Three call troop operations on the frequency modulated (FM) radio, "Saber Three, this is Red Two-Three, off at 0602, over."

Troop operations acknowledged the call, and at the same time on the UHF radio, I heard, "One-One, this is Two-Three X-ray [This was the weapons aircraft copilot]. Take up a heading of One Five Zero."

"One-One, roger out."

The weapons aircraft was responsible for navigation to and from the AO. During the mission, one of the weapons aircraft pilots kept track of where the team was at all times. Since there was only one pilot in the scout aircraft, he couldn't look at the map and fly the aircraft at the same time when he was low level.

There was no further radio traffic, so Captain Maier and I talked to each other on the intercom. This was just casual conversation as I queried him about how the troop used artillery and made an observation that it was unusual to have a forward observer (FO) assigned down to troop level.

He replied, "Well, the air cav troops make more contact with the enemy than any other unit in the division. Division headquarters learned when we first deployed over here that if you wanted to employ artillery against 'real targets' [rather than shooting at suspected enemy positions], most of the sightings of the enemy were made by the cav pilots. Therefore, they needed FOs more than some infantry battalion slugging through the jungle who couldn't see more than twenty feet ahead of them."

The sun rose over the horizon, and on UHF, I heard, "One-One, this is Two-Three. I called the fire-support base, and there is no artillery fire. You're cleared to descend and start the mission."

"Two-Three, this is One-One. Roger out."

"White, this is Two-Three, over."

I replied, "This is White, over."

"This is Two-Three. I'm going to drop to 1,500 [feet]; you stay at two thousand, over."

"This is White. Roger out."

One-One and Two-Three started their descent.

One-One flew to about 250 meters from the fire-support-base (FSB) perimeter and started his reconnaissance. With each circle around the FSB, he increased his distance from it. Even from my altitude, I could tell that, on occasion, he was below treetop level and was down in the trees. Occasionally, he would hover over a spot, looking at something on the ground.

In about ten minutes, I heard One-One call Two-Three on UHF, "Two-Three, this is One-One, over."

"This is Two-Three, over."

"Two-Three, this is One-One. I found some old trails but no recent activity. Looks clear to me, over."

"One-One, this is Two-Three, roger. Take up a heading of Two Eight Zero, and I'll inform the FSB we're departing, over."

"This is One-One. Roger out."

One-One stayed low level as he moved out on the new heading. I noticed that during the reconnaissance and even now, Two-Three kept One-One in front of him and appeared to always be in a position to shoot.

We performed the same routine at two more FSBs, finding no recent activity. There was very little radio traffic between the three aircraft as we performed the mission. Captain Maier and I talked on intercom as we flew between the FSBs and learned a little more about each other.

"One-One, this is Two-Three X-ray. Take up a heading of Zero One Zero and let's go top 'em off."

While that conversation was taking place on UHF, I heard on FM, "Saber Three, this is Two-Three, over."

"This is Saber Three, over."

"This is Two-Three. We're departing station at this time, en route to POL [petroleum, oil, and lubricants], over."

"This is Three, roger out."

We were heading for LZ English, our rearm and refueling point. It was a few miles northeast of LZ Two Bits. From my altitude, I could see it in the distance. In a few minutes, One-One was on the radio. "Saber White and Two-Three, this is One-One. We will be landing on One-Eight and are cleared to POL."

Keying my microphone, I said, "This is White. Roger out."

"This is Two-Three. Roger out."

Within minutes, we were on short final to English. As we hovered to our refueling points, I heard Two-Three calling operations on FM.

"Saber Three, this is Two-Three. We're down at POL, over."

"Saber Two-Three, this is Three Mike [This was the operations sergeant]. Roger out."

As I sat it down at the POL point, I reduced the throttle to flight idle, and Captain Maier climbed out of his side of the aircraft and moved to the gas pump. He picked up the gas-dispensing nozzle and allowed some gas to run into a glass jar sitting next to the pump. He picked up the jar, held it up, and looked at the gas in the bottle. He was looking for water in the gas. Not seeing any, he put the bottle down and moved back to the aircraft, dragging the hose with him.

The H-13 had two saddle gas tanks, one on either side of the engine. He climbed up on the skid and opened the fuel-tank locking cap, inserted the nozzle, and started filling the tank on his side of the aircraft. We didn't shut down the aircraft while refueling; this was called hot refueling. He had to make sure that the tank was topped off but, at the same time, had to make sure it didn't overflow onto the hot engine. When he had it topped off, he replaced the locking cap and, moving in front of the aircraft, came to my side of the aircraft, and repeated the process.

As he was replacing the nozzle into its holder next to the pump, I thought, *"He's got that down pat. He kept his sleeves rolled down, gloves on, and kept his visor down. I wonder how many hours he has flying in an H-13. More than my twelve, I'm sure."*

As he climbed in the aircraft, I heard on the UHF, "One-One is up." "Two-Three is up." and I said, "White is up."

"Saber flight, this is One-One. We're clear to hover."

One-One was at the POL point next to me, and Two-Three was down the field from us. The POL point operator stood in front of One-One and raised his arms horizontally. One-One picked it up to a hover and backed away from the POL point. The operator signaled for him to swing his tail to the right, and One-One hovered out of the POL point. It was my turn next, and soon I was behind One-One.

We held short of the runway, and in a minute, I heard on UHF, "Saber flight, we're cleared to take the active, departing on One-Eight."

I keyed my microphone and said, "One-One, this is White, roger, and I'll follow you out."

"One-One, this is Two-Three X-ray. Roger out."

As we cleared the perimeter of LZ English, I heard Two-Three on FM, "Saber Three, this is Two-Three. We're off of English, en route to the barn."

"This is Three. Roger out."

In another minute or two, I heard One-One say, "Saber flight, we are cleared straight into One-Eight." We shot our approach to the end of the runway, turned right, and hovered to our parking spots.

When my postflight inspection was completed, Captain Maier and I walked to the operations tent. The morning briefing was underway, and as I made my way to my chair, I heard Major Beasley say, "We are going to concentrate our efforts today in the southern part of the AO, northwest of LZ Bird." Rising from his chair, he moved to the map and pointed where we were going to work.

"We have picked up a lot of trail activity in this area in the last seven days. Each team that goes out today will concentrate in a four-thousand-square meter reconnaissance box. The three [operations officer] will assign each team their box. Scouts," turning his head and looking at each scout, "pay close attention for any signs of recent activity."

He continued, "Brigade has already cleared us to work this area, and there are no friendlies in or near the box. As far as we are concerned, these are free-fire boxes." Turning to Captain Maier, he asked, "Is there any artillery that can cover this area?"

Captain Maier consulted his map and made a couple of measurements and then said, "No, sir. We'll have to rely on Blue Max." (Blue Max was the call sign for the aerial field artillery [AFA] or sometimes referred to as the aerial rocket artillery [ARA]. They were gunships that carried the maximum amount of seventy-six rockets and were not equipped with miniguns or chunkers.)

Looking at Blue (the infantry platoon leader), he said, "I want you to continue stringing wire around our perimeter here until we determine if we're going to insert you.

"Any questions?" he asked as he looked around the tent.

There were no questions. As he turned to leave, we all stood and came to attention. He went behind the map board, and Captain Hasselgrove started to brief the next reconnaissance team, which was One-Five and Two-Four.

While they were getting briefed, I studied my map and started to relate features I had seen on the ground during the first-light mission to my map. I was starting to memorize certain locations in the AO and their corresponding general map coordinates. I went to the map and transferred the reconnaissance box to my map.

I turned to Two-Four and asked him, "What altitude will you be at when we get to the AO?" He replied as he looked at his map, "Probably around two thousand indicated."

What that meant was that his altimeter, which measured height above sea level, would read two thousand feet, but he would actually be at approximately 1,500 feet above the ground.

"Captain Maier and I will go with you," I said. "I'll stay out of your way and should be near 2,500 indicated."

"Roger that," he said.

We followed the same procedure that One-One and Two-Three had followed on the first-light mission, only this time as we cleared the perimeter, One-Five stayed low level, and I heard Two-Four X-ray on UHF say, "One-Five, this is Two-Four X-ray. Take up a heading of One Nine Zero."

As we entered the reconnaissance box, Two-Four called One-Five, "One-Five, you are entering the box."

"This is One-Five. Roger out."

I watched as he flew his H-13 low level through the box. He was flying from the north to the south and did not slow down on this first pass through the box. As he reached the other side, he turned and flew back to the north and then turned to the west and crossed the box in this direction without slowing down. Since no one had fired at him, I saw that he had noticeably slowed down. As I watched him, it seemed he was casting about, just like a bird dog trying to flush a pheasant or dove.

CPT Chole scouting over the jungle

I was circling over both of them and kept One-Five on my side of the aircraft so I could observe closely. He crossed back and forth across the area several times, and then I noticed that he had come to a hover.

"Two-Four, this is One-Five. I have a fresh trail down here. It looks like five or six people were on it within an hour or two. They are moving south, over."

"One-Five, this is Two-Four. Roger, over."

On the FM radio, I heard, "Saber Three, this is Red Two-Four X-ray. Spot report, over."

"This is Saber Three. Send it, over."

"White One-Five, at 1035 hours, at 09124768, spotted a recently used trail, which appears to have been used by five or six personnel moving south. He is continuing to observe, over."

"This is Three. Roger, over."

"This is Two-Four X-ray, out."

I watched as One-Five hovered down the trail. He was in an area that had no trees, and I could clearly see that he was hovering sideways with the trail on his side of the aircraft. Soon he picked up airspeed and started flying in ever-increasing circles.

"Two-Four, this is One-Five. I lost the trail and am trying to pick it up, over."

"One-Five, this is Two-Four. Roger out."

He had circled the area for about five minutes when suddenly his tail came up, and he did a tight pedal turn to the right.

"Two-Four, you won't believe this! I've got an NVA down here, trying to hide from me. His feet are sticking out from under this bush, and he thinks I can't see him."

As he was talking on the radio, I could hear his machine gun firing and then watched as his observer fired into the bush.

"Two-Four, this is One-Five. One NVA, KIA [North Vietnamese soldier killed in action]. He was wearing green uniform, Ho Chi Minh sandals, was carrying a pack, and had one SKS rifle, over."

"One-Five, this is Two-Four. Roger, over."

"This is One-Five, out."

I noticed that he was working back and forth across the trail and was moving generally toward the south. While he was doing this, I heard Two-Four X-ray send a spot report back to the troop. My adrenaline started pumping, and I kept my eyes glued to One-Five.

Within minutes, his tail jumped up again, and he started to jink left and right as he hauled ass out of the area. I noticed that a red smoke grenade had been thrown from his aircraft and was lying on the ground. "TWO-FOUR, I'M TAKING FIRE, TAKING FIRE!"

"One-Five, this is Two-Four. Stay clear. I'm rolling in hot!"

I watched as Two-Four nosed the aircraft over and started his dive (gun run) on the enemy. Within seconds, two pairs of rockets were on the way. He continued his dive, and then I heard the sound of his minigun kick in. The rockets impacted about thirty feet to the east of the smoke grenade, and now the minigun was chewing up the ground around the impact area. I watched in fascination as Two-Four continued his dive toward the ground. *"Break it off, break it off!"* I thought. At what appeared to me to be the last possible second, Two-Four pulled the nose up and started his climb to altitude. As he was climbing out, I noticed that his crew chief and the door gunner on the other side of the aircraft were leaning out of the aircraft as far as their monkey strap (a strap around their waist anchored to the floor) would allow them. They each had an M-60 machine gun in their hands and were firing free gun (which means it was not mounted on a pedestal) down the side of the tail boom back into the area they had just engaged.

"Holy shit!" I thought. *"I've never seen anything like that before! God, I hope they don't hit the tail rotor."*

As they climbed out, they started to take fire from their left rear. I saw tracers reaching out to claim their victim. Somehow they were not hit.

"Two-Four, this is White. You're taking fire from your left rear!"

"Roger, I see 'em."

At about one thousand feet above the ground, the C-model gunship executed a maneuver I had never seen before. It appeared that he stood the aircraft on its tail and then fell off to his right. If this had been a fixed-wing aircraft, the maneuver would have been a wingover. When the aircraft righted itself, he was once again diving on the enemy position, only this time from the opposite direction. I learned later that the gunship pilots simply called this maneuver "a return to target."

He punched off two more pairs and hosed the area down with his minigun again. This time, when he climbed out, no one fired at him. I heard Two-Four X-ray send a spot report back to troop operations, and at the same time, Two-Four was talking to One-Five on UHF.

"One-Five, this is Two-Four. You're cleared in to check it out."

"This is One-Five. I'm on the way."

"Saber Two-Four, this is Saber Six [Major Beasley, the troop commander], over."

"This is Two-Four, over."

"This is Six. I'm en route to your position. Give me an update, over."

"This is Two-Four. One-Five found a trail that had recent activity. He followed it and killed one NVA. He started taking fire from the southeast, and we engaged the area. Results unknown at this time, over."

"This is Six. Is there an LZ nearby, over?"

"This is Two-Four, roger. We can put 'em in right on top of them."

"This is Six. Roger out."

On the FM radio, I heard, "Saber Three, this is Saber Six. Launch Blue, over."

Saber Three replied, "Wilco (will comply), out."

Those two words, "Launch Blue," initiated a series of actions that had been practiced and honed to a fine edge since the troop had been in Vietnam. As soon as Captain Hasselgrove wilcoed the troop commander's message, he picked up the microphone for the PA system and announced, "LAUNCH BLUE!"

CHAPTER NINE
LAUNCHING BLUE

The first squad (Three-One) of the infantry platoon was stringing more concertina wire on the southwest side of our perimeter. All of the men were stripped to the waist. Four of them were driving pickets into the ground. They had taken two expended 105-artillery canisters and welded handles on them, and they were used to drive the pickets into the ground. One man would hold the picket while the other man would pound the picket into the ground. The remaining four men in the squad were stretching out the concertina wire between the pickets and then securing them to each picket. The squad leader was supervising and helping wherever he was needed. This was hot, sweaty work that required the wearing of heavy leather work gloves to handle the razor-sharp wire. Their weapons, ammunition, and load-bearing equipment were laid out within easy reach as they worked.

Blues and Scouts string Concertina wire

The second-squad leader (Three-Two) was getting a haircut from a Vietnamese barber the troop had hired. He was sitting on some ammo boxes in front of the platoon tent. The rest of the platoon was inside the tent, trying to stay out of the sunlight. Some were cleaning weapons, some were reading or playing cards, and some were asleep.

Captain Burnham (Three-Five) and Lieutenant Chilcoate (Blue) were in the operations tent along with the pilots for the next Pink team (One-Three and Two-Two) that were scheduled for the next mission.

Blue Lift pilots and their crew chiefs had preflighted the aircraft after their last mission the night before. Some of the pilots and crew chiefs were in their tent, and some were on the flight line, performing minor maintenance on their aircraft.

As "LAUNCH BLUE" sounded throughout the troop area, men came bolting out of tents and started running toward the flight line. The first squad dropped the wire and put on their shirts and load-bearing equipment, draped four bandoleers of ammunition and C4 (plastic explosives) on their bodies, grabbed their weapons and helmets, and started hauling ass toward their aircraft. Three-Two ripped the sheet from around his neck, and the ammo boxes went flying as he jumped into the tent to grab his gear. Lieutenant Chilcoate's RTO (Blue Alpha), Specialist Cryster, ran into the tent and, before Lieutenant Chilcoate could say anything, told him, "Three-One is on the way, sir." On the flight line, cowlings were being slammed shut, covers were being pulled off of intake, and exhaust ports and rotor blades were being untied and rotated. Warrant Officer Flanagan started running toward his aircraft, and one of the Blues passing him grinned and said, "You're getting slow, sir."

Before Captain Burnham left the operations tent, Captain Hasselgrove gave him the coordinates for the orbit point. Within three minutes, all of the aircraft were out of their revetments, the Blues were on board, Three-Five X-ray had received departure clearance, and all aircraft had performed their hover checks.

Captain Burnham got on the very high frequency (VHF) radio and said, "Blue Flight, this is Three-Five. We will be departing on runway One-Eight."

As the aircraft turned onto the runway, there was the characteristic drop toward the runway, then a shudder as the heavily loaded aircraft hit transitional lift and started flying toward the end of the runway. They climbed out at five hundred feet per minute.

As they were climbing to their en route altitude, Captain Burnham got on the radio and gave them a briefing on where they were going and what en route altitude and formation they would use to the orbit point.

"Blue Three-Five, this is Red Two-Two on Uniform [ultrahigh frequency radio], over."

"This is Three-Five. Are you with us?"

"This is Two-Two. Roger that. I'm out your right door."

Although Red Two-Two was planning on being a member of the next Pink team, when the Blues were launched, it was troop procedure that a weapons aircraft would escort the lift to and from the insertion. Since he was scheduled to fly the next mission, this was it.

While Blue and Blue Lift were scrambling to get airborne, Captain Hasselgrove was busy on the radio. He called the Third Brigade Tactical Operations Center (TOC) and spoke to the Bravo Troop liaison officer (LNO) and told him we were about to insert the Blues, for him to get permission to insert, to find out who the Ready Reaction Force (RRF) would be, and where they were located. He then called the Second Battalion of the Twentieth Artillery (Blue Max) and had them launch a section of aerial rocket artillery (ARA) to rendezvous with Blue Lift at the orbit point.

While all of this may have seemed complicated to a casual observer, it was the routine way of conducting business for this troop and, on many days, was repeated as many as five times a day. Everyone knew his part in this scenario, and the coordination that was required to make each insertion of Blues flow smoothly was, by this time, quite routine.

One-Five had returned to the area where Two-Four had engaged the enemy force. One-Five was going over the ground very slowly and methodically. Soon he came to a hover, and I heard, "Two-

Four, this is One-Five. You got two of them, and I have a heavy
blood trail also."

As One-Five was talking on the radio, I heard two short bursts
from his observer's machine gun. I thought, "*I guess he's making
sure they stay dead.*"

"One-Five, this is Two-Four. Roger out."

On FM, I heard, "Saber Three, this is Two-Four X-ray, over."

"Two-Four X-ray, this is Three Alpha, over."

"This is Two-Four X-ray. At 1045 hours, at 09114766, White
One-Five observed and engaged one NVA, resulting in one NVA
KIA. At 1050 hours, Red Two-Four, at 09144767, engaged an
unknown number of NVA, resulting in two NVA KIA, over."

"This is Three Alpha. I have good copy, over."

"This is Two-Four X-ray, out."

"One-Five, this is Six. Check out that area you are in for our
LZ."

"This is One-Five. Roger, over."

"This is Six, out."

While Major Beasley was on station, he did not interfere with
the team. It was Two-Four's responsibility to run the insertion and
to brief the incoming Blue Flight and Blue Max. Major Beasley
would brief Blue and tell them what he wanted them to do when
they were on the ground.

"Saber Red Two-Four, this is Blue Three-Five. We are two
minutes from the orbit point, over."

"This is Two-Four, roger. If Blue Max is not here by the time
you are at the orbit point, just orbit, over."

"This is Three-Five, roger out."

Each of the lift aircraft had headsets that were used by Blue
and each squad leader to get briefed by the troop commander
prior to the insertion. The UHF radio frequency was used as the
controlling air-to-air frequency and was monitored by all aircraft
involved in the operation. Blue Lift used very high frequency (VHF)
for communication between the lift aircraft. Blue Max used a
different VHF frequency to communicate between them, but they
were also up on the troop's UHF frequency. The scout aircraft

came up on the Blue FM frequency, so he had communication with them as soon as they were on the ground.

"Saber Two-Four, this is Blue Max One-Six on Uniform [UHF], over."

"This is Two-Four, over."

"This is Blue Max, with a flight of two. We have your lift in sight and are tagging onto the rear, over"

"This is Two-Four. Have you worked with us before?"

"This is Blue Max. Negative, we normally support cavalier [Charlie Troop of the 1-9], over."

"This is Two-Four, roger. Stand by, break. Three-Five, One-Five, and Two-Two, are you monitoring, over?"

"This is Three-Five, over."

"This is One-Five, over."

"This is Two-Two, over."

"This is Two-Four. This will be a four-ship LZ. White One-Five will mark with smoke. Three-Five, your base leg will be one eight zero, and your final approach will be zero nine zero. Land about twenty-five meters short of the tree line. Blue Max, as they turn on final, I want you to dump half your load into the tree line that will be directly in front of them. You should be over Three-Five as he starts his approach. When you have expended half of your load, return to the orbit point and hold. Two-Two, you take the right side, and I will be on the left side. Any questions, over?"

"This is Three-Five. Wilco, out."

"This is One-Five. Wilco, out."

"This is Blue Max. Wilco, out."

"This is Two-Two. Wilco, out."

"Saber Blue, this is Saber Six, over."

"This is Blue, over."

"This is Six. We have killed three NVA in this area. When you move out from the LZ, move out initially on a heading of one-three-five degrees. That should take you to the bodies. Search them, collect all packs and weapons, and follow the blood trail and see if we can catch up to the rest of them. Any questions, over?"

"This is Blue. Negative, out."

"White One-Five, this is Two-Four, over."

"This is One-Five, over."

"This is Two-Four. Go ahead and mark and stay clear."

"This is One-Five. Wilco, out."

White One-Five looked up and, in the distance, could see that Blue Lift was in a diamond formation. Blue Max was above the lead aircraft, and he could see that Two-Two and Two-Four were on either side of the formation well to the rear. He decided he would fly due north and picked up as much speed as he could wring out of his H-13. He told his observer to get ready to pop smoke. His observer grabbed a red smoke grenade off the wire that was attached to his console, pulled the pin, and held his hand out the aircraft. One-Five sped across the LZ and told his observer to drop it.

"One-Five, this is Three-Five. I have red smoke, over."

"This is One-Five. That's affirmative, out."

Blue Flight started their descent and turned on final. The Blue Max aircraft had twenty-four rockets hanging off each side of their aircraft in a rectangular rocket rack. We called that configuration a "hog" gunship. As Blue Lift turned on final, the Blue Max aircraft started their prep. They placed their fire into the tree line directly in front of where Blue Lift was going to land. Forty-eight rockets with ten pounds of explosives in each rocket went off in the tree line.

From my altitude of 2,500 feet, I could hear the explosions as trees fell, and the ground appeared to erupt with fire and smoke. I noticed that Blue Lift was on short final, and the Blues were standing on the skids. On either flank of the formation, Two-Four and Two-Two were walking a line of rockets toward the tree line. I saw the flight do a slight flare and then level. I don't know if they touched down; but the Blues jumped off the skids, ran a few feet, and threw themselves to the ground. I watched as the last rockets from Two-Four and Two-Two exploded.

I thought, "*Shit, they must be within bursting radius of the rockets.*"

In less time than it takes to explain it, I heard, "This is Three-Five, coming out and breaking left." As these words were spoken, Blue Lift was off the ground and turning left.

"One-Five, this is Two-Four. You're cleared back in."

"This is One-Five, on the way, out."

In the various tactics classes I had attended over the years, the concept of violent execution of a plan had been discussed, and I had thought I understood what that meant. Well, now I did understand!

"Two-Four, this is One-Five. The LZ is green [no enemy contact or fire], over."

"This is Two-Four. Roger out."

On FM, I heard, "Saber Three, this is Two-Four X-ray. The Blues were inserted at 1110 hours at I shackle." He then gave their location using the code contained in the SOI. "The LZ was green, over."

"This is Saber Three. Roger out."

As Blue Flight cleared the LZ, the Blues assembled and started moving in the direction of One-Five. One-Five was hovering over the body of the first NVA soldier that had been killed this morning. The Blues searched the body, collected the pack and weapon, and moved on to the other two NVA that had been killed by Two-Four. While the Blues were searching these two bodies, One-Five started to follow the blood trail.

"Two-Four, this is Six. I'm returning to Two Bits, over."

"This is Two-Four, roger out."

Everything had been executed according to the troop's standard operating procedure (SOP), there was no contact on the ground, and in accordance with Major Beasley's earlier conversation with me, I knew he would be back out to relieve Red over the Blues.

I was engrossed in the way the troop conducted this operation. Up to this point, everything appeared to be going the way everyone expected it to go. The violence, death, and destruction were "routine," and everyone appeared to be focused on what was going to happen next.

The question yet to be answered was "Were these three NVA by themselves, or was there a much larger force lurking nearby, ready to kill and destroy the Blues?"

The Blues started moving toward One-Five who had picked up the blood trail once again. I had switched my FM radio over to the Blues' frequency and was monitoring the conversations between One-Five and Blue Alpha.

"Two-Four, this is Red, over."

I hadn't heard anything on the UHF frequency in the last half hour and was jerked back from what was happening on the ground to my cockpit. I then realized that I hadn't checked any of my instruments since the insertion. I quickly scanned the instrument panel and noticed that everything was in the green. It also occurred to me that I hadn't thought about actually flying the aircraft since the insertion; I was just doing it, without consciously thinking of it.

"This is Two-Four, over."

"This heah is Red. One-Three and I are here to relieve y'all. What's going on, hoss?" drawled Red in his inimitable way. Captain Hughes was from Alabama.

Two-Four briefed him on UHF, and I heard One-Five briefing One-Three on FM. Following this exchange of information, the three of us—Two-Four, One-Five, and I—departed station and returned to LZ English where we topped off on fuel and then flew to the troop area at Two Bits.

CHAPTER TEN
THE REST OF THE DAY

As we left the flight line, walking toward operations, I overheard One-Five say to Two-Four, "Man, that was great shooting. You blew one guy's head off, and it looked like you put a rocket right through the other guy's chest."

Two-Four shook his head slightly and turned to look at One-Five. "How many guys have you killed?" he asked. "That was number sixty," replied One-Five. Two-Four did not indicate how many he had killed, but it occurred to me that if One-Five had killed sixty, it meant that in all probability, those sixty people had tried to kill him also. I was thinking of how he had hovered down the trail, knowing that at any second someone could pop up and kill him, and a better understanding of what it took to be a scout started to form in my mind. I looked over at his observer and thought, "*These guys don't have a choice in the matter. They go where their pilot takes them, and they do the actual killing in most cases. There has got to be a lot of trust in their pilot.*"

I went to my tent where I got my washbasin, shaved, cleaned up, and went to the mess hall for lunch. After lunch, I went back to the operations tent and caught up on what was going on in the AO. The Blues were still following the blood trail, and Major Beasley and One-Four were preparing to go out and relieve One-Three and Red over the Blues.

About a half hour after Six and One-Four had taken off, the LNO from the Third Brigade called and informed Captain Hasselgrove, our operations officer, that one of the companies from the First Battalion, Seventh Cavalry had contact and was requesting a Pink team. One-Two and Two-Five were the next team scheduled. Captain Maier and I went with them.

As we arrived on station, I switched my FM radio to the infantry-company frequency and monitored One-Two as he talked to the infantry company commander. Before leaving the troop area, we had coordinated on what UHF frequency we would use on this mission. It was SOP that the Red aircraft would send a spot report to the infantry battalion headquarters and our troop operations every half hour. This required him to change FM frequencies throughout the mission. If he wasn't sending spot reports, he would monitor the frequency of the company we were supporting.

The infantry companies very seldom operated outside the effective range of supporting artillery. Captain Maier was busy checking his map and determining which artillery battery he would call in the event it was needed. Once he had determined which battery he would use, he checked his SOI, got the proper frequency, and, when we had a break in radio traffic, asked to change the FM frequency. I said yes, and he made a communication check with the artillery battery and then switched the frequency back to the infantry company.

I noticed that the first thing One-Two did after he made initial contact with the company commander was to fly over each platoon in the company and verify where the friendlies were.

The lead platoon had engaged an unknown-size force about half an hour before we had arrived on station. The enemy had broken contact, and they wanted help in finding them again. One-Two started working the area immediately to the front of the lead platoon. He kept his airspeed up as he made this initial reconnaissance. Receiving no fire, he slowed his airspeed as he started a very slow and deliberate reconnaissance in front of the platoon.

I continued to monitor the infantry-company command frequency. As One-Two worked his way forward of the company with no contact, the company started to move out. There is no question that having a scout preceding the unit in its movement created a different mindset on the part of the infantry. This type of warfare demanded constant vigilance on the part of everyone. Ambushes, booby traps, and snipers took a very high toll if you were not alert and aware of your surroundings. However, having a scout in front of you and a gunship circling overhead changed the environment. A half hour passed with very little conversation on the radio. Suddenly, I saw the tail of One-Two's aircraft go in the air as he performed a very tight turn to the right.

"Two-Five, this is One-Two. I have a dude down here in black PJs and Ho Chi Minh sandals, over."

"This is Two-Five. Roger, over."

Prior to that moment, I had not paid any particular attention to how Two-Five was covering One-Two. As I assessed the situation, it became crystal clear that Two-Five had selected his orbit point very carefully. The infantry company was moving from the north to the south. One-Two was in front of them, and now I noticed that Two-Five had established a racetrack pattern to the west of One-Two. That meant that if he had to engage the area, he would not be firing over the heads of the infantry or would he be firing into them; rather, he would be firing perpendicular to their axis of movement. This reduced the chances for a short or long rocket falling on our own infantry. In addition, he would have the sun at his back on his first gun run. "*Way to go, Two-Five!*" I thought as I watched him orbit over One-Two.

One-Two called the company commander and gave him a spot report on what he had found. He continued to circle this individual, and then I heard on UHF, "One-Two! You're taking fire from your right rear!"

"This is One-Two, roger. Smoke is out." His nose dipped, and his tail came up as he started hauling ass toward the infantry.

"One-Two, this is Two-Five. Stay clear. I'm rolling in hot!" While speaking these words, two pairs of rockets exploded on the ground where One-Two had been just seconds before.

As he was moving toward the infantry, One-Two was giving a spot report to the company commander. Two-Five executed a return to target and punched off another two pairs of rockets.

"One-Two, this is Two-Five. That ought to stop them firing at you. Go ahead and check it out." One-Two called the company commander and told him that he was going back in to check it out. As he approached the area, he kept his airspeed up as he passed over the area that Two-Five had just shot up. He crisscrossed the area several times then slowed his airspeed as he methodically checked the area.

"Two-Five, this is One-Two. You got one. This guy had a pack, dressed in a brown uniform, and an AK-47. He's dead. I'm going to check on the guy I was looking at, over."

"This is Two-Five. Roger out."

While One-Two was moving toward his new area of interest, he called the company commander and gave him the spot report on the NVA that was killed. As One-Two was searching the area, the infantry company was moving forward toward his location. In about fifteen or twenty minutes, the infantry company reached the location he was working. One-Two led them to the body of the NVA soldier. The body was searched, and the infantry company gathered up the pack, weapon, and ammunition. We had been working over the infantry company for about an hour and a half, and on UHF, I heard, "White, One-Two, this is Two-Five. Time to un-ass the area, folks, and go get a drink for our steeds."

One-Two and I "rogered," and One-Two called the company commander and told him that we were departing. He went on to say that he had enjoyed working with them and, if they needed any more help, to give us a call. We returned to English, topped off, and returned to the troop area.

After I finished my logbook entries and the walk around of the aircraft, I walked up to operations. It was around two thirty in the afternoon, and sweat was rolling off me, and I was thinking, "*It will take a while to get reacclimatized to this type of weather.*"

When I entered operations, I noticed that Major Beasley was sitting in his chair, reading some correspondence. He looked up as I entered the tent and asked me, "How's it going, White?"

Taking my hat off and wiping the sweat from my brow, I said, "It's too damned hot. Did you arrange all of these activities for my benefit, sir?"

He looked at me and, in a very matter-of-fact tone of voice, said, "This is what we do. Day in and day out, sometimes it's busier, sometimes it's quieter." As if to punctuate what he had just said, the radio behind the partition came to life.

"Saber Three, this is Red, over."

"This is Three, over."

"This is Red. Blue is in heavy contact with an unknown-size force at Zero Niner Zero One Four Seven Three Five. Launch a section of Blue Max and the QRF. Have Three-Five bring them out to the original insertion point, over." As Red keyed the mike to send the spot report, we heard him firing rockets, and his door gunners were also firing.

"This is Three. Wilco, out."

"Three, this is Three-Five. I monitored; we're on the way, out."

Captain Burnham (the lift section leader) had coordinated with Captain Hasselgrove when he had returned from the original insertion of the Blues; and he knew the location, frequency, and call sign of the QRF. Within a minute, I heard the lift crank up and depart.

Normally, Blue Lift laagered at a site closest to the QRF PZ. After the Blues were inserted, Blue Lift pilots remained with the aircraft and monitored the troop operation's net with a portable radio communication (PRC) 10. As I was to learn, a lot of days, Blue Lift waited all day without inserting the QRF.

When Red relieved Six on station, One-One was the next scout pilot up. One-Five and Two-Three were the next team scheduled to go to the AO and were in the operations tent when the call from Red came in. When Blue Lift took off, Two-Three ran to his aircraft and took off after Blue Lift to escort them on the insertion. Captain Hasselgrove sent the RTO down to the weapons-platoon tent to get Two-Four ready to go on the next mission.

Captain Hasselgrove then called the brigade LNO and told him to bounce a section of Blue Max and to pass on to the Third Brigade that the Blues were in contact, and we were en route to pick up the QRF. He then switched frequencies and called the infantry battalion that was providing the RRF and alerted them to the fact that the Blues were in contact, and we were en route to pick up the QRF for insertion.

Simultaneously, Major Beasley stood up, turned to me, and said, "Let's go, White. You need to see how we do this, and I need to see what's going on."

As we approached the area, Captain Maier was telling me that a decision would have to be made soon if they were going to follow this up with the insertion of the RRF. If we called for the RRF, then the infantry battalion would take over the operation, and that meant that an artillery battery would have to be relocated so they could support the infantry company. He went on to explain that Major Beasley would make a recommendation to the battalion commander based on what happened within the next hour.

I asked Captain Maier, "Who's responsible for the relocation of the artillery battery?"

He explained that the infantry battalion commander was alerting the brigade that if he put the RRF in, he would need artillery support. The brigade would coordinate with the division G3 who, in turn, would give DIVARTY (division artillery) a "be prepared" order to airlift a battery. They would also issue a 'be prepared' order to the Chinook battalion to get ready to airlift a battery of artillery. The fire-support officer (FSO) at the infantry battalion would coordinate directly with the DIVARTY S3 as to where the battery would be located and about how much time they had to get ready. He went on to explain that another consideration for the infantry battalion commander and the brigade commander was what impact would this have on their current operations. If they put in an artillery battery, they would also put in another infantry platoon or company to provide security for the artillery battery, which would require more lift assets to insert the rifle company. The infantry would go in first to secure the LZ before they put in the artillery.

Listening to this, I thought and then verbalized what I was thinking, "Shit, they'll never get all that coordinated today, let alone in a matter of hours."

Captain Maier looked at me, grinned, and said, "If this were any other division, I would agree with you, but you forget this is the CAV! This is what we do. The brigade and battalion commander knew this was a possibility when they cleared the troop to insert the Blues out here."

Our conversation on that topic ended when we heard Red start to brief Major Beasley on UHF. *"Damn a bear!"* I thought. *"This shit gets complicated."* We had talked and practiced tactics in numerous classes and practiced them in field maneuvers, but I had not really realized how fast-moving airmobile tactics would be. *"Readjust your thinking, Bert. This is a graduate-level war fighting!"*

I had already switched my FM radio over to the Blues' frequency and was monitoring the radio traffic between Blue and the squad leaders. The Blue platoon had followed the blood trail into the tree line where it intersected a trail. The NVA soldier had got on the trail and was moving toward the southeast. Blue had one squad on the west side of the trail, one squad on the east side of the trail, and he and another squad followed to the rear of the squad on the east side of the trail. They stayed off of trails whenever possible because so many of the trails were booby-trapped.

As they advanced into the deeper part of the wood line, the sunlight diffused, and sound became somewhat muted. They would occasionally catch glimpses of One-One as he searched the ground in front of them. They moved cautiously forward. Suddenly, the unmistakable sound of an AK-47 firing shredded the air as the point man of the squad on the east side of the trail came under fire. The squad deployed, and as they moved forward, they too came under fire. Blue took the squad that he was with farther around to the left in an effort to flank the enemy force. As they came abreast of the point squad, a heavy volume of fire was directed at them that halted their movement.

Blue directed the squad on the west side of the trail to move forward about twenty-five yards in an effort to determine the location of the enemy flanks. As this squad moved forward, nervous fingers verified that the selector switch on their M-16 rifles was positioned on full automatic. This squad had moved about ten yards when the point man literally bumped into an NVA soldier as he stepped around a tree. Both men were startled, but the point man of this squad reacted first and pumped around five rounds into the NVA soldier. As the NVA soldier was falling to the ground, the point man caught movement out of the corner of his eye. Whirling to his right, he saw about ten NVA soldiers moving in his direction. They started shooting at him, and he dove for cover behind the nearest tree. Shouting back to the rest of the squad that they had ten NVA moving toward them, he started to engage the enemy soldiers. The rest of the squad moved forward and put down covering fire as the point man moved back to their location.

The enemy had been located; the determination had been made that this was too large of an enemy force for the Blue platoon to kill, and the QRF had been called for. The enemy force on the west side of the trail was maneuvering against the squad on that side, and Blue ordered that squad to withdraw but maintain contact. He then sent one man from the east side of the trail back to act as a ground guide for the QRF.

A single-ship LZ was selected as close to the tree line as possible. The ground-guide Blue had sent back popped smoke to identify the LZ. This time, there was no prep of the LZ. One by one, Blue Lift landed in the LZ and dropped off the infantry platoon QRF.

I noticed from my position overhead that these soldiers did not stand on the skids as they came in for a landing. As a result, it took them ten to fifteen seconds longer than the Blues to unload the aircraft. Once on the ground, the platoon assembled in the tree line and moved forward to join the Blues deeper in the jungle.

The two platoon leaders conferred briefly, and the QRF platoon swept around to the right side (west) since that appeared to be where the heaviest resistance was coming from. As they moved forward, Major Beasley had Red and One-One move about one thousand meters to the southeast of the contact area and act as a blocking force. Within ten minutes, the QRF platoon reported that they were in heavy contact.

While all of these maneuvers were occurring, the RRF had moved into PZ posture, and Blue Lift had returned to the troop area at Two Bits. Blue informed Major Beasley that they had contact with an estimated company-size force. Major Beasley called the brigade S3 and informed him of what we had and recommended that the RRF be inserted ASAP. The brigade S3 said, "Roger. Wait, out." Within a couple of minutes, the S3 was back on the radio, informing Six that the battalion commander would be airborne shortly and to go ahead and select an LZ for the use of the RRF.

Meanwhile, the QRF platoon had come under very heavy fire and requested some gunship support. This was one of the problems associated with operating outside of the supporting-artillery range. While rockets were very effective against troops in the open, unless you changed the fuse setting on the rockets, they were not very effective when shooting through the jungle canopy. When loaded, the fuse setting was always set as point detonating (PD), which meant they exploded when they impacted something solid. When firing through the canopy, very few of the rockets reached the ground before they exploded. While the fuse setting could be changed, it required a manual setting that would require the aircraft to land so this could be accomplished. However, if the rocket could penetrate to within five to ten meters above the ground before they exploded, a lot of shrapnel would be generated and would certainly wound and perhaps kill some personnel. Of course, there was always the psychological advantage of shooting rockets at someone. The noise of the rockets firing, coupled with the explosion, would cause many people to keep their heads down.

Since we had a section of Blue Max on station, they fired in support of the QRF platoon. While this was taking place, the infantry battalion commander arrived in his command-and-control (C&C) helicopter. Major Beasley was in charge of the operation and would remain so until the RRF was on the ground. At that time, command and control of the ground units would transfer to the battalion commander. The line of command and control was very clear-cut, and there was never a question of who was in control during each phase of the operation. When the infantry company was on the ground, by SOP, they would relieve the Blues who would move back to a PZ and be extracted if battle conditions permitted. It was clearly understood by everyone that the mission of the Blues was to conduct ground reconnaissance, locate the enemy, develop the situation, kill the enemy force if possible, and, if not, maintain contact with the enemy until a larger force could be brought in to destroy the enemy. When that mission was complete, they were pulled out and stood by to conduct more ground reconnaissance at another likely site.

While Major Beasley and the battalion commander were discussing the situation, One-Six and Two-One arrived on station and relieved Red and One-One. It was decided that this Pink team would continue to act as a blocking force to the southeast of the contact area.

Captain Maier alerted me that the RRF was arriving. I watched and listened as they inserted the first lift of the RRF. Since we had already cleared the area, this insertion was completed with no preparatory (prep) fires. They secured the LZ until the lift returned with the infantry company weapons platoon, which contained their mortars. By this time, the Blues had sent back a guide to take them to the Blues' position. When the relief of the Blues was completed, Blue called Six and let him know that they were on their way to the PZ. Six called Three and had him launch Blue Lift to come and pick up the Blues. Major Beasley and I then departed station since we were already past the time we would normally stay on station. By the time we arrived at the POL point at English, Six was already ten minutes into his twenty-minute low-fuel light.

After parking the aircraft at Two Bits, Captain Maier and I walked up to operations. Blue Lift had dropped off the Blues and was still at English, topping off. I was talking to Lieutenant Chilcoate (Blue) about the mission, and he casually mentioned that in another couple of days, he was returning to the States. I asked him who was going to replace him, and he said he thought Lieutenant Johnson from Blue Lift. I talked a little bit with Captain Hasselgrove and then turned my attention to my map. I spent a good deal of time trying to associate features on the ground that I had observed all day to their map features and locations. Before I realized it, it was time to eat supper and then attend the nightly briefing.

As the briefing started, I thought, "*This could be last night's briefing.*" We followed the same procedure, sat in the same seats, and listened as Major Beasley told us where we were going to concentrate on tomorrow. Following the briefing, I went to the operations chart and posted it for tomorrow's missions, by moving the guy on top today (One-One) to the bottom of the list for tomorrow and moved everyone else up one space. During the briefing, it occurred to me that I had not checked with the platoon line chief (acting sergeant Artimisi) about what the platoon maintenance status was before the briefing, and I had not preflighted my aircraft before it got dark. I would not forget that again.

I returned to the platoon tent and conducted my own meeting with the platoon and then sat down on my bunk. As I sat there, fatigue washed over me, and I realized that I had flown more today than any single day during flight school or my checkout in the OH-13. I had flown 7.6 hours today, and it felt like it. I was tempted to take off my boots and just lie down and go to sleep but decided against it. I undressed; grabbed some clean shorts, a towel, and wash cloth; and, stepping outside the tent, moved to the shower point that was near the back of the tent.

The shower point consisted of a canvas bag with a showerhead on it suspended from two poles. Sitting next to it were several five-gallon water cans that had been heated by the sun during the day. I hefted several of them until I found one that still had some water in it. I poured what was in the can into the canvas bag and soaked myself, then turned off the water (by twisting the showerhead), and soaped myself up. I noticed that a slight breeze was blowing, which had felt very good when I walked outside; but now that water was starting to evaporate from my body, I was getting chilled. I rinsed and toweled myself dry and felt better than I had since my arrival. Boy, that shower felt good!

I lay down on my bunk and, securing the mosquito net under the air mattress, stretched out on top of the sleeping bag. Clasping my hands behind my head, I lay there and reviewed all that I had experienced today. I replayed several things in my mind:

- *They really have their shit in one rucksack. Thirteen years in the army and I've never been in a unit that conducts tactical operations as well as this troop does. It is amazing how everyone knows what to do without being told, and yet, I don't believe they have a written SOP, or if they do, no one has told me about it.*
- *Adrenaline was pumping through everyone's veins; you could tell that from the sound of their voices, but they were cool under fire. In fact, it was hard to tell from the sound of some of these guys that anyone was trying to kill them.*
- *They seem to kill with detachment. Will I be able to do that? Can I do that?*
- *Everyone responds to Major Beasley. There's a difference when he is in the area. He gives the impression that everything is under control and that it is going just the way it's supposed to be going. At the same time, everyone but Red seems somewhat hesitant around him. Is it that they fear his criticism, or is it that they don't want to disappoint him? Well, I will learn more about that the longer I am here.*
- *They don't hesitate to shoot. They kill people so matter-of-fact, so deliberately, so quickly. Can I do that?*
- *There is a rhythm and tempo on the battlefield. I could feel it today. Understanding the flow of operations and how long it takes to get artillery and gunship support are important. Anticipating decisions you will be required to make, understanding the basic operating procedures of our own unit and the units that will be called upon to support our operations— all of these are important, and all of these are handled extremely well by the guys in this troop.*
- *What was it that Major Beasley and Captain Maier said? This is the CAV! This is what we do.*

And with that thought, I dozed off to sleep.

CHAPTER ELEVEN
LEARNING CONTINUES

From July through September, I learned to be a scout and an effective combat leader. There was so much compressed into those three months that it is difficult to choose what to write about because it was filled with excitement, learning, laughter, and one of the most tragic days of my life.

Following the first day of combat operations with the troop, I settled into a routine for the next few weeks where I flew from six to seven hours a day. I was following the advice of Joe Rawl to "get a hundred hours before you go low level." This was difficult for me to do because I was the scout platoon *leader*. All of my trainings and desires were to be with the scouts and to *lead by example*, which, of course, dictated that I go low level and share the risk they were taking. I couldn't lead the scouts by example if I was flying at a safe two thousand feet of altitude. However, I do listen to advice and, occasionally, even take it and apply it. I was convinced that the advice he had given me was sound and, in retrospect, believe it was the best piece of advice I received in two tours in Vietnam. I believed so strongly in it that I required each new scout pilot to do exactly the same thing. This was not good news for Captain Maier because he was always stuck flying with the "new guy."

In addition to learning what the H-13 would and wouldn't do, I was given an opportunity to observe each of my scouts in action. I also learned the troop's standard operating procedures (SOP). They did the things they did the way they did them because through trial and error, they had discovered what worked. The sequence, the routine, the method, the frequency with which we did—all of these made everything predictable for each member of the team.

We also knew that if we got shot up or shot down, every member of the troop would do everything he could to get us to safety. We knew that! Our focus and priorities were our crew, our platoon, and then the troop. I don't recall any conversations about why we were in Vietnam or the correctness of that policy. We were focused on doing our job and surviving. To be honest about it, our concern went no further than the troop or to whoever we were working with on that particular day.

Within a day or two of arriving at Two Bits, I flew my first mission in the An Lo Valley. The An Lo Valley was, as the name suggests, located between two mountainous ridgelines to the west of Two Bits. The villagers who lived in the valley had all been relocated, and the entire valley had been declared a free-fire zone. This meant that any Vietnamese we found in the valley was automatically Vietcong (VC) or a part of the North Vietnamese Army (NVA). There were no "friendly" people left in the valley.

We conducted a lot of missions in the An Lo Valley. During these first few weeks, I went on most of the missions. Captain Maier and I would fly at about two thousand feet, staying out of everyone's way, and occasionally, Captain Maier would shoot some artillery in support of the troop. At that altitude, we were well out of small-arms range, and I had plenty of time to concentrate on how the troop functioned. I was usually very relaxed as we bored these holes in the sky. It was on one of these missions that I received my biggest scare while in Vietnam.

We were circling over the Blues, and I had commented that we were picking up some turbulence every time we passed over the narrowest part of the valley, which was immediately below. It was something that was present but of no concern because it was there one second, and we flew out of it the next second. Suddenly, without warning, we were thrown toward the heavens and were increasing our altitude in excess of one thousand feet a minute. I lowered the collective with no impact on our ascent. I bottomed the collective, thinking, *"This will surely stop this meteoric rise."* It didn't. Suddenly, we lurched over to the right, and Captain Maier involuntarily grabbed the top of the doorframe. He felt as if he were being thrown out of the aircraft! I pushed the cyclic as far to the left as I could, again with no impact. I had lost all control of the aircraft, and it seemed to me that in another second, we were going to invert and be completely turned over. Adrenaline shot through every fiber of my body, and my heart rate skyrocketed. At the same time, everything seemed to move in slow motion. I glanced at the altimeter and noted that the hand was winding up faster than I had ever seen, and we were passing through 5,500 feet. It ended as abruptly as it began, with the aircraft suddenly pitching over to the left and us falling like a rock toward the ground; I moved the cyclic back to the right, and this time, the aircraft responded. Trained reflexes took over to level the aircraft; and an instrument scan showed we were dangerously close to stalling out as our forward airspeed had bled off to practically nothing, and we were in a steeper nose high attitude than any helicopter I had seen and still be flying. "*Level, trim, power,*" I said to myself as I struggled to get the aircraft under control. I pushed the nose over with the cyclic and slowly pulled the collective up and added power. Our descent had stopped, and we were flying normally.

I glanced over at Captain Maier who had visibly blanched and who was still hanging onto the doorframe. "What happened?" he asked.

"Beats the shit out of me," I responded.

Of course, what had happened was that we had flown into a thermal updraft with a velocity that you would expect to find in a thunderstorm. All that I knew at that moment was that I had had absolutely no control over that aircraft for more than a minute, and it terrified the shit out of me. Writing about it all these years later still elevates my heart rate.

There are several matters that stick in my mind about those first two weeks with the troop. I had noticed that there was a degree of familiarity between the enlisted men and the officers in the platoon that was unacceptable to me. I had served twelve years as an enlisted man, and there were certain standards of conduct that were acceptable and others that were not. I had been raised in an army where officers were expected to lead and set the example in all military matters. As an enlisted man, I expected certain things from the officers over me. I expected them to know their job; I expected them to set a good example on duty and off duty; I expected them to be technically and tactically proficient; I expected them to set and enforce standards; I expected them to look after their men particularly in the area of pay, family, mail, and food; I expected them to be able to make decisions (lead, follow, or get the hell out of the way); I expected the same respect from them that I gave to them. I did not want or expect to be their buddy. In fact, every new lieutenant who told me, when I was a sergeant, that he wanted me to call him Joe or Frank or whatever was embarrassed when I told him that "his job was to lead the platoon, not try to win a popularity contest." He was no longer in college; he was in the army.

There was, and as far as I am concerned shall always be, a gap that should not be bridged between an officer and an enlisted man. An officer who wants to be one of the "guys" does not understand that his rank is *always* a factor. He cannot take it off and expect the men he leads to forget he is an officer. It doesn't work that way. His men, for good or bad, are always judging him. There is a truism "Familiarity breeds contempt." As far as I was concerned, it did. The danger every leader faces when he decides he will disregard his position and rank and become "one of the guys" is that he exposes his faults and weaknesses. If you decide to party with "the guys" and can't hold your liquor, there is nothing dignified about you with your head in a toilet bowl. "The guys" wink and point at you and say, "That is our leader?" I could recount example after example of similar incidents, and many of them are far worse than this example. Everyone makes mistakes, everyone has weaknesses; but if you choose to willfully expose your faults to the soldiers you are supposed to be leading, then they will soon question your ability to lead, and you will have deserved their contempt.

I assembled the platoon about the third or fourth night and told them that enlisted men calling officers by their first name would not be tolerated. I paused to measure the impact my words were having, if any. I noticed that my little pronouncement was going down sideways with some of the people—officers and enlisted alike. One of the men spoke up and said, "Sir, my pilot and I share the same dangers every day. We depend on each other, we look out for each other, and I consider him my friend. I know you are new to aviation, but, sir, it is different with aircrew members."

I thought, "*No, son, it isn't. We will order you to do things you don't want to do and take you places you don't want to go. Discipline and a strong chain of command are essential in any army if that army is to win the war it is fighting. You lose discipline, weaken the chain of command, and lose soldiers by ignoring this time-proven principle.*"

I did not intend to debate the issue, and I responded by saying, "I understand that your previous platoon leaders have allowed this practice to go on, but I do not intend to allow it to continue. Does everyone understand the policy?"

I did not delude myself by thinking that this was going to be accepted easily by everyone. First of all, I was the new guy, what the hell did I know? I hadn't proven that I knew what I was doing or that I understood what they were up against. I am sure that some also thought that worse luck for them, I would probably never go low level, and they would be stuck with me for the whole tour. For me, this was an important issue that had to be resolved early.

Another matter, more important than the way we addressed one another, was the issue of armor plating. Huey aircraft all had armor-plated seats that the pilot and copilot sat in. They had protection from small-arms fire from the rear and the side. The H-13 was an aircraft from the fifties and had not been designed with armored protection in mind. There were no individual seats in an H-13. The pilot and his observer sat on a bench seat that extended the width of the aircraft. A piece of armor plating had been designed that was placed on the bench seat and protected the pilot and observer from small-arms fire from below. It didn't offer as much protection as the Hueys did, but hey, it was better than none at all. At any rate, I had noticed that the pilots were taking the armor plating from one aircraft and transferring it to their aircraft before they took off. When I asked why they were doing that, they informed me that we only had four sets of armor plating for the entire scout platoon. We had ten H-13s in the platoon and eight pilots. I was informed that the armor plating was on requisition. I checked all the logbooks, and sure enough, there was an entry that indicated that the armor plating had been ordered, but I noticed that some of these had been ordered over a year ago. I checked with Warrant Officer Larry Kohler, who was our maintenance officer, and asked for a status on these requisitions. He checked and discovered that we had no valid requisitions at our supporting maintenance and supply headquarters. We ordered another six sets of the armor plating, and I checked with Mr. Kohler every week until we received all of them.

During my first week as Saber White, a warrant officer by the name of Larry Brown came to see me one evening and indicated that he wanted to transfer out of Blue Lift and become a scout pilot. When I asked him why he wanted to do that, he told me, "I want more action." He explained that a lot of the time, they just sat around, waiting for the Blues to be inserted or extracted. Little did either of us know at the time what that conversation would lead to. He ultimately became our superscout; and over the years, we have briefly entered and exited each other's lives, and it has been a lifelong, warm, and rewarding friendship.

Captain Robert Rice and First Lieutenant Louis Porrazzo were my section leaders. Captain Rice and I had gone through flight school together, and although we had two very different personalities and did not "run" together during flight school, we genuinely liked and respected each other. If there was ever a man that could bring order out of the chaos of battle, it was Bob Rice. I used to marvel at how he could arrive on station over a raging battle and calm everyone down to the point where rational decisions could be made. His slight Texas drawl and demeanor on the radio exerted a mystical influence that soon brought order out of chaos.

Lieutenant Porrazzo was an infantry officer who had gone to flight school and ended up in this scout platoon as a section leader.

He was a hard-charging young man who knew what he wanted from life. He was going to make a career of the army and wanted to provide the best for his wife and soon-to-be child. He was very animated and full of enthusiasm for whatever he was called upon to do. When he focused on some problem or project, he was intent. He was an outstanding leader and scout pilot who truly looked out for the welfare of his men. I liked him from the first conversation we had, and in the next few months, our senior-subordinate relationship developed into friendship.

On 19 July, I logged over a hundred hours in the H-13 and decided that it was time to go low level. By this time, Larry Brown had been transferred to the scout platoon from Blue Lift, and he became the official pilot for Captain Maier. I kept the policy of the newest scout pilot being designated as Captain Maier's pilot until I left the scout platoon. I am convinced to this day that it was that policy that allowed us to have such a low death rate in the scout platoon. Several of the scouts were wounded, but none were killed while I was the platoon leader.

Since I was now going to be a "scout," I needed an observer. Sergeant (E5) John Larensen was selected. He was a quiet young man about my height, build, and weight. It is difficult to remember all of the details about Sergeant Larensen since he and I spent a relatively short period of time together as crew members. As I recall, he was new to the platoon, having come from division G4. He had extended his tour by six months so he would be eligible for a three-month early discharge from the army. The available scout observers probably had a drawing, and whoever received the shortest straw was elected to be my observer. Believe me when I tell you that no one wanted to fly with a new guy.

The night before, I had placed myself on the roster of rotation in the operations tent. As I recall, I believe I was going to fly the third mission that day. The mission that came up was to fly a reconnaissance in the northern part of the AO along the coast of the South China Sea.

I had not been in this part of the AO before. Prior to departure, I studied my map to get an idea of terrain features and general direction from the troop Area. I don't recall who was flying as the high bird, but as we cleared the perimeter, he gave me the heading to follow. As we passed over a rice paddy, I called and informed him that we were going to test fire the M-60. I told Sergeant Larensen to fire a burst, which he did. It functioned just fine.

We were flying toward the recon box, and I thought, "*Well, now we will find out if I can cut it. It is different flying low level; you really see what is here. I'm only a foot above the rice paddy. This is damn near like being an infantryman except we move faster and should be harder to hit.*" Another part of my mind added another thought, "*Yes, but you can't drop down behind a log, a tree, or get in a hole when they start shooting at you.*"

Pushing that thought aside, I concentrated on observing for any signs of enemy activity and paying close attention to what was going on around me. I also found that this type of flying was exhilarating. Within minutes, we were at the coast. We were to do a general area recon along the coast. It had been reported that the North Vietnamese were using this stretch of the coast as a resupply point, and there were supposed to be some caves along the coast that served as cache points. I started my search pattern across the recon box. I kept my airspeed up to about sixty knots on my first couple of passes through the area. I did not notice anything that looked suspicious. I encountered moderate turbulence on the bluffs that overlooked the sea, which caused some concern. So I flew a little higher to give myself a larger margin for error in case one of the wind gusts pushed me toward the ground. We spent about half of our available time searching along those bluffs; and either the enemy wasn't there, or my inexperienced eye could not detect them. We spent some time looking over a village located near the coast, and I noticed several males dressed in black PJs, working the fields near the village. I flew over to them and circled around each of them. As I approached each of them, the downwash from my rotors caused them to reach up and grab their hat (made of straw and conical in shape). One of them looked up at us as we circled him and smiled. Neither of the other two looked at us as we circled them. If I had been more experienced, the one that looked up and smiled at us would have received more attention. However, at this stage of my development, I noticed nothing suspicious.

I called the high bird and told him I didn't see anything to report. He rogered, and in a couple of minutes, he called and told me it was time to head for the barn. As we started back for the troop area, I noticed that I had a death grip on the cyclic. I hadn't noticed just how tense I had become as we performed the recon.

Each day for the next few weeks, I performed several recon missions, and I found nothing. During this same period of time, it appeared to me that everyone else was able to find the enemy as we continued to have contact on virtually a daily basis, and I was starting to be concerned about my ability to find the enemy. When I asked the other scouts how they knew that the guy they were looking at was a VC or NVA when he was dressed just like every other farmer in the field, their response was always the same.

"You just know it."

"Give me a break," I would say. "There has got to be something that alerts you to look a little closer at particular people."

"Well, first of all, they are military-age males, they have close-cropped haircuts, and they are wearing Ho Chi Minh sandals [sandals made from vehicle tires]." Sarcastically, I would say, "Hell, that describes half the population of Vietnam. What makes you suspicious of one guy and not another?"

"White, I don't know what to tell you, White. I just know it when I look at one of them."

What was frustrating to me was their inability to pinpoint how they, with such unerring accuracy, were able to isolate the NVA and VC dressed as civilians. What I didn't know was that they couldn't describe what they weren't consciously aware of. What I learned as I became proficient in detecting these personnel myself was not found at a conscious level but rather at a subconscious level. It might have been the way they looked at you—or didn't look at you. It might have been the way they walked. It could have been their posture. It could have been a slight bulge around their middle. It could have been a hundred things that on a conscious level didn't register. But our mind is constantly processing the input it receives at a subconscious level, and suddenly, you are drawn to one individual. If asked why this one and none of the others, you can only say, "I just know."

I hadn't passed the real test of my reaction to a firefight yet, but daily, I was learning what it was to be a scout pilot. I was learning to be very observant and to pay attention to what was present and what was missing on the battlefield. I discovered that you could see and follow footprints from the air, and I don't know why that surprised me, but it did. I noticed on the first-light missions that in the early-morning hours, with dew on the grass, anyone walking through the grass left a trail as bold as a yellow-painted stripe on a highway. I was also learning how innocent civilians reacted when we flew around them. Each day that passed, I learned more of what it took to be a good scout pilot.

During these first few weeks, true to his word, Major Beasley had me fly with Blue Lift and the Red platoon, and I went on the ground with the Blue platoon. There was still a lot to learn.

CHAPTER TWELVE

GETTING EXPOSED TO THE
OTHER TWO PLATOONS

The nightly briefing ended with Major Beasley telling Captain Hughes (the Red's platoon leader) and I that the next day I was going to fly as copilot with the Red platoon. I don't remember the name of the pilot or crew members I flew with the next day, but I do remember several aspects of that mission. The first of these was the size of the rotor blades that were used on the C-model Huey. These, as I recall, were called 540 rotors, and in comparison to the rotor blades used with the H-13 or the D-model Huey, they were huge and appeared to be half the size of a barn door. As we were hovering toward the runway, I recall the pilot mentioning that "on some days, when the DA [density altitude] is pretty high, we have to bounce these ships off the runway to get airborne."

I looked at him and said, "You literally bounce them off the runway?"

"Yes," he said. "As we start to take off, we fly off our ground cushion before we hit transitional lift, hit the runway, and bounce back in the air and into transitional lift."

Shaking my head, I thought, "*I'm glad I don't have to worry about that.*" Little did I realize that I would also have to do the same thing to get airborne when we had a high DA. (Density altitude was a combination of barometric pressure and temperature. High temperature coupled with high-pressure systems makes the air less dense). While we were sitting at sea level, on a high-density-altitude afternoon, our aircraft would perform as if we were flying at five thousand to nine thousand feet above sea level, i.e., sluggish and the rotors had less lift.

Prior to takeoff, we had reviewed all the switches that were required to arm the aircraft, and he explained what my job would be today. Primarily, I was to observe and would do a little flying. My prime function would be to do the navigating and make the spot reports back to troop operations. He would do the shooting, but in the event he was wounded or killed, he made sure I knew how to operate everything.

In addition to the pilot and copilot, the crew consisted of a door gunner and the crew chief. Each of these men was armed with an M-60 machine gun and, unlike their counterparts in the lift battalions, were not restrained by having to mount their machine guns on pedestals. Our crew chiefs and door gunners were trained to fire at the enemy in "free gun" mode. They fastened a belt around their middle (called a monkey strap) that was fastened to the floor and allowed them to literally hang outside the aircraft as they fired at the enemy. They were an additional set of eyes on either side of the aircraft and, of course, were able to place very effective fire on any enemy force firing on the aircraft from below or from the rear.

The pilot discussed how difficult it was to see the scout and mentioned that one of their biggest fears was losing sight of a scout just when the scout needed fire support. He assured me that if he ever lost sight of a scout, he would immediately call on the radio and let the scout know that he had lost him. He mentioned that one of his big complaints with the scouts was their unwillingness to get out of the way during a firefight. He also pointed out the characteristic "lift" of the scout's tail boom when they turned suddenly. "That," he said, "was a warning that they had found something unusual, and more than likely, it was an enemy soldier or a fresh trail. We always have to be in position to shoot."

I flew about two more missions with the crew that day and didn't fire a round. Within a few more days, I was flying with Blue Lift.

I was assigned to Warrant Officer Tom Maehrelein's aircraft as his copilot for the day. Mr. Maehrelein was eighteen or nineteen years old at the time and, like all young men of that age, was convinced he was immortal. He had picked up the nickname "Wonder Wart Hog" because it appeared he was always reading a comic book by the same name. A story was circulating within the troop that on one occasion, the flight was going into a hot LZ (a hot LZ is a landing zone from which you are receiving enemy fire), and Mr. Maehrelein was reading a comic book on short final into the LZ. Normally, the copilot would be poised to take the controls in the event the pilot was shot during the landing. At any rate, the day I was flying with Blue Lift, the Blues were to be inserted into the An Lo Valley.

After we took off, we formed up in a trail formation and proceeded toward the valley. We were flying at about one rotor-disc separation from the aircraft in front of us, and I commented that this was a lot closer than we flew formation in flight school.

"Close! This isn't close," he said. "I'll show you how we normally fly formation." We slowly—but very deliberately—closed up on the aircraft in front of us. Since we were flying slightly higher than the aircraft in front of us, it was possible to overlap their aircraft with our rotor. We inched closer, and I noticed that our main rotor was now overlapping the tail rotor of the aircraft in front of us. I thought to myself, *"Now that he has proven what an outstanding pilot he is, we will back off."* We kept inching closer to the aircraft in front of us, and now the tail rotor of the aircraft in front of us was only about three feet in front of our aircraft. *"This is crazy,"* I thought.

"Back off," I said. He was concentrating on flying, but I noticed a small smile tug at his lips. "Well, sir, I was just trying to show you what a close formation was." He slowly let the aircraft in front of us pull away until we had about one rotor-disc separation. I was pissed and apprehensive at the same time. At about this time, Three-Five came up on VHF and gave us the preinsertion briefing. We did one turn at an orbit point and started our descent into the LZ.

I got on the controls with my feet resting on the pedals, my left hand resting on the collective, and my right hand lightly on the cyclic. We turned on to short final into the LZ, and Blue Max started their prep by firing half of their load of rockets into a hedgerow that was located directly to our front. I could feel the concussion of the rockets as they were exploding in front of us. I watched the flight leader (Captain Burnham) as he flew a steady approach to his touchdown point. The flight leader made all the difference in how smoothly an insertion went. He was shooting an approach to the ground and flew it down the wire to the spot he had selected. He was bleeding off airspeed at a steady rate and did not change his angle of approach.

I noticed that the Blues on the two ships in front of us were standing on the skids. I looked over my left shoulder and noticed that our Blues had also moved out onto the skids. My head swiveled to the front as I heard and felt explosions going off much closer to us. Our two weapon ships were firing rockets on either side of the formation as we touched down. The explosions, the dust, and the smell of cordite filled the air, and on the radio, I heard, "Three-Five coming out, breaking right." All four helicopters lifted as one, and we followed the leader back to altitude.

Just prior to touchdown, I felt our helicopter shake a little bit, and then I realized that our Blues had jumped from the aircraft just prior to touchdown. We couldn't have been on the ground more than ten seconds. "*That,*" I thought, "*is what practice will do for you.*" Everyone knew what to do and knew what to expect from everyone else. "*Man, these guys are good!*"

Several months later, Mr. Maehrelein performed one of the most daring rescues, one that was truly above and beyond the call of duty, and shrugged it off as if he did it every day. During the Battle of Hue, one of our gunships was shot down in the middle of an NVA battalion attacking Hue. The crew had been captured and was being marched away. He shot an approach to the two men nearest his aircraft all the while drawing an incredible amount of enemy fire. As he descended, the door gunners started shooting the NVA soldiers below them. As he came to a hover near one the soldiers, the door gunner shot the NVA soldier, and the crew member ran to the helicopter and jumped in. Picking it up to a hover, he flew toward the other soldier; and again, the NVA soldier who was holding the crew member hostage was shot, and the soldier ran toward the helicopter and jumped in. By now, a battalion of NVA soldiers was shooting at his aircraft. He coolly picked it up to a hover and started flying toward the remaining two crew members. The NVA saw him coming toward them. They turned and shot both of the men, killing them. Mr. Maehrelein continued flying toward them as the door gunners killed the NVA. He then landed next to the body of the pilot and waited while the crew chief drug his body to the helicopter. He then hovered over to the other body and waited while his body was hoisted onto the aircraft. All the while, he and his crew were the target of every NVA soldier in or near this clearing. He flew out of there and returned with the men to the Phu Bai base. His reaction and demeanor was very low-key, but for the rest of us, it was a reminder that we left no one behind. He truly is one of my personal heroes from a group of men who were all heroes.

Near the end of the month, I went on the ground with the Blues. By this time, Lieutenant Chilcoate had rotated home, and Lieutenant Billy Johnson had taken his place as the platoon leader. This was to be a temporary assignment for him since he was due to rotate soon. We all felt that by the time he was to rotate, we would have an infantry lieutenant, who wasn't a pilot, to take his place.

Our first insertion that day was to check out a bunker that one of the scouts had spotted. The scout had said that it showed signs of recent use. As we were on short final into the LZ, the by-now-familiar sequence of events was occurring. Rockets were exploding in front of us and on either side, and the Blues had moved out on the skids. I hesitantly joined them and thought, *"A guy could get killed doing this shit."* At about one foot off the ground, everyone jumped off the skid and immediately bent over and moved away from the helicopter. I followed suit, and by the time I straightened up, Blue Lift was airborne and on the way out of the LZ.

On final into an LZ being prepared by our gun ships.

Short final, into the smoke and cordite.

Blues on the ground, Green LZ.

Lieutenant Johnson was with the squad in front of us, and as we moved off the LZ, he made a communication check with each squad. I was with the third squad and fell into my position in the staggered column we used as we moved into the underbrush around the LZ. Having spent ten years in the infantry as an enlisted man, I knew what my job was. We soon moved into an area that had been hit with air strikes at some previous time. Trees were blown down and lying in a haphazard manner, which forced us to climb over, under, or around them. Within a half hour of being inserted, my uniform was completely drenched with sweat. "Wait-a-minute vines" entangled my feet and arms as we slowly moved up the hill. The heat was oppressive out here in the small clearing we were crossing, and I once again thanked God for the decision to get out of the infantry branch and transfer to armor branch.

The scout was flying back and forth in front of us and, occasionally, would fly a circle around us, and at altitude, the omnipresent gunship was keeping an eye on all of us. We had been moving forward about forty-five minutes when Lieutenant Johnson called a halt. He walked back to where I was and asked, "How's it going, sir?"

I smiled at him and said, "If it got any better, I couldn't handle it."

He laughed, whipped out his pocket camera, and said, "I have to have a picture of this. Saber White humping it with the Blues!" We talked for a few more minutes, and he told me that the scout said we were about ten to fifteen minutes from the bunker. He walked back to the squad ahead of us, and we started moving out.

CPT Chole (Saber White) humping it with the Blues.

There was not much talking as we moved forward. I noticed that everyone seemed to keep the proper distance from one another, and while they weren't tense, they were very alert. I was searching the sector to our left and trying to see and hear everything that went on around us. "*Wouldn't it be ironic,*" I thought, "*if the first firefight I was in occurred on the ground and not in the air!"* When we reached the bunker, Lieutenant Johnson deployed the platoon around the bunker. He motioned me over to where he was standing at the edge of the bunker and said with some disgust in his voice, "Does this look like recent activity to you, sir?"

I looked into the bunker and noticed some dry leaves piled up at the entrance. It was obvious that this bunker hadn't been used in a long time. I looked around the immediate area and could detect no signs of recent occupation or use. I said, "Nope, it doesn't look like it has been used recently."

He vented a little bit about what a waste of time this was and that the scouts should get their shit together and know what recent activity looked like. I made no attempt to defend the scout platoon as it was obvious that this was a waste of time. He got on the radio and sent a spot report to the Red bird and asked where the nearest PZ was located. He got the platoon moving toward the PZ, and in another half hour or so, we moved into a clearing and got set up to be extracted.

I watched as each squad spaced themselves into the trail formation that Blue Lift was going to use on the extraction. Our squad split itself in half—with four men on one side and three of us on the other side—with about fifteen feet separating us. Each squad was separated in depth from the squad in front of it and in back of it by about twenty to thirty feet. As we waited for the lift to arrive, we all faced to the outside, observing the distant tree line. In a few minutes, we heard the unmistakable sound of a group of Hueys letting down from altitude. I looked to our rear and saw them turn on final. At the same time, each squad leader stood up in front of the squad and held his M-16 over his head horizontal to the ground. Each pilot knew which squad he was going to pick up and shot his approach to that squad leader. The Blues had done this so many times the spacing between the aircraft looked like it had been measured off with a yardstick. As the aircraft was settling to the ground, we jumped up and ran to the aircraft and climbed on board.

Put it here (Squad Leader designating landing point for his bird).

We sat on the seats and, within seconds, were airborne. None of us had seat belts fastened, and as we banked to the left coming out of the PZ, I momentarily had a vision of me sliding out the open door and falling to the ground. Centrifugal force held us in place, but I thought, "*You'd never do this in peacetime.*" As we climbed to altitude, the air outside got cooler, and it felt great. I pulled off my helmet, mopped my brow, and heaved a sigh of relief. I was thinking of the lister bag (a canvas bag filled with water that used the natural process of evaporation to cool the water inside the bag) hanging next to the flight line and how good that water was going to taste.

The crew chief handed the squad leader a headset as the aircraft banked, and it was apparent to me that we were not returning to Two Bits. It appeared we were flying to the southern part of the

AO. We were inserted a total of three more times that day, and at the end of the day, I was one whipped puppy. The heat and the adrenaline had taken it out of me, and as I dragged my body up the hill to operations, I reflected on how I used to be able to do things like this all day long. A voice inside said, *"Yeah, and you were ten to twelve years younger."*

CHAPTER THIRTEEN
FIRST KILL

Several weeks after I started to fly low level, Sergeant Larensen and I had just completed a last-light mission. We refueled at LZ English, had cleared the perimeter, and were en route to Two Bits. Our Red bird was over us, and we were looking forward to calling it a day.

We were zipping along over some rice paddies between English and Two Bits when I noticed one individual dressed in black PJs, coolie hat, and Ho Chi Minh sandals walking down this rice-paddy dike. I was going to continue toward Two Bits, but something in my mind said, "*Check him out.*" I called the high bird and told him we had someone who looked suspicious, and we were going to check him out.

We came around and flew back to this individual. We circled him, looked at him, and I decided he needed to be checked closer. I couldn't say why I was so suspicious, but I was convinced there was something about him that wasn't right. We came to a hover in front of him, and I noticed he didn't break stride as he approached us. We were about four feet above the rice-paddy dike, and as he approached, he was looking into the barrel of Sergeant Larensen's M-60 machine gun. He approached within three feet of the aircraft, stopped, smiled, and produced a card of some type and held it up for Sergeant Larensen to look at.

I keyed my intercom and told Sergeant Larensen to motion to him and have him lift up his shirt. Since his machine gun was hanging from a bungee cord (a heavy elastomer cord that was fastened to the top of the door frame. We hung the machine gun from this cord.), Sergeant Larensen let go of the hand guard with his left hand and motioned for him to lift up his shirt. The individual just stood there, looking at Sergeant Larensen and me, and made no effort to raise his shirt. I told Sergeant Larensen, "Make sure he knows what we mean." Once again, Sergeant Larensen pointed at him, then reached down, and lifted the edge of his shirt and again pointed at him. The individual just shrugged his shoulders and bent down as if he were going to walk under the helicopter. I hovered sideways away from him and lowered the collective so we were now about one foot off the rice-paddy dike and Sergeant Larensen's machine-gun barrel was now level with the man's eyes and about twelve inches from his face.

The man stepped off the rice-paddy dike and was going to walk around the front of the helicopter. I told Sergeant Larensen, "Put a short burst in front of him." I pushed left pedal, added some power, and kept abreast of him. Sergeant Larensen fired a short burst of about five rounds in front of him. He didn't look back at us; he pulled a grenade from under his shirt and started to run through the rice paddy. I told Sergeant Larensen, "Kill him."

Sergeant Larensen fired a long burst into his body. He preferred to use all-tracer ammunition since it was easier to adjust in on the target. We were so close I could see each round as it hit him. I was not prepared for the sensation of everything going into slow motion. I had always thought that slow motion, as depicted in the movies, was a technique that was used to dramatize a scene. I didn't think that it would happen in real life.

I was wrong. As the bullets tore into his body, I watched in horrified fascination the reaction of his body to each bullet. When the bullets slammed into him, he was lifted off the ground and did a complete somersault in the air. At the apex of this somersault, the last two bullets from the machine gun hit him in the head, and his head exploded with blood and parts of his brain being picked up by the rotor wash and being blown back into the cockpit. We were only about three to four feet from him. Sergeant Larensen was getting covered with blood, and I felt something hit my face. I reached up with my left hand and brushed at my face and noticed that what had hit me was part of his brain. I also noticed that as he was turning over in the air, his shirt flew up and revealed a pistol belt that held two hand grenades, and a green NVA uniform rolled around the pistol belt.

I watched as he fell on his back in the rice paddy. At that moment, everything went back to normal speed. I flew a circle around him and noticed that his eyes were open, and they appeared to be looking at me. His mouth was open, and the rice-paddy water was flowing into his mouth. I tore my eyes away from the body and quickly checked around us to see if there were any more NVA nearby. As the realization of what I had just done started to sink in, a chill swept over me, and in my mind rang the sixth commandment, "Thou shalt not kill!"

At that moment, the radio came alive, and the Red bird asked me what I had. I automatically gave the response I had heard so many others give, "One NVA KIA attempting to evade. He had a couple of grenades and an NVA uniform rolled around his pistol belt, over."

"Way to go, White. Let's head back to the barn, over."

"Call Saber Three and see if they want the Blues to be inserted to check the body," I replied. In a minute, the Red bird called back and told me that it was too late to insert the Blues. I rogered his transmission, and leaving that hapless soul lying on his back with his unseeing eyes gazing toward heaven, I turned toward Two Bits. As we flew toward Two Bits, neither Sergeant Larensen nor I said a word.

I conducted the platoon briefing that evening, vaguely aware that there was not only absolute approval but also a sense that I had crossed a barrier that had, to that point, separated me from them. *"A rite of passage,"* I thought.

I lay on my ammo boxes with the mosquito net tucked in and tried to go to sleep. I closed my eyes, and the images of this evening came rushing forward, and I watched the bullets tear his body apart once again. *"I wonder if he was married, had children. A few hours ago, he was a vibrant person, full of life—and just like that! I snuffed that life out. God, that could happen to me. Just like that, one minute alive and the next dead. Dear God, forgive me. I wonder if his wife and children will ever know what happened to him. We just left him lying in that stinking rice paddy. Dear God, forgive me.*" Tears were welling in my eyes, and I immediately snapped my eyes open and reached for a Lucky Strike. "*Get a hold of yourself, Bert,*" I thought as I inhaled a long drag from the cigarette. "*You are a soldier, and this is a soldier's job. This is what soldiers are paid to do.*" I had washed up when I returned from that flight, but I could still feel the spot on my cheek where parts of his brain had landed on me. I absently reached up and felt that part of my face as I thought about my responsibility as a leader. "*You're no better than anyone else in this tent. Lord knows that everyone here has killed a lot more people, and they're not falling apart. I am their leader. I can't show this type of emotion about killing the enemy. I cannot be perceived as having any hesitation in doing this. If I hesitate, they will hesitate, and hesitation will cost them their lives. If you can't do this, resign your commission and go tell Major Beasley you can't do it.*"

I pulled the mosquito net aside and ground the cigarette butt into the ground. I lay back and tried to go to sleep. As soon as I closed my eyes, the image of those bullets tearing that poor soul's body apart leapt to the forefront of my consciousness again. I opened my eyes and willed myself to think of something else. I started to think of my children and wondered if I would ever see them again. With a sense of unjustified certainty, I knew I would see them again, unlike the man I had killed today. Suddenly, Reverend Scafe, my pastor at the First Presbyterian Church in Bremerton, Washington, popped into my mind. In my mind's eye, I could see him calling me forward at a Sunday-evening church service, putting his arm around my shoulders, and praising my singing ability. I was a sophomore in high school at the time, and that was the first time in my life that anyone had publicly praised anything I had done. He was a kind man, and he had no idea what an impact that gesture had on my psyche. That thought was followed with "*I wonder how proud he would be of my actions today. THOU SHALT NOT KILL!*"

I found my pack of Luckys and shook out another cigarette. My waterproof matches were pushed between the cellophane wrapper and the pack of cigarettes. I used my fingernail to push them up to where I could pull them out, lit up a cigarette, and replaced the matches in the pack. I lay on my back in the darkness, staring up at the top of the tent, my left hand behind my head and my right holding the cigarette. *"All these years in the army and I never once thought how I would feel when I actually killed someone."* I recalled the bayonet classes I instructed while I was a young drill instructor at Fort Riley and Fort Polk. *"What is the spirit of the bayonet?"* I would yell. *"To KILL!"* the massed voices of the recruits would shout back. I taught it, I believed it, and yet, I had never considered the effect of the result on me and those men of that teaching.

What I was taught as a child and young adult in all of the Sunday-school classes and the churches I had attended presented me with the moral dilemma I was now struggling with. I was raised on the King James Version of the Bible, and the sixth commandment was very clear. I didn't realize that other versions of the Bible changed the sixth commandment to read, "Thou shalt not murder."

As I lay in the darkness, chain-smoking one cigarette after another, trying to overcome the horror of today, I realized that I had to resolve my feelings about this because this was just the beginning of the killing. As I listened to the breathing of the men asleep in that tent, I knew that every man in it had killed repeatedly, and there was no doubt that many in this tent had killed more than a hundred. *"God,"* I thought, *"this isn't like the movies! If every person [better change that to enemy soldier], if every enemy soldier I kill is an eyeball-to-eyeball kill, how will I handle it? How can I reconcile what I have been taught and believe with what I have to do? David slew Goliath and saved his people; Moses closed the Red Sea on thousands of enemy soldiers and saved the people of Israel. Surely, God forgave those two men."*

As these thoughts entered my consciousness, I started to come to grips with what I had to do and started to rationalize the killing. *"If we don't do this, who will? Millions of soldiers before me went through a similar experience. Freedom is not free, and this is the price that someone has to pay. These soldiers deserve a strong leader."* And on and on, it went throughout the night until I finally fell asleep.

In the morning, I awoke with a determination not to think of the enemy soldiers as human beings. I would not dwell on their death at my hands. To do so was to risk losing my sanity. From that day until the end of my second tour, I did not keep track of how many enemy soldiers I killed nor did I regard them as living, breathing human beings. They were merely something we shot at and, in most cases were shooting at us. I have tried to keep the death and carnage I brought to the enemy buried deep in my mind and made a conscious effort not to think of them. There are only two deaths I caused that I cannot bury: this one and the first woman NVA soldier I shot and killed.

In the months that followed, I killed from two to four enemies every time I went to the AO. When you do that much killing every day, you just turn it off in your head. I have been successful in that effort, but there are many of my comrades who have not been able to do that. Years after all of these happened, there are many brave men who are still struggling with the moral and, in some cases physical, dilemma their experiences in that war brought to them. We (the Vietnam veterans) were exposed to the same horror and carnage that all soldiers have faced when fighting a war. What separates us from the other veterans of previous and subsequent wars is our treatment upon our return from war.

We were reviled, spat upon, ridiculed, and shunned in general by the American public. The media and the "entertainment industry" depicted the Vietnam vets as a group of dope-crazed killers whom no self-respecting person would want to associate with and which no employer would want to hire. Jane Fonda, Bill Clinton, and others of their ilk will tell everyone today that they were merely protesting American policy and not the service members who were fighting and dying on the battlefield. That is a crock of bovine scatology (as General Schwarzkopf would say). When America sends her sons and daughters onto a battlefield, the time for debate about the correctness of the policy has long since passed. When the decision has been made and the troops committed to battle, the only proper debate thereafter should be centered around the question, "Have we committed an overwhelming force to defeat the enemy as soon as is possible?" I am convinced that most of the protesters of the Vietnam War were motivated more about the issue of their personal safety (not having to go) than any egalitarian idea presented as justification for their action. One need only look at the genocide that occurred in Cambodia, Bosnia, and Kosovo, and hear the deafening silence from this same group of cowards who, then and now, justify their actions during the Vietnam War as being based on the concept of equal political, economic, and legal rights for all human beings. You can only attain political, economic, and legal rights if you are willing to die to attain them. Freedom isn't free. Honorable men and women pay for the price of freedom; they are willing to sacrifice their reputations, fortunes, and their very lives to purchase that freedom.

I am proud to say that I am a Vietnam War veteran. I know that what I did all those years ago was the honorable thing to do, the correct effort to devote myself to. I prefer to spend my time with honorable men and women rather than associate with sunshine patriots who were not willing to sacrifice their reputations, fortunes, and, most certainly, not their lives to the ideal of freedom. As they say, "Talk is cheap."

CHAPTER FOURTEEN

GETTING INTO THE
SWING OF THINGS

The next few months settled into a routine of reconnaissance, screening friendly units, first—and last-light missions, insertions, extractions, bomb damage assessments (BDA), firefights, putting in air strikes, and the inevitable killing that accompanied all of these missions. It was a period of time during which my soul was tempered like steel. I would have lighthearted bantering conversations in the operations tent and, within twenty minutes of these conversations, was plunged into a life-and-death struggle with the enemy. I went from laughter to tragedy, and through it all, as a leader, I was conscious of having to set the example. Every leader develops a style of leadership that he is comfortable with, and over the years, I had observed many good leaders and a few piss-poor ones. From my life's experiences and my basic personality, I developed a style that worked well for me and appeared to suit those I led, as well as my contemporaries and seniors.

I tried to communicate clearly what I expected, I made firm corrections when those expectations were not met, and at the same time, I tried not to become personal in my corrections (attack the act not the actor). Most of these firm corrections were in the realm of tactical mistakes. I never had a problem getting the scouts to *engage* the enemy; my biggest problem was teaching them when to disengage and turn the fight over to another element. I kept emphasizing that the scouts' mission was to locate the enemy, develop the situation, and report. It was not their mission to try to kill all the enemies in the AO.

I am, by nature, a friendly, upbeat type of person. I have a tendency to look for the good in people and in whatever situation we find ourselves. I also know the value of a positive word of encouragement during stressful situations and the value of consistent behavior on the part of leaders. Those being led should be able to predict what a leader's response will be to different situations. When a leader does not meet the expectations of the led and reacts totally different than what they expect, the leader creates stress and uncertainty among the led. This is not good in a combat situation. I tried hard to be consistent in my behavior as their leader and remain calm during the most stressful situations. But if you are a son of a bitch by nature, be a son of a bitch all the time.

Smiling, patting on the back, establishing standards, providing firm corrections when necessary, recognizing that all people make mistakes, allowing people to do their job and giving them recognition for a job well done, giving the credit to your subordinates when your unit has done well, praising your subordinates to your superiors (don't hog the glory), accepting full responsibility when your unit screws up (don't blame your subordinates), and interceding on their behalf when they needed help were things I looked for in my leaders, and I hope I provided that kind of leadership to those I led.

Something we all got a kick out of was the 0600 greeting from AFN radio, "Good morning, Vietnam!" Shortly after I arrived in the troop, Bob Rice and I moved into a two-man tent, and in the morning, just before breakfast, I would walk into the scout tent and say, "Good morning, Vietnam! Another day, another opportunity to excel! Rise and shine!" This was invariably greeted with groans and vague threats of retaliation. Several of my common phrases—"Never a backward glance or a moment's hesitation, drive on!" "A thing of beauty by golly," and "Another day, another opportunity to excel"—were phrases I hoped helped establish a positive attitude in a place and at a time where there was very little that was positive.

Major Beasley was consistent in his behavior. As I indicated earlier, he was remote from most of the people in the troop and devoted more time being critical of what went wrong than emphasizing what went right. He was also concerned with enemy body count. On one occasion, when questioned by a higher headquarters, he had the Blues line up the bodies from one engagement and took a picture to prove that what was reported as enemy KIA was correct. The term "hard-nosed" comes to mind when I think of Major Beasley. He did not vacillate or hesitate, and as one of the led, I knew what to expect as he was predictable in his actions in various situations. He didn't expect to be liked or appear that he cared if he was liked. What he expected was for everyone to do their job and be aggressive in finding and killing the enemy. His leadership style worked for him and for us.

Major George Burrow was the troop executive officer (XO) and had an entirely different approach. He had a dry sense of humor and a keen wit. He had the ability to relate to people and took the time to just talk with them. I often thought he had an unenviable position during this period of time. In most organizations, you have the good guy and the bad guy, playing off of each other. Usually, the second in command is the bad guy and is the one that chews people out when they screw up. The leader is the good guy praising those who deserve it. Major Burrow was not given an opportunity to operate in that mode since Major Beasley was in control of everything and chose not to share any aspect of his command.

Major Burrow's sense of humor was deceiving in that it was often very pointed but, to me, always amusing and usually funny. As a part of the nightly briefing, the platoon leaders would give their maintenance status: how many aircraft were flyable, how many were operational but not mission ready, etc. Following the nightly briefing, the platoon leaders would update the mission board as described earlier. On more than one occasion, as I moved toward the board, Major Burrow would say, "Now we get the real status on the White platoon. White, why is it that every night you brief that everything is flyable and the next morning only two birds are up?" I would give some smart-ass answer, and we would laugh.

These lighthearted, humorous exchanges became an integral part of our reality, and we developed a bond that made our existence a little easier to endure. However, it was the first time we flew together that the bond was cemented.

Major Burrow and I arrived at the troop at about the same time, so we were both "new guys." Since he was the XO and was primarily responsible for the administrative and maintenance effort of the troop, he did not have the opportunity, at that point in time, to get out into the AO. He frequently asked various crews to take him along on missions, but nobody wanted to fly with a new guy.

CPT Chole in his OH-13, August 1967, LZ Two Bits.

On this particular day, the troop was supporting a battalion of the Third Brigade that was involved in heavy contact with an NVA regiment in the Sui Cau Mountains. All of the scouts had flown two or three missions that day in support of the operation, and there was at least one firefight with the enemy per mission. As the rotation was going, it appeared that I would end up flying last light around the various fire-support bases in the AO. Normally, we didn't find much on the last-light mission, and it was rare that we got involved in a firefight. Major Burrow and I were sitting in the operations tent, listening to the spot reports being sent back by the teams in the AO, and he said to me, "White, it looks like you're going to fly last light. How about taking me with you?" I checked the mission board and asked, "Can you shoot an M-60?" "Shit, I can shoot the eye out of a gnat at one hundred yards," he replied. I laughed and said, "All right, sir, I'll see you at the bird in about a half an hour. Don't forget your chicken plate [chest armor]."

After we cleared the perimeter of Two Bits, I called Bob Zahn, our high bird, and told him that we were going to test fire the M-60. I saw a box lying in an old bomb crater and told Major Burrow it was time for "old dead eye to demonstrate his marksmanship by hitting that box." He fired the machine gun, and by God, he hit the box! I was impressed and said, "Okay, a couple of other things to talk about how we are going to react if we meet the enemy. Make sure that if we are fired upon, you pull the trigger and return fire. I don't care if you see who is shooting; just get some return fire going. Be careful of where you are shooting when I'm in a right-hand turn. If I tighten up the turn, there is a good possibility the rotor blades will come between you and the enemy, and I don't want you shooting us down. If we get in a firefight with a large force, we won't hang around too long, so be prepared to drop a smoke grenade when I tell you" as I pointed to the smoke grenades hanging from the console. He nodded and said, "Got it."

"*This is an opportunity to show him what low-level flight really is!*" I thought as we dropped to within inches of the ground. He was dutifully impressed as we cleared a hilltop with the skids dragging through the grass. What I didn't tell him was that I had run out of power, and if the top of the hill hadn't arrived when it did, I would have had to push right pedal and fall back down the hillside and try it again. We were having a good time until I heard Major Beasley call me on UHF and tell me that I was to replace him on station over an infantry company in the Sui Cau.

We found the infantry company and flew around them twice. On our third pass around them, I was talking to the company commander and mentioned that we were flying over three bunkers, and he asked, "Are they occupied?"

As if to answer, two NVA soldiers in each bunker jumped up and started shooting at us with AK-47s. We were about ten feet above them, and I could feel the rounds hitting the armor plating we were sitting on, and the impact of each round threw us up against our seat belts.

Major Burrow looked at me and said, "You're damned right they're occupied! Them sons a bitches are trying to kill us!" The expression on his face and his reaction, with that epitaph, caused me to start laughing.

I was going to tell him to start returning fire when suddenly I heard Bob Zahn on UHF. "White, set it down! You're on fire!" That wiped the smile from my face, and I looked to the front and saw a clearing at the base of the hill directly below us. We flew to the base of the hill; and as we landed in the clearing, I reached up and pulled the fuel, shut off handle down, hit the quick release on my seat belt, and un-assed the aircraft. Major Burrow unhooked the machine gun from the bungee cord, hit his quick release, and was out of the aircraft on his side running to the right front. I ran about twenty-five feet away from the aircraft, hit the dirt, and looked back at the aircraft, expecting to see it explode.

I saw that Major Burrow had about 1,200 rounds of machine-gun ammunition trailing after him as he ran, and I started to laugh again. As I looked at the aircraft, I didn't see any flames, but there was plenty of smoke. I hollered to Major Burrow and asked him if he was all right, and he replied, "Yes!"

I yelled to him, "I'm going to check the aircraft!" I jumped up and ran to the aircraft. As I was inspecting the engine compartment, I noticed that one of the hydraulic lines had been shot, and the hydraulic fluid had sprayed on the hot engine, which had produced all the smoke that Bob Zahn had seen. I heard some AKs fire and saw the ground erupt around me. I looked up to the hilltop, and those sons a bitches were still shooting at us! As I jumped into the aircraft and attempted to start the engine, Bob Zahn made a gun run on their position, and the firing stopped for a couple of minutes.

I hollered to Major Burrow, "If this hummer will start, we're out of here!"

He replied, "Roger that!"

In the excitement and with adrenaline pumping through my veins, I just pushed the starter button and didn't check anything. It didn't start. I rolled the throttle back and forth between my hands and tried again. It still didn't start. A round came through the windscreen inches from my head and sprayed me with Plexiglas. "*Calm down*," I told myself. "*Go through the regular starting procedure.*" As I did so, I noticed that I had left the magneto switch in the "on" position when I left the aircraft, and I said, "Shit, no wonder it wouldn't start!"

I tried again, and the engine sputtered to life. It was missing; and obviously, something was wrong, but it was running. I turned on the radios and heard on UHF, "This is Three-Five. I have White in sight, and we are on short final."

I looked over my shoulder, and there was the most wonderful sight any pilot in the troop could see: Blue Lift on short final with the Blues standing on the skids, coming to the rescue. In my mind, I heard a bugler play charge as the cavalry rode to my rescue. I keyed the mike and told Three-Five to abort, that I had it running, and that I was going to fly it back to the troop area. He rogered and broke off the approach. I asked him to have one bird follow us back since the engine was really running rough.

Major Burrow climbed in, still trailing 1,200 rounds of machine-gun ammunition, and we got the hell out of there. After we flew back to Two Bits and Sergeant Artamisi (the H-13 line chief) inspected the damage, he shook his head and wondered how we ever got the engine started since one cylinder had a round through it. Then he had me crawl under the aircraft and look at the lift link. This was a link that connected the transmission to the airframe and actually allowed the engine to lift the aircraft. This link was approximately an inch and a half wide. It also had taken a round, and there was approximately one-eighth of an inch left on the link. I started to think what might have happened had that link let go and then decided I didn't want to think about it.

CH-47 lifting out my bird for some serious repair after
getting shot up.

About a month later, Major Burrow was reading a newspaper
when I walked into operations. He looked up at me and, with a
smile on his face, said, "Here, read this" as he handed me the
paper. It was his hometown paper, and I read this story about
Major Burrow being shot down in Vietnam. I started to laugh
when I read how we had repaired the aircraft after he was shot
down and flew it to safety. I looked over at him; he shrugged and
said with a smile, "Hey, what can I tell you?"

CHAPTER FIFTEEN
AMIDST THE KILLING

Acting sergeant Artamisi was the scout platoon's line chief and was responsible for ensuring that the OH-13s were in flyable condition. He was really a specialist fourth class, but we were short of so many crew chiefs at the proper rank that we made him an acting sergeant and put him in charge of all the OH-13 crew chiefs. Those crew chiefs, at times, performed miracles. Many of the OH-13s we had were more than twenty years old, and most of them were held together with safety wire and green tape. The scout aircraft were probably the most shot-up aircraft in the troop, but somehow or other, they kept them flying. They were magnificent men who took pride in their ability to keep those birds flying. Sometimes they didn't get shot up; the pilot's dented, bumped, and flat ass tore them up on some occasions. I was as guilty as any other pilot, and the worst I battered one up was on a first-light mission.

The day before my incident, Red Hughes was covering the Blues on the ground and was so engrossed in watching over them that he flew into the top of a tree with his gunship and knocked the chin bubble and radios out of his aircraft. That evening, he was getting razzed, and I am afraid I was the worst one when it came to kidding him. I was offering comments about "old men who couldn't see" and "the older you get, the less coordination and reaction time you have." "This is really a young man's game," etc. The next morning, it turned out that he and I were both scheduled to fly first light. It was unusual to have the scouts' and weapons' platoon leaders flying as a team. After the first-light mission, we were to fly up the An Lo Valley and put in an air strike. We took off before daybreak and were in the An Lo Valley as sunlight filtered into the valley. There was a layer of ground fog partially obscuring the valley floor, but you could see the valley floor through occasional breaks in the fog. While flying over one of those patches, I saw a fresh trail wandering through some grass. The enemy's movement through the grass knocked the dew off the grass, and the trail stood out like a superhighway across the bottom of the valley. I knew the enemy had passed this way within the last half hour since the dew hadn't reformed on the grass. I got excited and told Red that I was going to drop down and take a closer look and see which direction they were moving. I knew that the grass would be bent in the direction they were moving.

Maintenance never ends. Crew Chiefs and Observers patching up an OH-13 after a fire fight (Who has the Green Tape?)

The An Lo Valley had been sprayed repeatedly with Agent Orange to defoliate the valley. The trees that had lost their leaves bleached white and were not hard to see most of the time; however, against a background of fog, they could virtually disappear. As I dropped lower into the valley, I was concentrating on the trail so hard I wasn't thinking about flying. As I was studying the trail, Sergeant Larensen hollered, "Pull up! Pull up!" I glanced to the front and saw this huge white tree in front of us. I pulled back on the cyclic and cranked on as much power as that bird had and yanked the collective up under my armpit. Thank God, it was early in the morning with a low DA. As it was, the rotor chopped off the top foot of the tree, and we flew through the next four feet of it. That old bird shuddered, wobbled, and literally staggered through the air, and the Plexiglas bubble shattered into a million pieces and flew back into our faces. Thank God, we both had our visors down. The aircraft was still flying and soon regained its airspeed as I surveyed the damage.

The bottom half of the bubble was gone! I mean it wasn't there! The top half was now flapping in the breeze, threatening to let go at any minute. I pushed my intercom switch and asked Sergeant Larensen if he was all right. There was no answer, and I looked at him and asked the question again; but this time, I noticed that there was no sidetone, and I knew something was wrong with the radio or intercom. Red called and said we'd better get going, or we were going to be late putting in the air strike. Well, that answered that question. The radio was still working. I attempted to answer but, again, got no sidetone, and I hollered over the wind and engine noise and told Sergeant Larensen to answer him. Sergeant Larensen rogered his transmission, and we kept flying. I reached for my helmet and felt along my headset cord and discovered the problem. A piece of Plexiglas had cut my microphone cord, and I could not transmit from my side of the aircraft. I hollered at Sergeant Larensen, and when he looked at me, I waved my cut microphone cord at him and told him he would have to answer all radio calls. He rogered, and we flew to the orbit point where we were to meet the forward air controller (FAC) from the air force. The FAC was there, but the fighters weren't. I thought, "*Late again!*" It was my experience that they never showed up on time.

Soon Red called and said he was running low on fuel and that we would go to the nearest refuel point and top off. Sergeant

Larensen rogered, and Red gave us a heading, and off we went to refuel with the top half of the bubble still flapping in the breeze. As we flew toward the refueling point, I debated about telling Red what had happened, and then I thought about how I had razzed him the night before about his flying into a tree, and I said to myself, "*Naw, I won't tell him.*" There were two separate refueling points on opposite sides of the fire-support base, and after we landed, I frictioned down the controls and got out of the aircraft while Sergeant Larensen was refueling and told him I was going to swap sides with him so I could talk on the radio. As I plugged my headset in, I heard Red on the radio,

"White, since you are the only H-13 in refueling, I presume that it is you sitting over there with half a bubble, over."

I answered, "Well, if I'm the only one here, I guess that's probably correct, over."

"Oh, you didn't have the guts to tell me you flew into a tree, did you? You no-seeing, uncoordinated captain pretending to be a pilot!"

And that was just the beginning. He razzed me for the next hour and a half until we got back to Two Bits. In the process, I had to listen to him send a spot report back to the troop, explaining what had happened to White that morning. Of course, he didn't know, but he sure sent back an imaginative report. I knew it was going to be a long day and decided that what I needed to do was spend my day in the AO. I changed aircraft when we got back to the troop and did just that. When I returned that evening, I went to my tent, and lying in the middle of my bunk was the top half of my bubble. Attached to the inside was a homemade flag with a drawing of a hand flipping the bird and around it this inscription, "Fuck you if you can't take a joke." I started to laugh; and Red appeared, clapped me on the shoulder, and said, "What goes around comes around, buddy."

Some of our H-13s had skid-mounted machine guns. Arming these machine guns from the cockpit required the pilot to push a button that released a shot of nitrogen into the system. That, in turn, pulled the charging handle of the machine gun to the rear twice, which allowed the bolt to pick up a round and then seat it in the barrel. The system worked just fine. There was only one small problem: there was no way to recharge the nitrogen bottles in Vietnam. This meant that to arm the machine gun, we tied a piece of rope on the charging handle; and after we cleared the perimeter, we would lean out of the cockpit, grab the rope, and pull it to the rear twice. That armed the system, and we were ready for combat.

I shall never forget Larry Brown, who always wore a yellow scarf, leaning out of the cockpit, yellow scarf streaming to the rear and yanking on that rope. I thought as I watched, *"All we need are leather caps and goggles, and this becomes a World War I flying scene."*

Staff Sergeant (SSG) Wells arrived from Delta Troop, and Major Beasley told me that he was going to be assigned to the scout platoon as the platoon sergeant. The story that was circulating about him was that he was being transferred to us because he was out of control in D Troop. As the story went, his platoon was on an ambush patrol when a couple of the men from the platoon were captured and decapitated by the NVA. The next morning, their heads were mounted on stakes near the ambush site, and Sergeant Wells lost it. As far as he was concerned, any Vietnamese he saw was to be killed in retribution. It didn't make any difference if he was an NVA, VC, or civilian.

Staff Sergeant Wells was a big man: he was well over two hundred pounds and at least six foot one. I don't recall our initial conversation, but I had learned from years of experience that you couldn't believe all the stories you heard about an individual. I always made my own judgment about each individual, and I tried to keep it impersonal. The fact that he was a staff sergeant, and not under charges, made this story about him suspect in my mind.

Sergeant Larensen became CWO Joe Rawl's observer, and Staff Sergeant Wells became my observer as well as the platoon sergeant. He had never flown as a scout observer, and it would be my job to teach him all aspects of scouting from the air. He had been a ground cavalry scout, so the only thing we had to concentrate on was looking at this job from a different perspective and teaching him how to fly and land the aircraft. All scouts taught their observers how to fly and land the aircraft. With only two of us in the aircraft, if the pilot was shot or killed while flying, the observer had to know how to get the aircraft back and land it safely. This was important to both of them if they wanted to survive.

Our first day of flying together was memorable. Our first mission that day was around 1000 hours. It was already hot, and we had a steady breeze blowing from the southeast. After the preflight inspection, we both strapped in, and I started the aircraft. Our crew chief was standing in front of us and motioned me to bring it up to a hover. I knew the breeze was blowing from our rear and that we had a high density altitude, but I was not prepared for what happened next. As I raised the collective, I felt the back of the skids come off around, but the toes of the skids were firmly planted on the ground. As I applied more power, the rear of the aircraft rose higher in the air, but the toe of the skids did not budge. The main rotor was now dangerously close to striking the front of the revetment, and the crew chief anxiously started looking for a place to take cover. I lowered the collective and set the aircraft firmly back on the ground. I turned to Staff Sergeant Wells and said, "You'll have to get out of the aircraft. Between the two of us, we have too much weight in the cabin with this tailwind. Walk up to the main runway, and I'll pick you up on the runway."

With him out of the aircraft, the aircraft lifted off like it normally would, and I hovered up to the runway and picked him up. Sergeant Wells strapped himself in, and I picked us up to a hover. We had a crosswind, and I had all the power I could get out of the aircraft. I thought, "*Shit. I've never had to use this much power to hover!*" The tower cleared us to the active, and as I turned into the wind, I noticed that it didn't take quite as much power to hover. We started our takeoff, and as we approached transitional lift, I realized I didn't have any throttle left. I had wrapped it as far as it would go, and I knew we didn't have enough power to get into transitional lift. I thought, "*Well, the gunship guys bounce it off when they have to. Let's see if I can do it too.*" We hit the runway with enough force that by popping the collective slightly, we bounced back into the air and into transitional lift, and we were flying. On UHF, I heard one of the gunship crew members chuckle, then groan as if he were lifting something, and then announce to all who were listening, "It's diet time in the White platoon!"

We had been flying together for about a month when Major Beasley decided to conduct a search of a village that reportedly was a major VC village. We put the Blues on the ground at daylight and had two scouts on station. One was screening to the north of the village, and one screening to the south. Staff Sergeant Wells and I were on the south side of the village and flew a route that gave us good observation of the village as we flew an arc around the village from east to west and then back from west to east. Part of our flight route was over a cemetery, and on one of our passes over the cemetery, I saw something move out of the corner of my eye and did a hard left turn. Flying to the left took more power since you had to increase the pitch on the tail rotor, and you were flying in a direction that was counter to the centrifugal force of the main rotor. As I completed my turn and tried to apply more power, I discovered I already had full power. My throttle was at the stop, I heard the rpm bleed off; and I found myself in that situation of being out of airspeed, altitude, and ideas all at the same time.

The Vietnamese are buried within a five-foot-high mound that covers their remains. We were over the middle of such a graveyard, and there were burial mounds directly below and to the front. We had about twenty to thirty knots of forward airspeed, and it was clear that we were going to make a running landing.

I had just enough time to select a touchdown point that was between the rows of these mounds and hoped that the ground was firm enough to prevent the toes of the skids from digging in and causing us to flip over. A thought flashed through my mind, *"Wouldn't it be ironic to die in a Vietnamese graveyard?"* As we touched down, I lowered the collective and tried to get the rpm back to operating rpm. We were still sliding forward at about twenty knots, and the rpm was starting to come back up when I suddenly noticed a two-foot-high dirt wall about four feet in front of us. Adrenaline surged through me as I realized that unless I got the toes of the skids over the wall, we were going to flip over. I pulled back on the cyclic and up on the collective just as we reached the wall of dirt. The toes of the skids just cleared the wall, but we had lost any vestige of power. Our forward momentum carried us over the wall, and we slid to a stop with a jarring thump as the heel of the skids slid off the wall, and we fell to the ground.

Staff Sergeant Wells looked at me and said, "What happened?" I explained that we were downwind, had full power, had lost rpm, and fell out of the sky. He asked, "How do you know when we are losing the rpm required to fly?"

I pointed to the tachometer and then said, "That will tell you, but usually, the sound of the engine will tell you sooner." From that day forward, he kept one ear tuned to the sound of the engine. We could be in the middle of a firefight, and if the engine speed dropped fifty rpm, he would holler on intercom, "Rpm! Rpm!"

After we built up our rpm, I turned into the wind, took off, and continued our mission. As we were making our fifth or sixth pass around the village on the south side, an NVA soldier stepped out of the jungle, waving a white cloth attached to the business end of his AK-47. I couldn't believe it! This guy was trying to surrender to us. We circled around him, and I instructed Staff Sergeant Wells to pay close attention to the jungle this guy had just stepped out of. The question was, was he acting as a decoy to get us to commit troops to this area and then spring an ambush as our aircraft started to land? I called Blue and alerted him to what we had and then called our high bird and asked him to contact the troop and have them send one lift aircraft out to the Blues' location, pick up a squad, and have them come to my location to pick this guy up. As we waited for the Blues to arrive, we motioned for this guy to sit down in the middle of the cleared area he was in, and we then conducted a detailed search of the terrain all around this cleared area. Within twenty minutes, he was picked up by Blue and transported to the Blues location, and he was interrogated by the Kit Carson scout (a former NVA soldier who now was on our side) we had assigned to the platoon. I am sure that somewhere else in Vietnam at some time, enemy soldiers surrendered to other helicopter crews, but that was the only time it happened while I was assigned to the squadron on either my first or second tour.

On another occasion, we were conducting an area reconnaissance, and while flying across a rice paddy, we approached a tree line at the edge of the rice paddy, and I executed a cyclic climb without increasing power. As we dropped down on the other side of the tree line, we dropped down in front of an NVA platoon. These guys had the complete uniform on including their pith helmets and were armed with AK-47s. "*Holy shit!*" I thought. "*We're too close to them to try and avoid them; the best thing to do is attack!*" I had learned in earlier engagements that we had the element of surprise on our side and that if we attacked a large force aggressively, we would often be able to fly through them without taking hits simply because they weren't prepared for such an attack, which seemed to throw off their aim. So I increased power and flew directly toward them.

Staff Sergeant Wells started to engage them and had killed about five of them. We were within fifteen feet of them, and I was looking at two NVA directly to the front of us who were firing their AK-47s at us. I could see the heat waves coming off their barrels, and I thought, "*This is it. They are going to kill us. We can't escape this one!*" The M-60 machine gun stopped firing, and Staff Sergeant Wells hollered, "The fucking gun jammed!" I pulled in more power and broke right. As I was doing this, I called the gunship and told him to put down some fire. This all happened in a matter of seconds, and I watched with morbid fascination those two soldiers firing at us as we turned away from them. "*How can they miss? We are only about ten feet from them,*" I asked myself as we flew away. I watched the instruments as we evaded out of the area.

Staff Sergeant Wells had removed the barrel from the machine gun and was beating it on the side of the aircraft. "This motherfucking ammunition! I've got a ruptured cartridge in the barrel!" he shouted to no one in particular. We had about ten people all shooting AK-47s at us, and I expected us to go down or get killed at any moment. I could hear the rockets from the gunship start to explode behind me and heaved a sigh of relief. I checked my instruments once again, and everything was in the green. I checked my controls, and everything appeared to be working properly.

Staff Sergeant Wells, pushing the intercom button, said, "We're ready!" as he pushed the barrel quick release lever down into position. We turned back toward the enemy and noticed that there weren't many of them left standing, and those that were on their feet were running toward a hooch. Before we could reach them, they had disappeared inside. We flew around the hooch but couldn't see inside, so we hovered outside the door as Staff Sergeant Wells looked inside. Those inside fired at us, and Staff Sergeant Wells returned fire and noticed that they had a bunker built inside.

On UHF, I heard my gunship call me and say, "Hey, White, I've got an NVA hiding from you behind the haystack." I looked toward the haystack and noticed that my gunship was hovering behind the haystack also! I called him and asked him what the hell he was doing. He replied, "This guy is so sure you don't see him that he doesn't know I am behind him. Watch this." This particular gunship was armed with a forty-millimeter grenade launcher, and as I watched, I saw the gunner start pumping grenades at the guy behind the haystack and blew him through the haystack. I shook my head and said, "Okay, guys, I need you to get to altitude and blow this hooch away. We have at least two more NVA in a bunker inside the hooch."

They made two gun runs on the hooch and blew the walls off and had half the roof blown away. I told them to hold up for a minute while we checked the hooch. I was convinced that no one could live after that attack. Just as those thoughts had formed, out of the hooch walked a bloody and bleeding woman holding a baby in her arms. I couldn't believe it! We hovered over to the hooch and saw the bunker clearly now. The entrance to the bunker was clearly visible along with its two occupants. Staff Sergeant Wells fired into the bunker, and I could see the tracers hitting the two occupants. "*Damn, he really is getting better with that M-60,*" I thought as he put two long bursts into the bunker. I called my gunship and asked him if he thought he could bring the walls and the roof down. He replied, "Shit, get out of the way, White, and I'll show you some real shooting."

Sure enough, in two more passes, the hooch was on the ground and burning. We flew back to the hooch and hovered over the bunker entrance. We had a bunker buster on the seat between us, and I told Staff Sergeant Wells to grab the bunker buster, and we would make sure we killed everyone in the bunker. A bunker buster was a machine-gun ammunition box filled with C-4 explosives with a grenade in the corner and the explosives packed tightly around it. When the grenade pin was pulled and the grenade exploded, it set off about three pounds of C-4 and usually destroyed any bunker it was dropped into. I positioned the aircraft so we were heading into the wind, and Staff Sergeant Wells held the bunker buster out the door as we hovered over the entrance. He looked at me and said, "Ready?" I replied yes, and he pulled the pin on the grenade and dropped it into the entrance. As soon as it left his hand, I pulled in as much power as I could get, and we hauled ass out of there. We were about thirty feet from the bunker when it exploded. The concussion wave was like a giant hand pushing the helicopter even faster away from the explosion. Debris rained down, but fortunately, no debris hit our aircraft then or any other time we used the bunker busters.

We had killed all the enemies, approximately twenty, and started looking for the woman and child to medevac them. They had disappeared, and I believe they made it to a tunnel or bunker and waited for us to leave.

After that mission, Staff Sergeant Wells, Sergeant Artamisi, and I went over every inch of that aircraft and did not find one bullet hole in the aircraft. I couldn't believe it! That evening, as I lay on my ammo boxes, I replayed the day's events through my mind and, once again, was incredulous that not one bullet hit the aircraft. How could that be? It was as if a protective shield had been placed around the aircraft. As I drifted off to sleep, I uttered a silent "*Thank you, Lord.*"

Staff Sergeant Wells was my observer for the rest of the time I remained the scout platoon leader. We developed a great rapport and worked well together. In retrospect, I was thankful we had this time to train and work together in this AO before we moved north.

One other impression I am left with from this period of time was the impact the music from this era had on many of us. When we were not supporting a ground unit, I usually had the Armed Forces Network (AFN) tuned in on my FM radio. During one firefight Staff Sergeant Wells and I were involved in, "Proud Mary" was playing on the radio as Staff Sergeant Wells was killing some of the enemy as they were trying to kill us. It seemed that the machine gun was keeping time with the music: "Rolling [*short burst*], rolling [*short burst*], rolling down the river [*long burst*]." It was surreal and yet was a part of the whole experience.

Sergeant Artamisi was an excellent guitar player as well as a crew chief. Today, if I hear the song "House of the Rising Sun," I am immediately transported back in time and visualize myself lying on my ammo boxes at the end of the day with lights out, sides of the tent rolled up, one hand behind my head, the other with a cigarette, listening to Sergeant Artamisi sitting on the sandbags that surrounded our tents, singing, "*Momma tell your children not to do the things I've done, don't live your life in sin and misery in the house of the rising sun.*"

CHAPTER SIXTEEN
LOU PORRAZZO

As I indicated earlier, Lou was one of my section leaders. Lou was a new person to me, as was everyone else in the platoon, with the exception of Bob Rice and Lieutenant Williams. He was an infantry first lieutenant occupying an armor officer's position in an armor branch unit. This was not uncommon during Vietnam and would prove troublesome to many officers following the Vietnam War.

Many officers following Vietnam found that while they may have served two or three tours in Vietnam in aviation assignments, as far as their branch was concerned, they were not branch qualified. In other words, if you were an infantry officer and had not commanded an infantry platoon and had been an infantry company XO and commanded an infantry company, then as far as infantry branch was concerned, you had limited potential. This practice was not confined to the infantry branch; it was true in all branches.

To illustrate this, in 1975, I was the captain's assignment officer at armor branch. We had a requirement to fill a nominative position for an armor captain. This individual had to have commanded a platoon and a company, and it was desired that he also had some battalion staff time. I selected several files and circulated them to the other assignment officers and the branch chief. The captain with the strongest file happened to be an aviator, and while he hadn't commanded an armor or cavalry platoon, he had commanded a lift platoon and a lift company in an aviation battalion and had also served as the battalion S4. He was my recommended choice for the position. The branch chief called me in and said that this captain did not qualify since he had not commanded an armor-type unit. My response was that using that rationale, none of the other people qualified since they had not commanded an aviation unit. As valid as that point was, it made no difference. It was recognized that this problem was plaguing army aviators, and eventually, the army would establish a separate aviation branch. However, in 1967, this was a valid concern for all officers assigned to a unit other than that of their basic branch, and it was a concern for Lieutenant Porrazzo.

Lieutenant Johnson, who was commanding the Blue platoon, was scheduled to leave the troop at the end of July. As mentioned earlier, the troop commander had asked for a nonrated (not a pilot) infantry officer to become the Blue platoon leader. When it came time for Lieutenant Johnson to leave the troop, we had not received a replacement, and it did not appear there was to be one in the near future. Major Beasley asked me if I thought Lieutenant Porrazzo would be interested. Later that day, I approached Lou and asked him if he wanted to be the new Blue. He replied, "Hell yes!" He was excited about the possibility of commanding a rifle platoon and asked me to recommend that he get the job. He went on to say that he knew that that would leave us shorthanded in the scout platoon, but this was an opportunity he had hoped he would get. Later that day, I recommended to Major Beasley that Lou be selected as the new Blue. That night at the regular evening briefing, Major Beasley announced that Lou was going to be the new Blue.

While I was happy for Lou, I also realized that he was taking a job that was going to require some strong leadership ability. I felt that he was up to the challenge, but it was not going to be a piece of cake. The Blue platoon was filled with some of the hardest men I had ever encountered in my life. These guys were hard asses who would kill without provocation and without remorse. They had seen too much killing and done too much killing. Death was their constant companion and did not sway them. They were fearless on the one hand and, on the other, would not obey a stupid order that they knew might get them killed. Just weeks before Lou took over the platoon, three of the Blues, who were on an outpost around our perimeter at Two Bits, raped and murdered a mother and her daughter. A member of the Blue platoon turned them in and was promptly threatened by the rest of the platoon, and he had to be escorted out of the troop area to keep from being killed. No, this was not going to be an easy assignment, but I felt if any lieutenant in the troop could do it, Lou Porrazzo could.

During the next two months, Lou and I would have many discussions at night in my tent about some of his leadership challenges within the platoon. We would talk about them, and I would sometimes offer suggestions and, other times, just listen as Lou talked them out. These frequent sessions developed a bond and a friendship that was unique for me. While I was friendly and outgoing, I didn't let any one get too close, and I tried to remain detached but responsive to those around me. I found myself taking more and more interest in Lou and the Blues, and while there was only a seven-year difference in our ages (Lou was twenty-four and I was thirty-one), in many respects, there was an aspect of a father-son relationship that developed between us. I allowed him to become important to me and looked forward to those sessions where we would sit down and shoot the breeze about everything and anything.

As August passed into September, I could see the subtle changes that were taking place within Lou. His easygoing manner was still there, but there was a touch of steel that showed through occasionally. He had matured and developed into an outstanding combat leader. I often thought that he could have been the model for the Follow Me statue at Fort Benning's infantry school. In my mind, he was the epitome of what an infantry officer should be, and I was convinced he had a brilliant career ahead of him. He took care of his men, and they respected and took care of him. He knew his job, his men, and the mission of our troop. He was doing a great job, and I took a great deal of pride in what he was accomplishing.

During the first week of September, we were informed that a nonrated infantry lieutenant was going to be assigned to the troop as the new Blue platoon leader. I thought that was great news since that meant that Lou would return to the scout platoon and resume his section leader's duties again. Specialist Markewitz, who had been Lou's observer in the scout platoon, was ecstatic. He missed flying with Lou and the way Lou related to him. He really admired and looked up to Lou, and he couldn't wait for Lou to get back to the scout platoon. Lou, on the other hand, was not anxious to give up the job of being Blue. He had developed his own bond with the Blue platoon and had developed a taste for being a ground combat leader.

Lieutenant Eikenberry arrived in the troop several days later, and through no fault of his own, his appearance did not inspire confidence. He was small in stature and looked much too young to command the Blue platoon. Initial impressions are important and, in this case, worked against him. Lou was a solidly built man, and I guess it could be said that he was a man's man. He looked every inch a soldier, and he had *command presence*. It exuded from him even when he was in a noncombative setting. One of the things Lou and I talked about was how to issue orders. You issue an order with the expectation that it will be carried out in a very matter-of-fact way. It is not personal, and you don't expect to have to discuss it. You expect compliance. You don't say, "This is an order!" You just say, "Sergeant, take your squad around to the right." The manner in which the order is issued has an impact on a soldier's willingness to comply. If there is the slightest hint of indecision, hesitation, wavering, or the slightest hint of panic in the voice, a soldier will say to himself, "*Wait a minute. Is this the right thing to do?*" Command presence is hard to define, but being sure of yourself and communicating that verbally and nonverbally is a big part of command presence.

Unfortunately, for Lieutenant Eikenberry, he picked up the nickname of Little Boy Blue. This made it much harder for him to do his job, but he learned and survived his tour in Vietnam. At any rate, soon after his arrival, Lou asked me if it was okay for him to go on R&R in Hawaii as soon as he left the Blue platoon and before he came back to the scouts. I said, "Sure," and he soon made arrangements to meet his wife in Hawaii on 30 September.

During the last week of September, Captain Hasselgrove also went on R&R. While he was gone, I was given the additional duty of acting as the troop operations officer. Although I flew some missions during this period of time, I spent most of my time in the operations tent. On 27 September 1967, the Blues had been inserted several times but had no significant contact or results while on the ground. In between missions, Lou stopped by the operations tent, and we talked about him leaving for R&R the next morning. This was his last day as Blue, and he was enjoying this last day of command. We talked about his wife and the fact that she was pregnant and how scary it was to think about being a father. I told him about the joys of being a father, and while the responsibility seemed overwhelming before you became a father, after the fact, it wasn't as scary as it seemed before you became one.

It had been a relatively routine day. The last-light team took off, and within a half an hour, they sent back a spot report, saying they had found some NVA soldiers running around in the An Lo Valley. The decision was made to launch Blue to check this out. I stepped out into the company street and watched as the Blue platoon ran for the aircraft. Lou was running down the street, and I stepped in front of him and said, "Lou, what the hell are you doing! Let the new Blue take them out."

He looked at me and said, "I am still Blue until midnight, and if they are going to be inserted, their platoon leader goes with them."

I said, "Bullshit. You have got to give it up sometime, and Eikenberry will be the new Blue tomorrow. Sit this one out."

He looked at me, smiled, and said, "Would you give up your platoon before you had too?"

I smiled back, slapped him on the shoulder, and said, "You know I wouldn't, but damn it be careful!" He gave me a thumbs-up and started jogging to the aircraft.

Within fifteen minutes, the Blues had been inserted into a green LZ. Soon we received a spot report, telling us that the Blues were in contact with the NVA force. The next spot report was to tell us that Blue was a line one. Line one was a code word for killed in action. I grabbed the microphone and asked him if it was the new or old Blue, hoping with every beat of my heart that the response would be the new Blue. The response was "The old Blue."

It felt as if someone slammed a fist into my stomach. Tears welled in my eyes. I told myself, *"Get a grip on yourself. You can't cry in front of these men."* The next hour was a blur. Soon it was time to extract the Blues, and before I knew it, Lieutenant Eikenberry walked up to me and handed me Lou's dog tags covered with his blood. I took the dog tags and walked to my tent and mourned the death of my friend. As I write this, I realize that still, after all these years, I have never let him go.

I suspect that for every soldier that has been in combat, you do not remember all of the men from your unit by name, let alone the ones that died in combat. Instead, the grief and loss are centered on one individual, and for me, that individual is First Lieutenant Louis E. Porrazzo, Saber Blue.

SABER BLUE

We did not get to say goodbye
We parted with a smile.
You took the path that led on high
And walked that final mile.

You left behind a legacy
Of duty, pride and honor.
It shines brightly in my galaxy
Of heroes whom I honor.

You were my friend a shining star
A man whose death I mourn.
And yet I hear from afar
The sobs of a child unborn.

Saber Blue, we pray for you
And remember all your zest.
A son, a husband, friend and leader of the crew
A man who gave his best.

In God's own way, he's chosen you
To scout it out ahead.
Farewell, goodbye, adieu
Lou Porrazzo, my friend

OH-13 flight line, August 1967, LZ Two Bits. Standing left
to right: SGT Leathers; SSG Crosby; CPT Chole. Kneeling
left to right: WO Brown; WO Graham; CWO Rawl

Blue 36 and 37 enroute to another insertion.

C Model gun ship with a "Chunker"
(40mm grenade launcher) mounted on the nose.

Red 24, C Model "Hog" gun ship (48 Rockets)
refueling at LZ Two Bits.

WO Kaufmann talks to SSG Wells as he refurbishes
the white painted strip on top of our gas tank
(This helped the gun ship pilots keep track of us)

CHAPTER SEVENTEEN
MOVING NORTH

The death of Lou Porrazzo was the most heart-wrenching experience for me in two tours in Vietnam. But then, I wasn't the only one in the troop his death had a tremendous impact on. Specialist Markowitz, his crewmate and observer in the scout platoon, was terribly upset and shaken by the death of Lou. Theirs was a close relationship, and I am not sure if he ever came to grips with it. Everyone in the troop who worked with Lou was upset a little or a lot. The next morning, the first-light team took off as usual, and the war continued.

Upon reflection, I have often wondered what impact the fact that there was no time to grieve had on men who had a friend killed in combat. I know one result was a conscious effort not to get too close to other men you served with. You didn't want to learn about their family, dreams, or aspirations. After their deaths, it was always easier to pack up their personal belongings if you weren't close to them. Of course, a result of this distancing was the almost-cold and callous approach many of us adopted when a crewmate was wounded or killed. All we were interested in was getting a replacement for him so we could go on with our job. We couldn't deal properly with their deaths, so we didn't deal with them at all. I can't speak for other people, but for me, it got to the point that in some cases, I didn't even want to learn their names. But of course you did; and when they were seriously wounded or died, they took a little more of you with them, and the shell you were building around your emotions got a little thicker.

As I write this, my mind goes back to Fiftieth Company at Officer Candidate School (OCS) at Fort Benning, Georgia. The one thing that was constantly stressed was "Control your emotions, candidate!" We were publicly chewed out, ridiculed, and harassed by our tactical officers (tacs) who made every effort to stress us to our limit. It was part of the program, and the deliberateness of it either broke you or you did learn to control your emotions. Our tacs were not battle-hardened veterans; in most cases, they had just graduated from the class in front of us. They, however, passed on what they had endured, and the entire process became institutionalized. It was mentally and physically tough, but I am thankful that I had the opportunity to be prepared for my job as a combat leader by this program. When we turned Blue (became the senior candidates), we were visited by a congressional delegation that had a profound impact on this program. The year was 1963, and after their visit, we were informed that much of the institutional conditioning were considered cruel. The strict timetable we had to live by, the nightly spit shining of the barracks' floors, the public chewing out, and the "demeaning humiliation" were to stop. And, thus, the program was changed, and as a result, Lieutenant Calley graduated from a radically different OCS than I and thousands of men before me had. This was my first exposure to the social scientists and the impact they were to have on the army during and after the war. What they failed to grasp, then and now, is that war is brutal and barbaric. What we are training officers to do is to lead a unit in combat and have that unit kill as many of the enemy as efficiently and effectively as they can, conserving ammunition during the process and not getting themselves killed. Death is their constant companion, and if they don't have the mental toughness to make the right decision under stress, then they should not be commissioned as an officer.

For me, the mental conditioning I received in OCS taught me to compartmentalize my emotions and allowed me to develop as an effective combat leader. Those who have never experienced combat may wonder if this is a good thing to learn, but as a combat leader, you must learn it. So in the final analysis, the combination of a very tough OCS and my experience during this first tour reinforced the value of being able to control my emotions, and I learned that lesson well.

Prior to Lou's death, we had been alerted that we were going to move north. They were moving the marines from around Chu Lai north to reinforce the marines at Khe Sahn and Da Nang. Intelligence had indicated a buildup of NVA forces in First Corps area, and the Third Brigade of the First Cavalry Division was to replace the marine force at Chu Lai. Since we were a part of the "slice" of division units that supported or operated with each brigade, we were going north with "our" brigade.

On 1 October 1967, we struck our camp at Two Bits South, loaded our tents on trucks and helicopters, and flew north to Chu Lai. When we arrived at Chu Lai later that day, we discovered that no one was expecting us. There was no fuel, no maps, no ammunition, and no welcome from the Marine Air Wing or the staff of Task Force Oregon that later turned into the Americal Division. In fact, we were told there was no room at the inn (Chu Lai base) and for us to go away. Major Beasley told the Task Force Oregon G3 that he wasn't going away. His mission was to deploy the troop to Chu Lai, and by God, that's what he was doing. Since neither the air wing nor the Task Force Oregon staff would give us permission to land at Chu Lai proper, Major Beasley selected a troop laager site outside the perimeter of Chu Lai. One sand dune back from the ocean, we set up camp. Within two hours of closing at Chu Lai, Major Beasley had procured some maps of our new AO and had coordinated with the G3 on the locations of all friendly units in the AO. He decided that he and the platoon leaders would do a recon of our new AO just to get a feel for what we were going to operate in. We had no intention of doing battle with anyone; we didn't have the radio frequencies of any artillery units or ground infantry units. We were just going to get familiar with the AO.

Major Beasley and Red in their C-model gunships, Captain Burnham in his D-model lift ship, and I in my H-13 took off to get a look at this new AO. We overflew the entire area at altitude and saw what looked like a formation of Hueys sitting on top of a hill. I dropped down from altitude for a closer look and discovered it was, in fact, a formation of Hueys that had been destroyed on the ground. We called this site Million Dollar Hill.

I called Major Beasley and told him I was getting a nosebleed from flying at altitude and that I preferred to stay low level on the way back to Chu Lai. He gave a short laugh and said it was okay to stay low level. They all thought I was joking, but in fact, I had started the day with 367 hours of pilot time in the H-13, 267 of which were low level. Flying nap of the earth was my environment and the place I felt most comfortable flying. It was interesting to note that I had flown more time in the three months I had been in country than I had during the year of flight school.

We were flying generally east southeast on the way back; and while not consciously looking for the enemy, I was scanning the area ahead of us and below us, looking for any type of movement, texture changes in the vegetation, or any sign of recent activity such as a trail. As we cleared the trees that bordered a stream and flew over the streambed, I couldn't believe what I saw. Directly beneath us was a platoon of NVA soldiers—in full uniform, complete with pith helmets—taking a break. Staff Sergeant Wells started firing the M-60 machine gun and was yelling, "Come right! Come right!" Some of these soldiers had their boots off, and their feet were dangling in the stream, some weapons were stacked against a tree, and one soldier was pointing at us as if to say, "Gee, look at that." It was apparent they had never encountered a U.S. Army Air Cavalry Troop before. We killed all of them. By this time, Major Beasley and Captain Hughes had discovered two more platoons and were engaging them with rockets and miniguns. We weren't prepared to follow up on this contact. We had no QRF or RRF, no more maps, no rearm and refuel points established, and no communication to brigade headquarters. To be honest about it, since we had the only maps of the area, no one at the troop could have found us if any of us had been shot down. None of these items entered our minds.

We had found the enemy, and we were going to kill them. The adrenaline was pumping, and the lust for battle consumed us. We flew through them, around them, and over them, and killed at least fifty of them. That was our introduction to Operation Wallowa; and the NVA received an introduction to Bravo Troop, First Squadron, Ninth Air Cavalry. It wasn't until Major Beasley ran out of ammunition that it occurred to any of us that perhaps we should hold off on this until we had some people to reinforce us or perhaps rescue us. Major Beasley ordered all of us to altitude. One of the gunships had taken a few hits, but none of the crew members were wounded or killed. The flush of victory competed with the rush of adrenaline, and we were, literally and figuratively, flying high as we headed back to Chu Lai. I scanned the FM frequency until I found the AFN station and heard James Brown singing "I Feel Good." That pretty much encapsulated our feelings.

While we were in the AO, some of the men had located the Marine Corps Air Wing Officers Club. That evening, we went to the club to celebrate our victory. On the official level, we were not welcome at Chu Lai; on a pilot-to-pilot basis, we were welcomed. Sometime during the evening, one of the marine pilots asked if we were carrier qualified. We responded no, and a cheer went up from the marines. Tables were hastily pulled together. Now we had what passed for a carrier flight deck. Two or three marine pilots grabbed one of our pilots, lifted him off the floor, turned him horizontally, and threw him down the tables. Bottles and glasses went flying as he roared down this impromptu flight deck. They took great delight in qualifying each of us. I still find it interesting after all these years that the comradeship that developed between the army pilots and the marine-corps pilots never did develop between us and the staff of the Americal Division.

We were stuck on the beach for two days until a typhoon came roaring in from the South China Sea. Major Beasley tried to get permission for us to move onto Chu Lai, but that was denied. In his travels around the air base, he had discovered a new marine-corps hangar under construction and, upon his return to the troop area (which was already ankle deep in water), instructed us to fly our aircraft to the hangar. He instructed Major Burrow to get the rest of the troop loaded on vehicles and moved to the hangar. We took off in gale force winds and hovered to the hangar, tied down our aircraft as best we could, and then went to the hangar. The hangar was locked, so we shot the lock off and moved in.

The next day, the squatters from B Troop were discovered in the hangar and told to get out. Major Beasley stood firm and announced we weren't leaving until a troop area was located for us on Chu Lai. I wasn't privy to all of the discussions, but there was certainly a flap over this major and his ragtag outfit that had stolen a marine-corps hangar. The marines refused to allow us on their part of the base. From their point of view, we were an accident waiting to happen, and they wanted no part of us. This, as far as the marine corps was concerned, was an army problem. If we needed space, get it from the army. The American Division didn't want us either, but they were ordered to get us space. We ended up establishing our troop area on the American Division's main helipad.

To many people, the concept of refusing space on the Chu Lai airfield by the marines is conceivable, but to be refused space by another army unit is inconceivable. All I can say about that is the army is made up of all kinds of people. Some have power, some don't. If the person with the power chooses to be an ass, then all sorts of people suffer. I don't know who was refusing us the space, but I suspect it was the American Division G3. When Major General Tolson, commanding general of the First Cavalry (airmobile) Division, learned of this, a greater power was applied, and we moved onto the helipad.

When we flew and drove our battered aircraft and vehicles to the helipad, the division staff was aghast. Right across the street from the helipad was the division headquarters. It was bad enough that we landed nine fully armed C-model gunships and ten OH-13 aircraft, with machine guns and grenades hanging from wires and no revetments to park them in; but when they glimpsed the Blue platoon with bandoleers of machine-gun ammunition draped across their bodies, grenades and packages of C-4 explosives hanging from them, blue bandanas around their necks, and a cold steel look in their eyes, they couldn't believe it!

We soon discovered they had an Officers Club located next to the division headquarters. This club looked like it had been taken from some Hollywood movie set. It sat high on a bluff that overlooked the South China Sea. It had a thatched roof with a gentle sea breeze circulating through the open windows of the club. There were ceiling, fans, a jukebox, tables and chairs, a mahogany bar, Red Cross girls, nurses, good food, and was as far removed from combat as was thinkable. The only thing missing was a neon sign over the door spelling out "Rick's American Café" and Humphrey Bogart to greet us when we arrived. It sure was a different world than the world we lived in. After we saw the club, we understood why the staff officers were shocked to see us camped outside their headquarters.

Having settled the issue of our base camp, we next selected a forward operations base (FOB). The First Battalion, First Armored (1-1) was located at the east end of the Que Son Valley on an established fire-support base they operated from. We colocated at this fire-support base and named it LZ Porrazzo. Every morning, we would fly to LZ Porrazzo, kill as many of the enemy as we could find, and, in the evening, fly back to Chu Lai. The contrast between the fighting with its blood and gore and that Officers Club made it an unreal world. Our attitude toward the Americal staff was colored by that contrast. The division G3 kept telling us not to fly over the division headquarters when we took off or landed, but since the prevailing wind was from the east, which meant we would just about always take off over division headquarters. If the winds were calm and we could take off east or west, we always took off over their division headquarters.

CHAPTER EIGHTEEN

ANOTHER BEGINNING

The move to Chu Lai found us facing an entirely different enemy than we had become accustomed to in the Bong Song plains. We were now facing the Second NVA Division that consisted of three regiments of infantry and two local force (VC) battalions. This division had been virtually unopposed since the end of World War II and had been moving freely during daylight hours. It took the Second NVA Division two months and approximately 577 soldiers killed and seventy soldiers captured by B Troop before they stopped moving during the daylight hours. During our first two months in this AO, Bravo Troop averaged killing 288 NVA a month.

For example, during our first two weeks of operation in this AO, every scout crew averaged killing three NVA on every mission. As a scout crew, we averaged three to five missions a day; therefore, each scout crew was killing from nine to fifteen enemies every day. This was eyeball-to-eyeball combat with the enemy, it was a life-or-death struggle on every mission, it was the pilot and observer against one to fifteen NVA at a time, it was individual combat that was as barbarous as any in the annals of history. This was humanity regressing to a precivilized struggle for dominance—kill or be killed and survival of the fittest, quickest, and most agile. And every day, these crews greeted each dawn with the thought that today would surely be the day they would die.

You may ask, "Why would anyone do that?" I cannot answer for anyone else, but for me, there were several components to answer that question. First, I had come to grips with my own mortality. Death is a certainty and not optional as so many people today seem to believe. It is only the timing that is uncertain. Second, if you believe as Saint Thomas Aquinas so clearly explained, that God is the archer and we are the arrow, then you believe that you have been set upon the course whose ultimate destination is known only to God. The flight path of this arrow will be buffeted by the winds of decisions you make or fail to make along the course, but you travel the course, secure in the knowledge that you will not die until you have hit God's target and not one second sooner. That is not to say that you do dumb or stupid things along the course; rather, you do what is called for and in moderation. So for me, I was not afraid of dying, and while death was a constant companion, it was not the overriding concern. The timing of my death was and is in God's hands. And lastly, this was my job. I was the scout platoon leader with the emphasis on leader. You may shove from the rear, but you certainly do not lead from the rear. If you think of your unit as a string and you want it to go in a straight line, I defy you to push it in a straight line. On the other hand, if you grasp it and step out smartly, it will follow in a straight line. Our troop commanders and platoon leaders in this remarkable troop were all leaders in that sense of the word. While I was in this troop, I knew of no leader that put his personal safety ahead of the mission, and that was the key to our phenomenal success.

The month of October saw changes in the leadership structure of the troop. Captain Jim Hughes (Red) completed his tour on the fifteenth of October and was replaced by Captain Erle Thomas. Captain Thomas was a man of slight build with an entirely different personality than Red Hughes. Where Captain Hughes swaggered with a cigar firmly clamped in his teeth, Captain Thomas walked quietly and, as I recall, did not smoke at all. The phrase "good ole boy" popped in your mind when you thought of Captain Hughes, and Captain Thomas was the antithesis of that image. Captain Thomas was quiet and thoughtful but just as effective as the weapons platoon leader he was replacing.

Major William Ryan joined the troop just before we left Two Bits and was designated the new troop operations officer on the day we arrived at Chu Lai. He replaced Captain Hasselgrove who had completed his tour and was returning to the States. Major Beasley was getting short and was going to return to the States at the end of October. I found it strange that they would bring in a new major who had date of rank on Major Burrow's. The intention was that Major Ryan would replace Major Beasley as the troop commander, and Major Burrow would remain the troop XO. I believe that the overriding consideration was the fact that Major Burrow was an infantry officer, and Major Ryan was an armor officer. Air cavalry was an armor-proponent unit, and the armor branch did not want to fill one of the few command slots it had in air cavalry with a nonarmor officer. At any rate, Major Ryan started to learn our procedures as the troop operations officer.

As I think back on that particular period of time, I can only imagine what he must have felt. It had to be overwhelming. We had just moved into an area of operations where our contact with the enemy had risen to an all-time high, and the violent execution of operations for which this troop was known had raised several more notches. To be thrown unsuspectingly into a unit that had more daily contact with the enemy than any other unit in the First Cavalry Division, a unit that inflicted more casualties on the enemy than any battalion-size and some brigade-size units in the division at that time, and be expected to command it with no loss in efficiency was a daunting thought.

I knew from my own introduction to this unit that it took time to become accustomed to the managed violence, to learn the procedures that this troop had developed that made it such an effective fighting unit, and to capture the spirit that made this troop so unique. I recall thinking at the time that Major Ryan had a lot to learn in a very short time. I didn't dwell on it because I had more-than-enough action to keep me occupied.

While the scout platoon had ten H-13 aircraft, we never had ten scout pilots. I believe that the maximum number of scout pilots on hand while I was the scout platoon leader was eight. During the beginning of Operation Wallowa, I believe we were down to five or six pilots in the platoon. The crews had to be given a day off occasionally, and on those days, we were down to only four or five scout pilots operational, which meant that on some days you flew more missions than you normally would.

It was on such a day that the rear area at Chu Lai called and informed us that the weather was deteriorating, and a typhoon was moving up the coast toward us. They recommended that we leave as soon as possible and try to beat the storm back to Chu Lai. Since none of the scout aircraft had instrumentation to fly IFR, Major Beasley instructed us to take off immediately and follow the road (QL-1) back to Chu Lai. There were only four scouts present in the AO that day, and I told them that we would fly in a trail formation back to Chu Lai. I took off as the lead aircraft, flew to QL-1, and turned south toward Chu Lai. The farther south we flew, the worse the weather became. We were soon flying through a driving downpour of rain, and the wind gusts were becoming severe. I had all of my lights on, including my landing lights. I told everyone to tighten it up since it could be disastrous if anyone lost sight of the aircraft in front of us.

Soon, I could see nothing in front of me, and my visibility out either door was down to about fifteen feet. I slowed down to a creeping hover and told everyone that if he lost sight of the aircraft in front of them to set it down on the road below us and wait at least fifteen minutes before he tried to continue. I noticed that I was indicating sixty knots airspeed but knew I was barely moving forward. Suddenly, the aircraft shuddered, and I saw that the airspeed indicator was coming back through one hundred knots. We were experiencing wind gusts of up to fifty knots, which greatly exceeded the safety tolerance for this aircraft.

The heavy wind was blowing rain through the open cockpit, and we were getting drenched. Since I was already sweating profusely, the rain was not uncomfortable. I called Chu Lai tower and informed them we had a flight of four inbound over QL-1. They informed me that the airport was closed and that we could not land at Chu Lai. "*Great! Fucking wonderful!*" I thought. As I saw it, we had two options: land where we were or press on, disregarding Chu Lai tower. I opted for the latter. I asked for a communication check on FM, and when they answered, I noticed my automatic direction finding (ADF) needle swung ninety degrees to my left, which told me that we were directly to their west. I turned east and started flying toward the airfield. This took us off the road. We were now flying cross-country, and I didn't have a clue where we were. As I slowly hovered forward, I noticed, at the last possible second, a tree line immediately to my front. I warned everyone behind me and increased power enough to clear the trees. When I did that, I lost sight of the ground and, except for the trees, could see nothing outside the aircraft. As we cleared the trees, I quickly lowered my collective until I caught sight of the ground below me. I kept on hovering forward. Staff Sergeant Wells was trying to see through this driving rain directly ahead of us and kept rubbing his eyes as if that would allow him to see farther ahead.

We kept inching forward, and then I noticed we were now flying over a smooth surface. "*This has to be the main runway,*" I thought and heaved a sigh of relief. While we still had a ways to go, and it was far from the safety of being on the ground, at least I was familiar with the obstructions around the runway and had a general idea of where we were. That was a hell of a lot more than what I had known one minute before. As we continued flying generally east, I kept looking for some landmark I recognized but could see nothing that was more than ten to fifteen feet from the aircraft, and what I saw I did not recognize.

I called the other scout aircraft and learned they were all still with me. I didn't recognize anything below me and, in desperation, called the troop rear area and asked if they heard us. The RTO stepped outside the tent and, in a moment, replied that he thought he heard us southwest of their position. I knew we had cleared the main airfield perimeter, so I turned toward the northeast. We soon were flying over some buildings and tents, and I hoped we wouldn't fly into some antenna. I saw a road beneath us and turned farther north and continued hovering up this road. I knew there were telephone and power lines alongside the roads here, so I increased my height until I could just barely see the road.

In a few minutes, the RTO was on the radio, telling me in an anxious tone that he had just caught sight of us and to turn west. *"If he could see us, we have to be damn near over them,"* I thought. I turned west, lowered my collective, and, as I got closer to the ground, could see our helipad! *"Thank you, Lord!"* I silently said to myself as I hovered into my parking place.

Shortly after we landed, the wind slackened in velocity, and the rain let up a little bit. Within a half hour, the rest of the troop landed, much to the relief of everyone.

On 13 October, Staff Sergeant Wells and I had just completed a reconnaissance mission in the northwest portion of the AO. We had found and killed a small force of enemy soldiers. Since we had found them at the tail end of our time on station, we didn't have enough gas to fly back to LZ Porrazzo, so we had stopped at LZ Baldy to refuel. This had been the second straight mission we had flown without a break, and I opened a can of C-rations while Staff Sergeant Wells was refueling the aircraft. As I was eating, the radio came to life, and the operations officer called to inform me that there was a unit in contact that needed some help. Since we were the closest team, they wanted us to go to their aid as soon as we were finished refueling. I called my gunship, who was also refueling, and asked him if he had enough ammunition on board to fly another mission immediately. He replied that he did. I called Major Ryan back and informed him we would be airborne in about three minutes. He then gave me the location, frequency, and call sign of the unit in contact. I called my gunship and asked if he had a good copy on the message from Three. He replied, "Roger that." I stuffed my face with the remainder of the C-rations as Staff Sergeant Wells climbed on board. As he was strapping in, I told him to open a can of Cs and chow down since we were going on another mission. As we departed Baldy, I gave him the information that I had. He nodded his head as he opened a can of C-rations.

When we arrived at the location that had been given us, we found no firefight and no unit in contact. I called operations back and asked them to verify the grid location of the unit in contact.

They read back the coordinates they had given us earlier. Many ground units had difficulty reading maps in this terrain, and realizing that, I came up on their frequency and called them. They responded to my first call; and yes, they were in contact, and their point squad was pinned down and had taken casualties. While he was talking, I noticed that my radio direction-finding needle had swung to the left. I turned left, centered the needle on the gage, and started flying in that direction. Every couple of minutes, I would call him, and when he responded, I verified if we were going in the correct direction. Within minutes, we were in the vicinity of their location. This was verified when we started to receive fire from three or four positions in a hedgerow directly below us. Staff Sergeant Wells returned fire, and I heard the platoon leader on the ground start to shout into the radio, "I see you! We are right in front of you! Behind the rice-paddy dike." I looked ahead and saw them. I turned right and flew to the rear of the enemy then flew an elongated flight path until I was able to approach the friendly position from the rear without receiving enemy fire. As I was moving to his position, I asked him to give me a current SITREP (situation report).

He explained that they had been moving across this rice paddy toward the dry ground to their front. When his point squad was about ten feet from the hedgerow, the enemy opened fire and killed or wounded everyone in the squad. While he was explaining this, I saw the point squad pinned down in the open with the rest of the platoon hunkered down behind a rice-paddy dike to their rear. It was obvious that the lieutenant was in a state of near panic. I told him, "Okay, calm down. We'll get them out of there. I'm going over for a closer look." I had noticed that the machine gunners were also behind the dike, and I told him, "Get the machine guns set up on either flank on top of the dike."

He said, "There is so much fire." To which I replied, "Lieutenant, get the machine guns set up. That point squad needs covering fire. Do it NOW!" He replied, "Roger," and in a few minutes, I saw the machine gunners start to move.

Staff Sergeant Wells and I then flew toward the west until we were out of small-arms range and then turned and flew back toward the point squad following the hedgerow. While we were flying toward them, I called my high bird and asked him if he could see the point squad. He replied, "Roger that. White, they are awfully close for rockets. I'll cover you with my minigun."

I replied, "Roger that shit." We were flying at about three feet above the rice paddy, right in front of the hedgerow. We started to take fire from the hedgerow, and Staff Sergeant Wells poured fire right back from his M-60. The enemy was on the right side of the aircraft; and below me, on the left side, was the pinned-down rifle squad. One of the squad members looked up at me and waved a hand, without raising it off the ground. I heard the minigun on the gunship start up, and the enemy fire slackened just a bit. I continued down the hedgerow until the firing stopped. We now knew where the enemy positions were located, and I thought, *"How are we going to get them out of there?"*

I called the pinned-down squad leader and asked him what his status was. He replied, "Three killed and everyone else wounded." I asked him if they could all run if they had to. He replied, "You damn right, if it will get us out of here alive!" We all realized they would die unless we got them out of there soon. The problem was that they were in the open, only about ten feet from the enemy, who were in prepared positions. We needed smoke to get them out of there.

I asked Sergeant Wells how many Willie Peats (white phosphorous grenades) we had with us. We had a mixed box of grenades on the seat between us (frags, concussion, and some WP). He counted and replied, "Four."

I said, "Well, the only way to get them out of there is to use smoke. Here's what we're going to do. When we fly back up the hedgerow, you throw the WP in front of the enemy positions ten to fifteen feet apart. As soon as the smoke starts to build, we'll fly over the point squad and cover their withdrawal. Our gunship can punch off a few rockets to keep the enemy down."

Sergeant Wells looked at me and said, "You realize that I can't fire the machine gun until I get rid of the grenades?"

I said, "Yeah, I know." What was unspoken between us was the fact that once we started this run, we were very, very vulnerable. With our machine gun firing in the enemy's direction, it at least threw off their aim and made them nervous. Without our return fire, they had clear shooting at us.

While I was briefing the gunship, the platoon leader, and the squad leader on what we were going to do, Staff Sergeant Wells was getting the grenades ready. He had secured the machine gun out of the way and had straightened the safety pins on the grenades. He had three WP grenades between his legs and was holding the other one in his hand. I called the pinned-down squad leader and told him that as soon as we were over them, they were to haul ass back to the platoon. He said, "Roger that shit!"

While all of our gunship pilots were good shooters, this was going to require some very precise shooting. When you consider that many of our gunship pilots used a grease-penciled X on the windscreen as their aiming point, it was remarkable how accurate they were.

As soon as everyone was ready, we started our run. As we approached the pinned-down squad, we started to receive heavy ground-to-air fire. Staff Sergeant Wells tossed one, two, and three; and then the last grenade was out, and as far as I could tell, we had not been hit. I turned left and turned back toward the point squad. I heard and felt two rockets explode. Then I heard on the radio, "Goddamn it, White, get the fuck out of the way! You're flying into my rockets!" I had turned back toward the point squad too quickly and was where I shouldn't have been. As soon as these words were uttered, one rocket exploded beneath us, and another rocket exploded directly to our rear. The concussion wave from the rockets hit us and threw us forward. Our high bird broke off his gun run and was climbing back to altitude as fast as he could to get ready for the next run.

Nothing appeared damaged, and we flew to the lead man of the pinned-down squad. The smoke was billowing out from the grenades, and while Staff Sergeant Wells was firing into the hedgerow, I was on the radio, exhorting the squad to "go! Go! Go!"

We hovered sideways over the squad, firing into the hedgerow until the last man was safely behind the rice-paddy dike. Our gunship had executed a return-to-target maneuver and was walking rockets down the edge of the hedgerow. Smoke, debris, and explosions filled the air. Major Beasley had arrived on station, and he and our high bird gave another lesson on what was meant by violent execution of a plan. I heard on the radio that the medevac bird was not going to come in unless he had gunship cover. I called the medevac crew and told them I would escort them in. I looked up and searched the sky for them and finally saw a speck that was the medevac aircraft. I said to Sergeant Wells, "He's so high I bet he has a nosebleed." We laughed as I started a climb to altitude, and the medevac started his descent. I had them come up on UHF and briefed them on where they were supposed to land. We joined up with them and flew between them and the hedgerow, firing our machine gun.

"Saber White, this is Medevac, over."

"This is White, over."

"Are you in an H-13 on our right, firing a machine gun, over?"

"That's affirmative, over."

"Are you supposed to be our gunship cover, over?"

"We're not supposed to be. We *are* your gunship cover, over."

Sergeant Wells turned to me and grinned. and I grinned back. Just as they were touching down, an excited sounding voice came on the net and said, "They're out in the open! They're assaulting our position!" I was watching the hedgerow and didn't see anything. Then I realized that I was hearing another platoon in the same company that was located somewhere else. Well, the medevac bird heard the same call and immediately pulled pitch to get out of there. It took us about five minutes to convince him to go back and pick up the casualties. After the medevac was complete, we returned to LZ Porrazzo and finished lunch. I don't recall which infantry unit it was, but it was the most satisfying mission I flew on my first tour. We flew two more reconnaissance missions that day before we called it a day and flew back to Chu Lai.

We had two methods of flying back to Chu Lai. We either sent the scouts ahead, and we swept the inland waterway with the scouts generally on line and about a thousand meters between us. The gunships were in a gaggle behind us, and Blue Lift was behind them, or we flew back as Pink teams followed by Blue Lift. On most sweeps on our way back to Chu Lai, we didn't find much, but on some occasions, we would find the enemy and get our last kills for the day along this inland waterway. There was a big lake northwest of Chu Lai, and when we reached that point, we normally climbed to altitude and entered the traffic pattern for Chu Lai.

That evening, as I entered the operations tent for the nightly briefing, Major Burrow said, "Hey, White, you're a fucking hero! That infantry unit you supported today wants to put you in for a medal. I told them we would take care of it." And he did. I received my first Silver Star for that action.

The awards and decorations policy for the troop, and squadron for that matter, was restrained. We were involved in so many firefights and killed so many enemies that it took an extraordinary event to receive an award of some kind. What might be considered extraordinary in most units was considered routine in B Troop. The men in this troop were the most courageous men I have ever served with; and yet, courage was the norm, it was what was expected from all of us—it was our job. To face what these men faced on a daily basis and then to accomplish what these men did required more than courage; it required a sense of dedication and fearlessness that you seldom find in an individual and rarely find in an entire unit. Bravo Troop was one of those units.

The next morning, Major Beasley informed me that Major Ryan had to start flying in the AO and get some experience since he was going to assume command of the troop in two weeks. Therefore, I was going to be pulled from the scout platoon; and the next day, 15 October 1967, I was going to become Saber Three, the troop operations officer.

CHAPTER NINETEEN
OPERATIONS

Having worked in operations while Captain Hasselgrove was on R&R, I was familiar with my new duties. This was going to be entirely different from what I had experienced up to this point. As the operations officer, I would seldom, if ever, be required to engage in close combat with the enemy, and I would concentrate more on coordinating and directing the efforts of the teams in the AO rather than actually participating in the operations myself. As I settled into the new routine, I found myself feeling uneasy about my position. My duties were no problem; I was totally qualified for it, and I knew exactly how to coordinate every aspect of what we did. What bothered me was the fact that I was no longer sharing the daily danger with everyone else and felt guilty about my relative secure position.

There were eight enlisted personnel assigned to the operations section: an operations NCO, a communications NCO, two clerks, and four radio telephone operators (RTOs). The fact that we were in combat did not alter the fact that flight records had to be maintained on all aviation personnel; radios had to be manned twenty-four hours a day; the operations map had to be kept current with all unit locations, boundaries, and the location of all artillery in the brigade AO. Daily, weekly, and monthly reports had to be prepared and submitted, and of course, we had to post all changes to radio frequencies as they occurred and distribute the daily "key list" for our secure radios. We did not lack for things to do, and truthfully, the troop could not have operated as smoothly as it did without this type of behind-the-scenes effort. However, it was a complete change of pace and orientation for me that required some time to adjust to. What I found ironic was the fact that I was now assigned a D-model Huey to fly, and I found that I preferred to fly the H-13! My checkout on the Huey was accomplished, flying back and forth between Chu Lai and LZ Porrazzo. I now flew at altitude (1,500 to two thousand feet above ground level [AGL]) and gained an entirely different perspective of Vietnam. It is a beautiful country with lush green vegetation and sparkling white beaches. I often thought, *"If this country wasn't at war, it would be a beautiful place to vacation. When this war is over, maybe I will return as a tourist."*

At Chu Lai, we operated out of our tent where we conducted our morning and evening briefings.

MAJ Burrow in front of the Operations tent at Chu Lai, October 1967

At LZ Porrazzo, the operations section operated out of a bunker that was partially dug into the ground.

Operations Bunker, LZ Porrazzo, October 1967.

We maintained an operations map at each location but did the routine administrative work back at Chu Lai. Essentially, the operations section at LZ Porrazzo consisted of me and an RTO who also maintained the daily staff journal. In this journal, we recorded each spot report that we received from the teams in the AO and all other messages received from the Third Brigade, the squadron, and the Task Force Oregon (Americal). We also had a poster hanging in the bunker that pretty much expressed the troop's attitude. It showed a vulture sitting on a bare tree limb, head down and swiveled so it glared at you. Under the picture was this caption: "Patience my ass. Let's go kill something."

All significant activities were recorded; and at the end of each day, we did a recapitulation of daily significant events and kept a running total of all types of statistics, e.g., how many friendly and enemy were killed in action, wounded, or captured; how many meals we consumed; how many bags of mail we received and sent out; how much ammunition was consumed; how much fuel was consumed, etc. As we compiled these statistics, it occurred to me that it would be a good idea to write up our more significant actions. Since I was going to do the writing, I arbitrarily selected thirty or more enemies killed in a day as significant. I also decided that any operation that illustrated a reconnaissance technique that I wanted to emphasize would also be written about.

As I wrote up these significant actions or techniques, I would have the pilots come in at the end of that day's operation and draw a sketch map of the contact area and try to gather just a few more bits of information from them. I did not attempt to go back in time; I started recording these significant actions from the day I became the operations officer. These reports are the basis of the narrative accounts I will offer in the next few chapters.

As I settled into the position of operations officer, I established a routine for myself. Captain Bob Rice, who was now Saber White, and I shared a GP small tent and had an opportunity to discuss a lot of things in the mornings and in the evenings. I was able to keep up with how the guys in the scout platoon were doing and observed; once again, how once you leave an organizational unit (such as the scout platoon), you really were no longer considered as being relevant to what they were doing even though you were still in the same unit. This is not unusual and is something many a person with a big ego has difficulty in accepting. The truth of the matter is, we are all replaceable, and we only count when we are actively involved in either making decisions or carrying out decisions for that organizational unit and actively contributing to the results of that particular organizational unit.

My days settled into a routine that I held to as long as I was with the troop. In the morning, I would stop by the operations tent and read the staff journal from the night before going to breakfast. After breakfast, I'd talk to the troop commander and get any additional guidance for that day's operations, prepare for, and give the morning briefing. Following this briefing, I would go to my aircraft and fly to LZ Porrazzo and get the forward operations ready to function for the day. Once at LZ Porrazzo, I would call the Third Brigade S3 and our troop liaison officer, who was located at the brigade's Tactical Operations Center (TOC); get an update from them; brief each team before they departed for the AO; stay on top of what each team was doing; coordinate what the teams could not coordinate; keep a constant status of the fuel and ammunition available at LZ Porrazzo, Ross, Baldy, and Colt; make sure the operations map had the current boundaries and artillery locations; and ensure we had the proper frequencies and call signs for everyone that operated in the Wallowa AO. When the troop was in contact with the enemy, I tried to anticipate what, where, and when we needed new teams; the QRF and RRF; and any special equipment in the AO. At the end of the day's operation, I would follow the troop back as we conducted our nightly sweep down the inland waterway to Chu Lai. Back at Chu Lai, it was always a hasty supper, then prepare for the nightly briefing, discuss with the troop commander to receive guidance and make recommendations for the next day's operations, conduct the nightly briefing, check on the administrative effort of the operations personnel for that day, and, if we had wounded in the hospital at Chu Lai, go with the troop commander and visit them. On a few occasions, I would go to the Officers Club and have a drink, return to the troop area, take one last swing through operations, and then head for my tent. There was very little variation in my routine, and it went on day after day after day.

I soon got to know our squadron commander, LTC Robert H. Nevins, on a more personal basis. The rest of the squadron was still at Two Bits, and he would fly up occasionally to touch bases and fly with us. While I was the scout platoon leader, I had talked to him on the radio occasionally but had never met him in person. One thing I admired about him was the fact that he let everyone do their jobs. He would check in with you when he arrived on station, and then he would observe but never interfere with what a team was doing. This built confidence in the team members and was rare with most senior officers.

My observation was that most battalion and brigade commanders could not resist interfering with operations that were in progress. It was particularly bad when a unit was in contact. Sometimes you would have them stacked up over a contact area three deep and each of them issuing different directives to the guy on the ground who was doing the actual fighting. On one occasion, while we were still operating out of Two Bits, Colonel Nevins was on station with us as we were supporting a unit in contact. We had worked out a plan of attack that we (the ground unit and the troop) were executing. Suddenly, this voice on the FM radio (the battalion commander) starts asking questions and giving the ground commander a hard time in the middle of the firefight. I got on the radio and told him to stay off the net until this action was completed. He got irate and demanded to know who the hell I thought I was. I was about to tell him who the hell I was when I heard Colonel Nevins on the radio, telling this guy to meet him on UHF. We heard no more from this battalion commander while we were on station and, in the process, completed our mission as planned with no further loss of friendlies. While I hadn't met Colonel Nevins personally at that time, he shot to the top of my list of commanders to work for.

I discovered that, in person, he was very personable, animated, and a man who could make a decision. He was the type of leader who inspired confidence in his subordinates and *delivered* for his subordinates and his seniors. The confidence everyone had in him was not misplaced. Under his leadership, the squadron achieved some of its greatest successes while in Vietnam. What also struck a responsive cord with me was that he was a "bottom line" type of person. He didn't have any hang-ups about procedures as long as the results we were after were achieved. That's another way of saying that it didn't have to be "his way or his technique." If someone had a better idea or way to do something, he was willing to try it, and if it worked, he gave that person full credit for achieving the results we were all striving for and never tried to pull off any credit for himself. If it didn't work, he took full responsibility for it not working and never offered the excuse that he had received bad advice or that someone else hadn't carried out the plan correctly. If the term "command presence" could be applied to anyone, Colonel Nevins was the man. He set an example in leadership that was an inspiration to all with whom he came in contact and, in my mind, was one of the few great leaders in Vietnam.

CHAPTER TWENTY

THE BATTLE AT PHU 'O' CHAU

The inland waterway, as we called it, was a river that started near the port town of Hoi An and worked it's way southward to just north of Chu Lai where it emptied into a lake. It was very close to the ocean, and in the north, the river was separated from the ocean by ten to fifteen thousand meters of low sandy hills. As it snaked its way southward, the river drew closer to the ocean and, in places, was only separated by narrow strips of land that were in places only a one hundred meters wide. Along this inland waterway were numerous little villages, and the waterway teamed with commerce that was carried on by the use of sampans.

The area also teamed with NVA and VC forces. On our nightly sweeps down this waterway, we would invariably find and kill from two to ten enemy soldiers. The Third Brigade S2 had reports of numerous NVA and VC forces located along this waterway. Major Beasley decided to conduct area-reconnaissance missions from the brigade's northern boundary down the waterway to the south. We started a detailed reconnaissance on the seventeenth of October beginning at the northern boundary.

I knew that if the scouts were going to find concealed positions or troops, we had to restrict the reconnaissance to a relatively small space. Our standard reconnaissance box was two thousand meters by two thousand meters. We plotted a series of these boxes down the length of the river and started our reconnaissance on 17 October. As we worked our way south down the river on the seventeenth and eighteenth, we were picking up signs of increased enemy activity. On the nineteenth, just south of the village of Phu 'O' Chau, the troop engaged and killed nineteen enemy soldiers. Twelve of these soldiers were very near to the river itself, and it appeared to us that there was a concentration of enemy troops in the immediate area.

Based upon our findings and recommendations, the brigade decided to conduct a sweep, search, and destroy operation near Phu 'O' Chau the next day, 20 October 1967. The concept of the operation was to have A Troop 1-1 Armored Cavalry start a sweep south of Phu 'O' Chau and drive the enemy forces north toward Phu 'O' Chau. While this sweep-and-search operation was being conducted, elements of the 1-7 Infantry Battalion would be air assaulted into positions north of them, but still south of Phu 'O' Chau, and sweep south toward the 1-1 Armored Cavalry.

Our part of this operation was to conduct a screen to the front and along the right flank of the 1-1 Armored Cavalry and to provide initial reconnaissance and security of the landing zones (LZs) to be used by the 1-7 Infantry. Once the infantry was on the ground, we would conduct reconnaissance to their front and screen their west and east flanks. The operation would begin at 0630 hours with the 1-1 Cavalry starting their sweep north, and the 1-7 infantry would air assault into LZs 3 and 9 at 0800 hours.

At 0630 hours, a Pink team arrived on station and started reconnaissance in front of A/1-1 Cavalry. As the troop and the Pink team moved forward, there were signs of recent enemy activity, but the enemy could not be located. This team moved farther north and checked LZs 3 and 9 in preparation for the air assault of the 1-7 Infantry. At 0800 hours, A/1-7 Infantry air assaulted into two green LZs. This initial Pink team returned to LZ Porrazzo, and at 0745 hours, Captain Erle Thomas (Red) and a scout aircraft started to screen the right flank of A/1-1 Cavalry along the river. The vegetation in this part of the AO consisted of palm trees, rice paddies, hedgerows, and scrub brush. This terrain offered much better observation than what we found farther to the west where bamboo thickets turned into thick jungle. At 0825 hours, Red observed some movement to the rear of the scout. Upon closer investigation, he observed several NVA soldiers attempting to avoid detection. He immediately engaged them with rockets and machine guns. They returned a heavy volume of fire, hitting his aircraft and causing some damage to his radios. He disregarded the enemy fire and pressed his attack upon the NVA, killing four of them and wounding another. The scout returned to the contact area and started a detailed search of the area. Red was at altitude, covering the scout, when his door gunner shouted on intercom that he saw two VC trying to run from the contact area. Red came around to the left, and as he straightened out, he saw them in front of him. He called the scout and told him he had two VC in sight and was going to engage. He rolled in on a rocket run and punched off two pairs of rockets. One of the rockets hit one of the VC in the back, and the other was blown to pieces by the explosions of the other three rockets. The scout checked the bodies and confirmed that two more VC was KIA.

That team had to return to Porrazzo to rearm and refuel. Red had to change radios and have his aircraft checked. Major Beasley, in his gunship, and another scout, Warrant Officer Larry Brown, went to the area and started to screen in front of A/1-7 Infantry. At 0930 hours, Major Beasley observed some people moving along a trail but could not determine if they were civilians or the enemy. He directed Mr. Brown (warrant officers are referred to as mister) toward their location, and as he came upon them, they were on the pilot's side of the aircraft. As soon as the enemy saw his aircraft, they immediately fired at him. They were armed with AK-47s, and everyone fired at him on full automatic. His aircraft took many hits, and pieces of metal and Plexiglas were flying around inside the cockpit. He came hard right and pulled in as much power as he could. At the same time, he was talking to Major Beasley on the radio.

"Six, this is One-Four! Those sons of bitches really laced me! They're dressed in green and khaki uniforms, and they all have packs and weapons!"

Major Beasley replied, "Roger, I'm rolling in hot." As he was speaking, two pairs of rockets were screaming toward the enemy. He executed a return to target and punched off some more rockets that exploded in their midst. Three enemies were KIA, with the rest running and finding whatever cover they could.

"One-Four, this is Six. What's your status?"

"Six, this is One-Four. We're okay. We were just nicked, but they shot the shit out of this aircraft. I think they got my hydraulics. I better fly it back to Porrazzo, if this bird will make it."

"Roger, take up a heading of two one zero."

They departed station and started their return to LZ Porrazzo. Back in operations, we had been monitoring their conversation on UHF, and when we heard that One-Four had been badly shot up, I had Warrant Officer Jere Anderson (One-Three) take off to replace One-Four on station. As Major Beasley and Mr. Brown approached LZ Porrazzo, Mr. Brown told Major Beasley that he could make it to Porrazzo by himself and that he and One-Three should "go get them sons a bitches!"

An inspection of his aircraft after he landed revealed that it was unsafe to fly and could not be repaired at Porrazzo. Later that day, a CH-47 picked up the aircraft and slung it to our direct-support unit for repairs.

Meanwhile, Major Beasley and Mr. Anderson had returned to the area of contact and started to hunt down the survivors of the earlier attack. Mr. Anderson soon picked up a blood trail and followed it to a bunker. He marked the bunker with a smoke grenade, and Major Beasley fired the rest of his rockets at it. He had expended all of his rockets, but the bunker was still standing. The difficulty was trying to shoot a rocket inside the bunker entrance. Mr. Anderson hovered in front of the bunker entrance and started to receive fire from the bunker. His observer had an M-79 grenade launcher with him and launched a grenade into the bunker entrance. The firing from the bunker stopped, and Mr. Anderson hovered closer until his observer could look into the bunker. His observer could see one NVA dead and another one wounded.

While this was going on, Major Beasley had called for a replacement for himself since he had to refuel and rearm his aircraft. Warrant Officer Griffith Bedworth (Two-One) relieved Major Beasley on station and continued the screen with Mr. Anderson. As Major Beasley was returning to LZ Porrazzo, he spotted one

NVA in khaki uniform with web gear, attempting to hide from him. Since he had fired all of his rockets, he came to a hover over the treetops, and his door gunner killed the enemy soldier below him.

Soon after arriving on station, Mr. Bedworth's crew saw two more NVA in a bunker and engaged the bunker with his chunker (nose-mounted forty-millimeter grenade launcher) and killed one more NVA. A/1-7 started to move toward the bunker when Mr. Anderson saw three more NVA with camouflage on their backs about fifty meters north of the bunker. Mr. Bedworth engaged this force with rockets this time and killed two NVA soldiers and wounded another one. Alpha Company swept this area and captured the three wounded soldiers and confirmed all the previous kills in this area.

Major Beasley decided that we needed two teams in the AO at the same time: one to screen the advance of A/1-7 Infantry and another to screen the advance of A/1-1 Cavalry. Major Beasley and Chief Warrant Officer Joseph Rawl (One-Five) screened around A/1-7 Infantry, and Captain Thomas (Red) and Warrant Officer Russell Kaufman (One-Six) screened around A/1-1 Cavalry.

No sooner had Red and One-Six arrived on station than Red saw three NVA in khaki uniforms, attempting to avoid detection. He engaged them with rockets and machine-gun fire. They immediately returned fire, and soon a hail of fire was directed at Red. He completed his first gun run and did a return to target and engaged them again. He killed the three of them and had One-Six check the area. As Mr. Kaufman checked the area, he saw a lot of recent trail activity in the immediate area. He followed the trails to a hedgerow and decided to do some reconnaissance by fire. He flew about ten to fifteen feet in front of the hedgerow, and his observer fired into the hedgerow with his M-60 machine gun. The enemy obviously thought Mr. Kaufman could see them because they returned fire. The volume of fire was surprising, but one thing these scout crews knew was that when you're in the middle of them, your best chance of survival is attack, attack, attack. His observer concentrated his fire on the part of the hedgerow where the heaviest fire was coming from. Several of the enemy broke and ran. Red saw them running from the hedgerow and rolled in and blew all four of them away. By the time the firefight was finished, the One-Six crew had killed twelve of them, and Red had a total of seven on this fuel load. At the same time, about three hundred meters to the north, Major Beasley and Mr. Rawl were continuing their screen for A/1-7. As they were searching the area, Mr. Rawl found an NVA dressed in a green shirt with black shorts and with a pack and weapon, trying to hide in a water hole. He engaged him, resulting in one more NVA KIA.

As A/1-1 Cavalry and A/1-7 closed the distance between them, it was apparent that we only needed one team to work that area. The next team to go out was Two-One (Mr. Bedworth) and One-Three (Mr. Anderson). At 1345 hours, One-Three saw some bushes move, and looking closer, he saw that they were attached to an enemy soldier. His observer fired, and suddenly, they were receiving fire from other "bushes" in the area. The enemy fire was very heavy, and Mr. Anderson could feel the aircraft getting hit. He pressed his attack on the enemy and killed two of them, and two more ran away, trying to save themselves. They didn't get very far because Two-One rolled in and killed one of them for sure, and the other one disappeared into the underbrush. We then heard on the radio,

"Two-One, this is One-Three. I have control problems with the aircraft. We better head back to Porrazzo."

"This is Two-One. Roger that. Take up a heading of Two One Zero. Are you okay?"

"This is One-Three. Yeah, we're okay, but this bird has more vibrations than the Beach Boys, and they ain't good vibrations!"

After landing at LZ Porrazzo, the crew chief inspected the aircraft, and it had more hits than Mr. Brown's aircraft and had to be slung out by CH-47 also. That was the second scout aircraft that had been badly shot up, and this was before 1400 hours.

White (Captain Rice) decided that he would fly the remaining scout missions for the day, and at 1430 hours, he and Major Beasley observed six NVA attempting to evade them. White immediately engaged them and became the target for intense automatic-weapons fire. He pressed the attack upon the enemy and killed three of them. The remaining three attempted to escape to nearby bunkers and/or hide in the brush. When they broke and ran, Major Beasley rolled in on a rocket attack and killed one more of the enemy soldiers. The other two escaped into the brush and probably died of their wounds. We only counted four killed because we couldn't find the other two bodies.

Major Burrow (the troop's executive officer) was in another gunship, observing the action, when at 1550 hours, he observed an NVA in gray uniform with pack and weapon, attempting to evade out of the area. Major Burrow engaged him with rockets, resulting in another NVA KIA.

Major Beasley and Captain Rice broke station to rearm and refuel. Major Beasley flew back to LZ Porrazzo, and Captain Rice flew to LZ Baldy to refuel. After refueling, Two-Eight (Warrant Officer Zahn) joined White as he took off from LZ Baldy, and they returned to the contact area. As they arrived in the general area, Two-Eight saw another NVA with pack and weapon and engaged him with rockets, resulting in one more NVA KIA. At 1630 hours, White was doing a very low and slow reconnaissance, and as he flew over a trench line, he saw four enemy soldiers crouched down, trying to hide from him. He executed a tight right turn so the enemy was out his right door, and his observer was able to shoot down the length of the trench line, killing all four of the enemy soldiers.

Since midafternoon, we had found no enemy soldiers between A/1-1 Cavalry and A/1-7 Infantry. All of our contacts after 1400 hours were to the north (rear) of A/1-7. It was becoming apparent that they were attempting to escape to the north.

At 1725 hours, White and Two-Eight observed three more NVA. White executed a tight right turn and immediately became the target of intense enemy fire from the NVA. He pressed the attack and killed the three of them. As it turned out, this was our last contact for the day.

We wrapped up the day with no one in the troop wounded or killed; three aircraft shot up, which were grounded temporarily for repairs, and fifty-one of the enemy had been killed. In my brief summation in the after-action report of this battle, I concluded by saying, "By continuous reconnaissance of the battle area, we exerted maximum pressure on the enemy, keeping him off balance and affording him no opportunity to recover [a defensive posture]."

CHAPTER TWENTY ONE

THE BATTLE AT HUONG MY

Following the battle at Phu 'O' Chau, we continued to apply pressure on the enemy along the inland waterway. This was accomplished by conducting more reconnaissance and search-and-destroy operations in the area. The 5-7 Infantry Battalion was conducting ground sweeps throughout the general area, and based on prisoner interrogation and other sources, the brigade S2 concluded that the enemy force in this area consisted of one or more NVA battalions and possibly the Third NVA regimental headquarters.

On 23 October, it was decided to make a concerted effort in the vicinity of the village of Huong My. The plan was for 5-7 Infantry to conduct a sweep of this area from the west toward the east, hopefully flushing the enemy and driving them against the banks of the inland waterway. Our mission in this operation was to screen in front of the advancing infantry and along the banks of the inland waterway.

At 0645 hours, One-Four (Warrant Officer Brown) and Two-Five (Warrant Officer John Fieg) arrived on station and checked in with the battalion S3 who asked them to concentrate on the area in front of the center company. One-Four came up on the company frequency and let the company commander know that he and Two-Five were on station and to let the platoons know that he would be working in front of them. He also reminded the company commander to call him if they decided to shoot any artillery while he was working to their front. He also told him that he would remain on their frequency while he was on station. Before he started his reconnaissance, he identified the current location of each platoon and then started working toward the east.

At 0710 hours, One-Four observed two enemy soldiers. They saw him at the same time and immediately ran into a bunker. In one of the more bizarre incidents of this war, the occupants of the bunker literally threw these two out of the bunker in a vain attempt to keep their bunker's location a secret. It was too late for that effort since One-Four was right outside the entrance. As these two soldiers came flying out of the bunker, One-Four engaged and killed both of them. He then hovered over the entrance, dropped a smoke grenade, and had Two-Five roll in on a gun run. Mr. Fieg made two rocket passes on the bunker and destroyed the bunker. One-Four hovered over the debris but could not determine how many enemies were killed since those inside the bunker were buried under the rubble and were not visible from the air.

At 0800 hours, One-Four observed two VC dressed in black clothing, which we referred to as black pajamas, with weapons, and engaged them. They ran to another bunker nearby and were safe from Mr. Brown. One-Four marked the bunker with a smoke grenade, and Two-Five engaged with rockets, destroying this bunker also. This time, when One-Four checked after the rocket attack, he found that one of the two that had jumped into the bunker was dead. The other one was not visible, and Mr. Brown presumed he was underneath the rubble. Since many of these bunkers had connecting tunnels, it was possible he had escaped, so we did not carry the other VC as KIA.

After this engagement, they continued their reconnaissance, and at 0830 hours, One-Four saw two NVA in blue uniforms and engaged them, resulting in two NVA KIA. At this time, Captain Rice (White) and another gunship arrived on station to relieve Messrs. Brown and Fieg.

This replacement team picked up the reconnaissance effort from One-Four and Two-Five and continued searching the area. Captain Rice soon had a call from the infantry company commander, asking his assistance in locating a sniper that was slowing the progress of the platoon on the left flank.

This type of search required a very low, slow, and detailed reconnaissance effort. He flew various search paths, looking at the suspected terrain from every angle. It required an hour and a half of this type of flying before White noticed that the texture of one of the bushes was out of pattern with what he was flying over. He came around, and he and his observer looked very closely at the bush. The sniper hidden under the bush apparently thought that they saw him and made a sudden movement to fire at the scout helicopter. He never really completed the movement because the observer killed him before he could turn fully over.

This team had expended one fuel load, looking for the sniper, and it was time to return to LZ Porrazzo and refuel. Captain Thomas (Red) and Warrant Officer Brown (One-Four) replaced this team on station and continued the reconnaissance.

This was Mr. Brown's second trip to the AO that morning, and he knew what he was looking for: bushes tied to the backs of the NVA soldiers. It didn't take him long to spot five more enemy soldiers, which he immediately engaged. They also tried to evade to nearby bunkers, but he and his observer killed four of them. The bunkers they were trying to reach were located inside the hooches that made up this little village they were next to. One-Four hovered in front of most of the hooches and looked inside them. They all had a bunker constructed in the corner of the hooch. Red and One-Four continued to work the area around this fortified village, and within five minutes, One-Four detected three more enemy soldiers with packs and weapons. They were within one hundred meters of where he had killed the previous four. He engaged them, and since they had watched what he had done to their comrades, they immediately returned fire. This heavy volume of fire did not slow him down, and he pressed his attack until he had killed these three also.

It was apparent that we had found the major force in the area, and Red called the S3 of the 5-7 Infantry and made a recommendation that they move the battalion toward this location. While Red was talking to the Third Battalion, One-Four found two more NVA who immediately started firing at him. Keep in mind that in most of these contacts, the scouts were generally no more than five to thirty feet from the enemy, and two or more soldiers firing their AK-47s on full automatic could put up a hell of a lot of firepower. The key to survival for the scout crew in this type of close combat was to attack the enemy, relying on the shock effect of the noise of the helicopter and the volume of fire that the observer and the skid gun placed on the enemy. One-Four pressed the attack, and two more NVA were killed.

Delta Company of the 5-7 Infantry was the first ground unit to reach the area in which we were operating. As they moved into the area, they became decisively engaged with the enemy. One platoon was pinned down and could not move. As this was taking place, Red observed two NVA and rolled in on a rocket and machine-gun attack. As he dove toward the enemy, his aircraft became the target for very heavy automatic and semiautomatic fire. His copilot was hit in the left arm, and his aircraft was hit in several places. He launched two pairs of rockets and watched as the rockets exploded at the feet of the enemy, killing both of them. His copilot was bleeding profusely, and his aircraft was not responding as it should. He called One-Four and had him proceed toward LZ Baldy. As they were leaving station, he called me and gave me an update and also informed the battalion S3 that they were leaving and that another team would be out to support them ASAP.

Captain Rice (White) led the next team to go to the AO. The 5-7 Infantry asked for support from the brigade, and one company from the 1-7 Infantry was air assaulted into a position just north of D/5-7 Infantry in an effort to relieve some pressure on this unit. D/5-7 called for artillery, and the battalion had air strikes diverted to strike the fortified village that Red and One-Four had found.

Our role changed from screening for the infantry to that of providing an aerial blocking force around the area of contact. We could not and would not fly in an area that had artillery and air strikes actively being placed on the ground. We moved out well to the flanks and to their front in an effort to contain the enemy and prevent their escape from the engagement area.

Normally, all three radios were turned on, and the pilots learned to listen with a "third ear." In other words, you listened at a subconscious level to all of the radio traffic and responded to what was important. We tuned to the ground unit on FM; we used UHF for communications between the scout and the gunship and tuned in the forward air controller (FAC) on VHF. An observer listening to and watching all of these would often get confused as to what was happening. Hell, it was complicated, but as a participant, you had to keep it sorted out. Your life might very well depend on your ability to understand what was going on. As you worked with the different ground units, you learned their radio call signs and the call signs of the supporting units, and you really learned to listen with that "third ear."

At 1310 hours, White saw five more enemies with bushes on their backs, attempting to evade from the contact area. He engaged and was immediately engulfed in return fire. He pressed the attack upon them and flew a tight circle around them while his door gunner killed all five.

The actions of the enemy changed in the afternoon. Until this last contact with White, the enemy had generally waited to fire until they knew they had been observed. From this point on, they started firing at us as soon as they saw a helicopter in their immediate area. All contact with the enemy after 1300 hours met with very heavy automatic and semiautomatic fire.

Red and One-Four replaced White's team on station, and at 1600 hours, One-Four found three more enemies attempting to evade from the contact area. As soon as they saw him, they engaged him. One-Four flew into their midst and killed the three of them. A half hour later, Red observed five enemies with packs, weapons, and camouflage on their backs, scurrying to get out of the area.

"One-Four, this is Red. I got five dudes to your right front that think they're invisible. These suckers are mine!"

With that announcement, he rolled in and punched off four pairs of rockets, and his copilot engaged with machine-gun fire. One pass and they were all dead. One-Four flew to the area and hovered over the bodies.

"Red, this is One-Four. Good shooting! There's not much left of them. You've got five confirmed KIA."

Major Ryan in his C-model gunship was on station, observing Red and One-Four. Ten minutes later, he observed two more NVA attempting to evade, and he rolled in, firing rockets and machine guns, and killed those two.

Major Beasley and White replaced Red and One-Four on station. Most of the enemies were attempting to escape to the northwest out of the AO. The combination of the ground sweep by the 5-7 and the air assault by the 1-7 had cut off any chance of these forces reaching the inland waterway. Our contacts with the enemy in the afternoon had concentrated in this area, and as the afternoon wore on, these contacts continued.

Between 1800 and 1815 hours, Captain Rice (White) located another nine enemies trying to flee and immediately engaged them. Major Beasley was White's cover bird, and from altitude, he observed some green uniforms laid out to dry next to a hooch. When White had completed killing the nine NVA, Major Beasley directed him over to the hooch to check it out. White hovered in front of the entrance and immediately drew fire. He looked inside and saw a bunker that the fire was coming from. We then heard,

"Six, this is White. There are two NVA inside this hooch, inside a bunker, over."

"White, this is Six. Roger. Clear the area, and I'll blow them fuckers away."

"This is White. Roger out."

With that, he moved farther to the west about five hundred meters and held off to the side.

Major Beasley rolled in with rockets and, on the first pass, sent two pairs to the target. They blew the hooch away, and on his next couple of passes, he concentrated on the bunker. From his altitude, it looked like the bunker had been destroyed also.

"White, this is Six. You're clear to check it out."

"This is White. Roger, out." Captain Rice flew back to the bunker and came to a hover over the debris. "Six, this is White. That was good shooting. We have two NVA KIA."

That was the last action for the day. On this day, 23 October 1967, we had killed another forty-three enemies. We had suffered one person wounded and ten aircraft shot at, one of those was hit but was flyable.

CHAPTER TWENTY TWO
THE TROOP, THE BLUES, THE MEDIA

Late in the afternoon of 31 October 1967, Lieutenant Colonel Nevins flew up from LZ Two Bits. The troop was assembled into a formation, and Major Beasley handed the troop guidon to Lieutenant Colonel Nevins who handed it to Major Ryan, and command of the troop passed with the guidon. Colonel Nevins praised the troop for what they had accomplished in the short time they had been in Operation Wallowa and praised Major Beasley for his "outstanding leadership" while he was the troop commander. Major Beasley offered a few comments followed by Major Ryan who made a few comments also. The troop was dismissed; Major Beasley shook hands all around, got in the passenger compartment of one of our D models and took off for An Khe. Lieutenant Colonel Nevins got in his aircraft and took off for LZ Two Bits, and the rest of us went back to the war.

Major Ryan lasted one week and two days as the troop commander. On 9 November 1967, while making a gun run, he and his aircraft were severely shot up, and he was medically evacuated out of country. The squadron was notified, and Colonel Nevins immediately made Major Burrow the troop commander. There was no change of command ceremony. That morning, when he woke up, Major Burrow was the troop XO; and that evening, I briefed him as the troop commander, and we went about our business as if nothing had happened.

This was possible because everyone knew Major Burrow, and Major Burrow knew the troop and the procedures we used. There was no change in what we did or how we did it. As future events proved, he was the right man at the right place, at the right time. He was the most fearless man I have ever known. His personal safety never figured into the decisions he made, and he was a leader that believed in the axiom "Lead by example." While he was with the troop, he was shot down thirteen times; and after he was pulled from a rice paddy or jungle, he would return to the troop, get in another gunship, and return to the battle.

Warrant Officer Larry Kreps was his copilot and was with him on most of these occurrences, and yet, he and the crew chief and door gunner on Major Burrow's aircraft absolutely believed in, and were devoted to, the man. I believe everyone that was in the troop at that time has a "Major Burrow story" they love to tell. It got to the point that whenever he went to AO, I would alert the Blues that he was airborne, and they would prepare to go rescue him.

During the month of October, the troop had killed 350 of the enemy, and we became the place to send the media. The division and the brigade public information officers (PIO) saddled with the demands of the print and TV media, got them out of their hair as quickly as possible, and the place to send them was to Bravo Troop, the first of the ninth. We had reporters from all the networks: ABC, CBS, NBC; and from *Life*, *Time*, AP Wire Service, etc. Most of the print reporters were reasonable, but the TV reporters were unrelenting, unreasonable jerks as far as I was concerned. They were all trying to "structure" a story that would win them a Pulitzer Prize. They had no interest in us or the reality of the war we were fighting. They were all looking for an angle, a gimmick, something bloody or something spectacular, and something that would get their piece on the evening news. Every one of the TV reporters that spent time with us wanted us to stage "events" for them to shoot. Major Burrow told each of them that we weren't about to hang our asses out so they could get some pictures, and he refused to create any "events" for them. As I recall, one camera crew from CBS said that if we weren't going to cooperate, they would leave. What really got me about these arrogant bastards was that they thought we cared if they left.

Since Major Burrow refused to stage events for them, they had two choices: hang around until something happened or leave, which is what I hoped they would do. Since we had no room for them on our scout or gunships, their only hope was that we would put the Blues on the ground. This AO was full of enemy personnel, and we were very careful about putting the Blues on the ground. That meant the media spent a lot of time sitting around or trying to dream up stories that would make the evening news.

Every troop had a few soldiers who where good with verse, and they would dream up new verses for familiar songs. One song was about Ho Chi Minh hanging from a palm tree, sung to the tune of "The Twelve Days of Christmas." One of the "news" crews thought this would be a good human-interest story, so they asked a couple of guys to line up near the operations bunker and sing it while they filmed it. As I was watching this, I was disgusted and thought, *"Now they want to make a musical out of this fucking war."* My disgust turned to laughter when I heard these pilots break into "superscout," sung to the tune of "The Green Berets":

> Puckered assholes in the sky
> Superscouts my fucking eye
> Men who mean just what they say
> Fuck off all night and kill all day

This was followed by several other verses, with each more graphic than the one before.

The camera crew did not think it was funny, but we roared with laughter. We knew that that was one piece of film that would never make it on the evening news.

One story about Bravo Troop did make the ABC evening news, and fortunately for the crew that filmed it, they never returned to the troop.

We had a contact in the valley. One of the scouts had observed four NVA leaving a hooch in this village. He engaged them; there was a short firefight, resulting in four NVA KIA. He had reported that it would be a good place to insert the Blues to check out the village further. We launched the Blues, and a news crew went with them. We selected an LZ near the village and did our normal prep of the LZ. The Blues reported a green LZ and started to move toward the hooch where the scout had killed the NVA.

It was apparent after they swept the small village that there were no more NVA present. At the request of the "news" crew, some of the Blues threw a few grenades and rounded up some farmers that they paraded in front of the cameras. All of these were filmed as if this were part of some big operation. Having completed the search of the NVA bodies and having collected the weapons and packs they were carrying, the Blues burned the hooch the NVA were leaving, moved to a PZ, and were extracted.

What appeared on the ABC news the next evening was a picture of the Blues setting fire to the hooch with a crying woman standing next to it. There was no mention of the fact that the hooch had been used by the NVA or that this was in response to a firefight between the NVA and our scout pilot. Some draft-dodging editor back in New York had decided to make his own statement with this film and manufactured one more piece of evidence that helped turn the American public against our involvement in Vietnam and, in the process, portrayed the American soldier as callous spoilers of the Vietnamese country. This was the first instance where I had actual knowledge of an event being deliberately distorted by a major network in pursuit of their own (or their employees) political agenda. It was certainly not the last instance; and during the months of October, November, and December 1967, the American public was fed steady streams of tripe about the imminent fall of Khe Sahn, more of that later.

There was one freelance reporter who earned our respect and admiration. Catherine Leroy was a vibrant young French woman who sought us out to capture our experiences on film. She spent two weeks with us. Her unassuming manner and willingness to share our hardships and danger soon earned everyone's respect. Her concern for all with whom she came in contact and her unfailing good humor made her one of the most beautiful persons I have known. One of the things I admired about her was that she didn't hang around "the brass." She has always reminded me of Ernie Pyle, in that her focus was on the soldiers who were fighting the war and getting their perspective on what they were doing. In between missions, you would always find her with the Blue Lift or the weapons-platoon or scout-platoon crews.

Catherine Leroy listening as I brief a team going to the AO

She sold her pictures of us to *Life* magazine. She left us in search of other stories and, in a few months, was taking pictures of the battle for Hue and became another casualty of the Vietnam War, we were told. When we learned of her death, it was as if a member of the troop had been killed. It wasn't until I was preparing this book that I learned she hadn't been killed but had been captured and subsequently released.

We also had two army combat photographers that would spend time with the troop. I don't recall both of their names, but they were exceptional soldiers and won our respect for their bravery under fire and their willingness to share the danger. When they were with the troop, they usually spent their time with the Blues.

While the troop was at Duc Pho, they took a picture of one of our lift ships hovering over a pinnacle and a group of Blues jumping from the skids to the ground. On the ground in the foreground was an RTO whose name I do not recall, Lieutenant Ted Chilcoate (Blue) with his back to the camera, Staff Sergeant Wilkerson (Blue Mike) just landing on the ground, the soldier getting ready to jump was Sergeant Bob Lackey, and behind him was Specialist Chryster who was to be shot in my aircraft on 13 November and the last soldier I can't identify. Warrant Officers John Flanagan and Jim Pratt were the two pilots of the aircraft. This photo won the DOD Photograph of the Year Award for Staff Sergeant Breedlove in 1967 and became, in many respects, the symbol of the army in Vietnam. It has been used as a cover for many publications and has appeared in many magazines. In my mind, it is fitting that the soldiers of Bravo Troop 1-9 Cavalry have come to represent all soldiers who fought in Vietnam. This picture was also used by the U.S. post office to represent the decade of the sixties.

Duc Pho April 24, 1967. Left to right, Unknown, LT Chilcoate, SSG Wilkerson, SGT Lackey, SP Chryster, Unknown. Pilots, Jim Pratt and John Flanagan (US Army photo)

As you, no doubt, have discerned, I have no use for television "reporters"; my advice to anyone who watches television news is to take what you see and hear them say with a large dose of skepticism. The "news" department in every television market is fighting for market share. The bigger their market share, the more they can charge for advertising. They are not interested in reporting on bland ordinary events. They want to show the blood, the gore, the conflict in any event, not in the interest of truth but in the interest of attaining a larger market share.

Another aspect of this issue is the personal bias of the person doing the reporting or the editing. There is no such thing as a neutral observer. Everyone has a belief about right and wrong, and that belief colors what we see and what we say. It colors every aspect of human activity from personal conduct to the global conduct of nations. You either approve or disapprove, but you are not neutral. If you are a reporter and you personally don't approve of an action or a policy, you have the opportunity and the means to distort a situation to support your point of view. That is exactly what happened when we burned the hooch.

CHAPTER TWENTY THREE
13 NOVEMBER, A DAY TO REMEMBER
THE BATTLE AT DONG SON

During the first week of November, the brigade began an operation in the southwestern part of the AO near Hiep Duc. The intent was to drive the enemy from the high ground around Hiep Duc down onto the plains where the brigade would have a better opportunity to maneuver against them and kill them. We supported the units with several Pink teams each day, and while we had instances of heavy contact with the NVA forces, no tactically significant battles developed. The enemy was still doing all it could to avoid closing with our forces. The airmobile warfare pressed upon them by our troop, and the rest of the brigade were taking a heavy toll, and they were trying to learn how to combat us.

While the majority of the brigade were conducting this operation, we covered the rest of the brigade AO with Pink teams. The ideal reconnaissance box was an area that was two thousand meters by two thousand meters square. A Pink team could do a thorough job of conducting reconnaissance within this box in an hour-and-a-half period. If we expanded the size of the box to three thousand meters by three thousand meters, we would probably find the obvious, but we significantly reduced the chances of finding a well-concealed enemy position or unit. I developed a reconnaissance plan that consisted of a series of reconnaissance boxes that were located throughout the brigade AO. The AO was approximately one hundred miles wide from the east along the coast to the most westerly point in the mountains and approximately fifty miles in length from our northern boundary to our southern boundary. We systematically covered the AO by first having a team conduct reconnaissance in the east, then the center, then the west. We also conducted first—and last-light reconnaissance around all of the fire-support bases in the AO. I kept track of when we last conducted reconnaissance in each box and was able to ensure we did not overlook any part of the AO. I should point out that these missions were self-generated. We did not sit around, waiting for brigade to ask us to conduct reconnaissance. This was the primary reason the troop was so successful in Vietnam.

Major Burrow returned from the nightly brigade briefing on 12 November and indicated that the brigade commander was concerned about reported enemy movement through the brigade AO. To get a better intelligence picture of this movement, he needed his interrogation teams to talk to personnel who lived in the AO. He wanted Bravo Troop to pick up some personnel for interrogation. With this guidance, Major Burrow prepared the troop to conduct several "snatch" missions. The concept was fairly straightforward. We would have five infantrymen (Blues) on each Blue Lift ship, and these ships would remain at altitude while Major Burrow and a scout would select the individuals to be picked up. Once selected, Major Burrow would direct a single lift ship to drop down from altitude; the Blues would jump off the ship, gather up the selected individual, get back on the ship, and the ship would then rejoin the others at altitude. We would repeat the process until we had a sample from throughout the AO. In addition, Major Burrow decided that this formation would be escorted by one more gunship from the Red platoon.

The next morning, 13 November 1967, we took off from Chu Lai and flew to LZ Porrazzo. Due to scheduled maintenance, previous battle damage, and shortage of crews, we had four aircraft from Blue Lift and my Huey for a total of five D-model Hueys. Four aircraft from the White platoon (OH-13s) and four from the Red platoon and Major Burrow's aircraft for a total of five C-model gunships. We started out the day with fourteen flyable aircraft at LZ Porrazzo.

LZ Porrazzo, Jim Pratt's bird the morning of November 13, 1967

Our first-light team had completed their mission, and we had responded to a brigade request to conduct reconnaissance in an area of interest they wanted checked when we first arrived at Porrazzo. When everyone had returned to Porrazzo, we launched our first "snatch" mission. Major Burrow had decided that we would begin our operation along the inland waterway. Major Burrow, a scout, another gunship, and four Blue Lift aircraft with their Blues on board took off at 0930 hours and headed toward the inland waterway.

Within twenty minutes after takeoff, the scout had selected a couple of suspicious-looking individuals and informed Major Burrow that these guys were likely candidates. Major Burrow concurred and directed the first lift ship to go in and pick them up. At 0953, Lieutenant Hirning dropped out of formation and started his descent. In what was to become the pattern for the day, the scout circled the individuals, holding them in what was to become the LZ. On short final, Lieutenant Hirning called the scout, who moved out of the way, and increased the size of his circle to include the lift aircraft and the Blues inside the circle. As the aircraft touched down, the Blues jumped off the ship and ran toward the suspects.

There was fear and surprise written across their faces. Just minutes before, they had been walking peacefully across this field, and while they had heard the choppers, they paid no attention to them. Suddenly, a small helicopter appeared from nowhere and was now circling around them. One of the men in the helicopter was pointing an M-60 machine gun at them and was motioning for them to do something. They both stopped and stared at the helicopter that was only about fifteen feet from them and was flying circles around them at about three feet off the ground. They first heard, then saw, a much larger helicopter approach them. As they watched, they saw some soldiers climb out on the skids, and it appeared that this helicopter was going to land on them. It landed right next to them, and before it touched down, the three soldiers standing on the skids closest to them jumped and ran toward them, motioning for them to get down. Before they could comply, they were grabbed by the soldiers and thrown to the ground. Their tunics were ripped open; they were searched, had their hands tied behind their backs, and roughly pulled to their feet and propelled toward the helicopter.

You can imagine what they were thinking as the helicopter took off. It was unlikely that any of these detainees had ever flown before, and now their first flight was in a helicopter with them lying on the floor with both doors open, and their hands were tied behind their backs. The helicopter climbed quickly to two thousand feet and rejoined the rest of Blue Lift. These detainees were terrified, and that was just fine with us.

Within a few minutes, the scout had spotted several more personnel, and as Warrant Officer Flanagan landed, five VC jumped from their concealed position and started to run away. The Blues fired at them, hitting several and possibly killing two of them. The other three threw down their weapons and surrendered to the Blues. They were searched, bound, and loaded on the aircraft. We didn't attempt to find the other two, and Mr. Flanagan took off as soon as the Blues were on board. As he was taking off, Warrant Officer Covey was landing about five hundred meters away, and his Blues picked up two more detainees. The scout and Major Burrow were busy selecting personnel, and at 1005, Lieutenant Hirning swooped down to pick up one more detainee. As soon as he was airborne, Warrant Officer McAnally dropped from the sky and picked up another one. Mr. Covey landed again and picked up three more detainees.

We continued our search along the inland waterway but didn't detect any other likely candidates for interrogation. At 1030 hours, Major Burrow directed Blue Lift to fly to LZ Baldy and land at the brigade heliport where the detainees would be picked up by the MPs and transported to the prisoner-of-war detention facility for interrogation. By 1100 hours, everyone had returned to Porrazzo, and we sent a Pink team to conduct reconnaissance in one of our previously selected areas. We settled down to our routine of sending a Pink team to the AO about every hour and a half.

Around 1330 hours, the brigade S3 called to let us know that out of the twelve detainees we had picked up that morning, one of them was a VC company commander, two of them were VC platoon leaders, another one was a VC assassination team leader; and two more were confirmed VC, but their rank and position were unknown. We all felt pretty good about that and whooped it up a little bit at the news.

Major Burrow decided we should do the same thing later in the afternoon, but this time, we would do it in the valley near where the rest of the brigade was conducting their operations. At 1500 hours, we started our second "snatch" operation for the day. The team composition was the same as it had been in the morning: one scout crew, four Blue Lift ships with their Blues, and Major Burrow and Warrant Officer Zahn as the two gunships escorting them. The headquarters section of the Blues remained at LZ Porrazzo.

At 1515 hours, Lieutenant Hirning dropped down to pick up three VC. As he landed, they tried to evade and were engaged by the Blues who killed two of them and picked up the third one. This third one appeared to be spaced out on dope and was definitely in la-la land.

At 1520 hours, Major Burrow observed one individual standing in the middle of a rice paddy by himself. The scout was working a little farther to the north and didn't see this individual. Major Burrow directed the next lift ship to drop down and pick this guy up. As Warrant Officer McAnally was on short final, he started to receive very heavy automatic—and semiautomatic-weapons fire. He aborted the landing, broke left, and started a climb out to altitude.

Major Burrow started his gun run on the enemy positions, and Mr. Zahn moved to a position to start a daisy-chain behind him. Major Burrow could see the enemy's heavy machine-gun position, and he lined up his sights on this position as he dove on them. Suddenly, he started to receive fire from his right front and, in particular, from that heavy machine gun. Green tracers started to fly past the aircraft. *"Holy shit,"* he thought, *"they're as big as basketballs! That has to be a fifty-seven-millimeter antiaircraft gun!"* Suddenly, there was a loud oscillating tone in his headset. He glanced at his caution panel and saw the master-caution light on and looked at the Christmas-tree display and saw that the transmission chip-detect light and the engine-oil light were on. Mr. Kreps reset the master caution, which killed the light and the loud oscillating tone.

Major Burrow looked at Mr. Kreps and said, "We're going down!" He picked a spot just short of the dry ground and shot his approach to the end of the rice paddy, cut the power, entered autorotation, and prayed that the transmission and engine would hold together until they were on the ground.

"Two-Eight, this is Six X-ray. We're taking hits, and we're going down!" Mr. Kreps transmitted on the radio.

"This is Two-Eight. Roger. We're with you, buddy. We'll cover you!"

"Three, this is Two-Eight X-ray. Six is going down!"

When those words came over the radio back at Porrazzo, Captains Rice and Thomas tore out of the operations bunker and ran to their aircraft and, in the process, alerted everyone that Six had been shot down. Within minutes, the three remaining gunships and three remaining scout aircraft were airborne. I called Lieutenant Eikenberry to get the rest of the Blues rounded up and ran to my aircraft as they climbed on board. As we climbed to altitude, I heard Two-Eight announce that Blue Lift was on short final into Six's location.

Warrant Officer Zahn was flying a "hog" gunship and had forty-eight rockets on board. He prepped the LZ on the right side as Blue Lift was on short final and suppressed the enemy fire from that side as they landed. Two-Eight became the target for the fifty-seven-millimeter AA but was not hit. The Blues were on the ground and ran to Major Burrow's aircraft. Two-Eight was out of position to cover Blue Lift as they came out of the LZ, and as they lifted off, the hedgerow on the right side of the LZ erupted into a wall of automatic and semiautomatic small-arms fire. Lieutenant Hirning's aircraft was badly shot up; and it soon became apparent that he was losing fuel at a high rate, but fortunately for him and his crew, they had just enough fuel to return to LZ Porrazzo. His aircraft would be nonflyable until we had the fuel tanks replaced.

While en route to the contact area, I called the Third Brigade TOC, explained the situation, and had them move the Quick Reaction Force into pickup-zone posture and get the Ready Reaction Force moving toward a pickup zone (PZ). When I arrived on station, I remained at altitude until I got a handle on the situation. Bob Zahn (Two-Eight) had expended all of his ammunition and was returning to Porrazzo to rearm and refuel. I called Red and told him to send one of the three gunships that was with him back to Porrazzo. Then I talked to White and learned that Captain Maier (our FO) was in one of the scout aircraft on station. I wanted him and Captain Rice to remain on station and for him to send the other two scouts back to Porrazzo. I then told Warrant Officer McAnaly that he was in charge of Blue Lift and to take the flight to LZ Ross and top off and to standby there to pick up the QRF.

We were beginning to sort it all out. Routine and our standard way of doing business were taking hold. Captain Maier remained at altitude and was busy getting some artillery laid to support us; Captain Rice (White) was low level, trying to get a handle on where all the enemies were located. Captain Thomas (Red) and his other gunship were in a position to provide fires in support of Major Burrow and the Blues.

By this time, the Blues were receiving heavy fire from their front and right flank and were pinned down in the rice paddy. I talked to Major Burrow and informed him I had the rest of the Blues on board my aircraft and that I was coming in to drop them off and to extract him and his crew. Based on the volume of fire that was being shot at the Blues, I decided this would be a low-level approach. We came in from the north. As we cleared the last vegetation between us and the Blues, we were about ten feet off the ground and were now in the open with Major Burrow's aircraft about five hundred to eight hundred meters directly ahead. We now became the focal point for all of the enemy's fire. The closer we flew toward the Blues, the more intense the fire became. We were now receiving fire from directly ahead and from our left and right.

I could feel and hear bullets hitting the aircraft, and the closer we flew, the worse it got. Bullets and Plexiglas were flying around inside the aircraft, and then the Blues I had on board started shooting back from inside the aircraft. We had eight Blues on board the aircraft, and they were all shooting out the open doors on full automatic. The adrenaline surged into everyone's system, and those two minutes of my life were burned forever into my memory. In two tours in Vietnam, I never again experienced that amount of fire directed toward me. It was apparent that we couldn't make it, so I broke off the approach and banked hard left to get the hell out of there.

The crew chief came up on intercom and told me that Specialist Chryster had been shot in the neck and was losing a lot of blood. I turned and looked over my shoulder and saw the blood pumping out of his neck. The wind picked up the blood and was blowing it around inside the cabin. What is unbelievable to me is that I can't remember the other pilot who was flying with me that day. At any rate, he called LZ Colt and informed them that we were inbound with a critically wounded soldier and have the medics meet us at the pad.

I called Major Burrow and told him it was a tad bit too hot for us. In a typical understatement, he replied, "Yeah, I noticed."

Bob Lackey, one of the Blues on the ground, wrote about this action in a book entitled *Hunter-Killer Squadron*, which was edited by another Blue, Matthew Brennan. He said, "Our headquarters squad tried to come in and get on the ground with us, and hundreds of rounds of ammunition were being shot at this single ship. Amazingly enough only one man was hit. My friend Jimmy Chryster was shot through the neck and killed. This was not a good place for us to be."

While we were inbound to Six's location, Captain Thomas (Red) rolled in to give us some covering fire. He was shooting at the enemy on our left side when another fifty-seven-millimeter AA weapon opened up. I recall hearing on UHF that Red had been hit and was going down. It registered with me, but I was rather occupied at the moment, and it wasn't until we were on the way to LZ Colt that I called the other Red bird and asked for a status on Red. He told me he saw everyone in the aircraft get out all right, but they were pinned down in the open next to the aircraft. Bob Rice (White) came on the net and informed me that he had Captain Maier registering some artillery, and he thought they could hold off any enemy attack with artillery fire. Captain Maier was demonstrating that he was one hell of an artilleryman as he adjusted the artillery fire to within fifty meters of Red so that it was between Red and the enemy. This prevented the enemy from reaching Captain Thomas and his crew and, undoubtedly, saved their lives.

The medics were waiting when we landed on the pad at LZ Colt. We got Specialist Chryster out of the aircraft and into their hands. He had lost a lot of blood but was still fighting to stay alive. We left the aircraft running, and as we turned to takeoff, the pilot that was flying with me tapped the fuel gage to get my attention. All of this action had taken place within fifteen minutes after we had taken off from LZ Porrazzo. When we left Porrazzo, we had a full tank of fuel, and we were now down to half a tank. That meant only one thing: we were losing fuel. And my first thought was that it was pooling under our aircraft as we sat on the pad. We pulled pitch and returned to LZ Porrazzo and discovered that our fuel tank had indeed been hit. This meant that this aircraft was not flyable until we had the fuel tank replaced also. This turn of events left us with three lift aircraft flyable, and with the two gunships shot down, we only had three gunships flyable. The scouts had survived the heavy volume of fire and still had their four aircraft flyable. That, however, was soon to change. Since the troop commander, the weapons platoon leader, and I had all been shot down, Bob Rice (White) took charge of the situation in the AO and prepared for the combat assault of the brigade QRF.

The priority of our effort at this point was to get Red, his crew, and his aircraft secured. The QRF would be inserted into Red's position, followed by the rest of that company (the RRF). After I had landed back at LZ Porrazzo and determined that my Huey was no longer flyable, I ran to the operations bunker and got an update from Bob Rice (White). I then called brigade and was told by the brigade assistant S3 that none among the brigade commander, the battalion commander, or the brigade S3 could be reached to authorize the insertion of the QRF or the RRF. Controlling my temper, but in my most assertive manner, I told this captain that we were following the division SOP on this. He didn't need anyone else's approval to get the RRF moved into PZ posture as soon as we had the QRF picked up. I also told him that we only had three Hueys left and for him to round up some more Hueys. There were several resupply Hueys in the AO, and they were directed to join our lift ships at LZ Ross and to assist in the insertion of the QRF and the RRF. Of course, I had no authority to commit the QRF and the RRF to battle, and there was nothing in the division SOP that said it could be done. But I sounded like I knew what I was talking about, and the assistant S3, to his credit (from my point of view), did what was required and got the QRF and RRF alerted and moving toward a PZ.

A hasty analysis of the situation revealed a couple of significant items:

1. The fifty-seven-millimeter AA weapons indicated the presence of a heavy weapons company.
2. Heavy-weapons companies usually form part of the security for a headquarters of some type. We learned later that we were fighting the Third NVA regimental headquarters.

A platoon from B/3-5 Infantry was the QRF located at LZ Ross. Our depleted lift section led by a nineteen-year-old warrant officer, Loren McAnally, proceeded to LZ Ross where he was joined by the resupply birds from the 227th Assault Helicopter Battalion. The QRF was loaded on board the aircraft, and they returned to the area of contact.

Bob Rice selected the LZ for the insertion of the QRF and coordinated with all elements in the area. While waiting for the insertion of the QRF, he placed several sections of aerial rocket artillery and continued shooting artillery into enemy positions. He was running out of gas and would not be able to cover the insertion of the QRF and the RRF. I informed him that I would replace him on station, and I bumped one of the scout pilots from his H-13 and took off with his observer for the AO.

After Captain Rice briefed me, I overflew Red's position. Red and his door gunner were on one side of the aircraft with the copilot and the crew chief on the other side. They were all lying in the rice paddy. As I flew over Red, he grinned and gave me a thumbs-up gesture. I was receiving sporadic fire from the enemy as I flew over his position, but it paled in comparison to what I had received just a short while earlier.

I heard Mr. McAnally on UHF, indicating that he was off of LZ Ross with the QRF on board. I gave him the LZ briefing and popped smoke for him as he turned onto final. A section of aerial rocket artillery (ARA) birds from the 2-20 Artillery Battalion and one of our gunships prepped the LZ for them as they were on short final. As the QRF touched down, a heavy volume of fire was directed at them and the gunships from the south and west; but at 1715 hours, the QRF was on the ground, and none of the lift section had been hit. The combined lift section returned to LZ Ross to pick up the rest of B/3-5 Infantry. While the lift had escaped being hit, another of the troop gunships was hit and had to return to LZ Porrazzo where it also was deemed nonflyable.

While waiting for the RRF to be inserted, I contacted the assistant brigade S3 and told him that as soon as we had this company on the ground, we were to insert another company into

Major Burrow's position. This took him by surprise, and he was hesitant. I reminded him of the division SOP and the policy of "piling on" once we had found the enemy. "Well," I said, "we have found the enemy, and now we need to pile on." He was not enthusiastic about committing another company to this battle, so I went on to explain the rest of my plan. After this next company was inserted into Major Burrow's position, we would then have two companies in line across the north side. The next logical step was to insert a third company to the rear of the enemy and encircle them with our forces. This would allow us to keep them in position while we systematically destroyed them. The assistant brigade S3 was a captain who was now getting a little nervous committing a battalion-size force into an operation that had not been approved by the brigade commander, the battalion commander, or the brigade S3.

I reassured him by telling him that, surely, by the time we had the next company ready to go, the command element would have returned. "Go ahead and have the next company move to a PZ posture, and I will get back with you after we finish the insertion of Bravo Company." With that, I switched frequencies and talked to the QRF platoon leader who had made it to Red's position. I asked him to inform Red that he and his crew were to get on the next lift ships that came in.

Within minutes, I heard Mr. McAnally call off of Ross inbound for the next insertion. This time, the QRF was already on the ground, and as the lift turned on to final, a heavy volume of fire from the enemy started, then decreased as the QRF returned their fire. At 1732 hours, we completed the insertion of Bravo Company 3-5 Infantry. Red and his crew got on Mr. Flanagan's aircraft and were returned to LZ Porrazzo.

I talked to the Bravo Company commander and told him to take up a hasty defense where he was and be prepared to link up with the Blues on his right flank or another infantry company we were trying to get in. I called the brigade TOC and spoke to the assistant S3 who gave me the location of Alpha Company 3-5

Infantry who was now in PZ posture. I called Mr. McAnally and gave him the location of where to pick up the next company.

I then called our operations and had them send a Pink team out to cover Bravo Company. After saying that, I realized that we were down to two flyable gunships, and perhaps both would be needed on the insertion of Alpha Company. I called operations back and directed them to get White on the radio. Bob Rice and I talked it over and decided that two White birds could cover and screen for Bravo Company. He said he and Mr. Rawl would be right out. The two Red birds were sent to escort the lift, and I flew over toward Major Burrow's location to select the LZ for the insertion of Alpha Company.

The middle of the rice paddy was not the place to be. The closer I got to Major Burrow's location, the more fire I was drawing. I changed my flight so that I would approach the area from the southeast, which put me over the enemy positions, but, at the same time, somewhat restricted their field of visibility. The only clear landing zone was the rice paddy itself, north of Major Burrow's position. Having selected the LZ, I concentrated on getting out of small-arms range. We had overflown several enemy positions that we marked with smoke grenades and, in the process, had received a heavy volume of fire directed at us. I don't know how many of the enemy my observer killed before we broke clear, but it was quite a few.

I called Warrant Officer McAnally and learned he was inbound with Alpha Company, and I flew out to mark the LZ for him. He informed me that when he went in to pick up Alpha Company, it was a red PZ. They had taken fire when they picked them up, and he knew they would take fire when they dropped them off.

As the smoke grenade cleared the aircraft, I could once again hear and feel bullets hitting my aircraft. I scanned my instruments and noticed that all my instruments except the tachometer dropped to zero. Everything sounded all right, and as I cleared the LZ, I headed northeast and called Warrant Officer McAnally. I got no response, and after a routine check, I determined I had no sidetone in my helmet, and it was apparent that my radios were dead also.

Since I couldn't talk to anyone, I was now ineffective as far as this insertion was concerned and immediately flew back to LZ Porrazzo, praying that the aircraft would hold together. If we went down, there was no way of informing anyone, and we would be on our own. It was an anxious few minutes until we had the LZ in sight. After landing, I noticed that the battery cables had been hit, among other things.

While this was going on, the insertion was met with a heavy volume of automatic and semiautomatic fire. The fire was so intense on the LZ that Warrant Officer McAnally decided that the only way to get out was to do a pedal turn and fly out the same way they came in. As they were flying out of the LZ, Warrant Officer John Flanagan heard that dreaded oscillating tone in his headset and saw the master-caution light illuminate. The oil-pressure and chip-detect lights were on, and he knew they were doing down. At approximately the same time, one of our last two gunships was heavily hit and was forced to make an emergency landing also. Warrant Officer Mike Covey piloted the lift ship right behind Mr. Flanagan. His copilot that day was Warrant Officer Larry Brown (our superscout pilot) who had volunteered to fly with the lift that day since they were short a pilot. When John Flanagan called that he was going down, Mike Covey responded that he would pick him up. They were about eight hundred meters north of the contact area and were able to land behind some trees and brush that, fortunately, did not have any enemy soldiers in the immediate area. As they sat there, waiting for John Flanagan and his crew to scramble aboard, Larry Brown turned to Mike Covey and said, "Shit, this was supposed to be a day I could take a break from all the action. Some fucking day off!"

One of the lift ships from the 227th followed our gunship to the ground and picked them up. The enemy was much closer to them, and they took fire all the way to the ground. The fire was so intense that they didn't bother to shut the aircraft off when they landed. They un-assed the gunship and ran as fast as they could to the waiting lift ship. As they took off in the lift ship, they noticed that the engine was still running, and the rotors were still turning.

The crews were dropped off at LZ Porrazzo, and the remaining lift ships and our one remaining gunship went back and picked up the rest of Alpha Company (again from a hot PZ) and flew back into the firestorm to complete the insertion of Alpha Company. On this last insertion into this hot LZ, another gunship and lift bird (both from the 227th) were hit and rendered nonflyable.

While this insertion was going on, I was on the radio back at the operations bunker, trying to convince the assistant S3 to move a third company into PZ posture. By now, the brigade commander, S3, and battalion commander for the 3-5 were back at the command post (CP). I was informed that no further troop movements would take place until the command group had an opportunity to assess the situation. I told the S3 that if he didn't make the decision now, we would soon be out of daylight, and the back door was wide open. A decision was made not to make a decision, and by the following morning, most of the enemy had escaped.

Night was falling; and we had one gunship, two scout aircraft, and two lift ships still flying. We had lost nine aircraft in today's operation. At this point, they were all repairable; but we soon were told that satchel charges had been placed in Warrant Officer Flanagan's lift ship, and it was blown up where he had put it down. As darkness fell across the Que Sahn Valley, Major Burrow and the Blues were still on the ground in the rice paddy, and we still had three gunships that needed to be recovered in the AO.

We had a crew rigging Red's bird for recovery when they were suddenly attacked by recoilless rifle (RR) fire. The second RR round hit the aircraft, and it exploded and burned where it was sitting. Within a few more minutes, Major Burrow's aircraft was also attacked by RR fire, was hit, exploded, and burned where it was sitting.

As darkness fell, I decided that I would keep the crews for the flyable aircraft at LZ Porrazzo, and I sent the rest of the crews back to Chu Lai. Those of us who remained spent the night near the radio and made communications checks with the Blues throughout the night.

LZ Porrazzo, Jim Pratt's bird the morning of
November 14, 1967 preparing to sling it back for repair.

In the morning, the battalion commander of the 3-5 Infantry
flew directly over the site of our battle of the previous day. Bob
Lackey gives this description of the events of that night and the
following morning:

> That was one of the scariest nights of my life. There was
> nowhere to crawl off to sleep. I spent the night standing
> almost neck deep in rice paddy water and trying to sleep. It
> was a wonder I didn't fall over from exhaustion and drown.
> Eventually, a large force (Alpha Company, 3-5 Infantry) of
> ground troops humped in to our location. The next morning
> a helicopter flew over at about nine hundred feet, which
> was absurd. We heard the "*Whop-whop-whop*" of chopper
> blades and looked up until we saw it. We had lost all these
> helicopters the previous day and night, and here was a Fourth
> Infantry Division colonel flying over to take a look. Across
> the rice paddy was this huge gray rock, and behind it, two
> barrels reached up and went "*Boomb-boomb-boomb*" (This
> was one of the fifty-seven-mm AA guns). The AA gunner
> was an absolute pro because all three rounds broke around
> the colonel's helicopter.

One knocked off the tail rotor. The pilot did a very good job of trying to autorotate, but he was too high up and it was too much of a strain on the transmission. He got down to about three hundred or four hundred feet when the transmission locked and the rotor stopped turning. The chopper started spinning violently around the mast. At about 250 feet off the ground, the crew chief was thrown out of the ship, and we watched the guy screaming and falling to his death. Then the main rotor blade snapped off. The ship nosed over, headed straight down to the ground, crashed, and blew up on impact. That was the sequence of events as I remember them. The helicopter lost both main rotors, then crashed, and exploded. It hit about ninety yards from where we were standing. We could see the crews, their faces, the flailing of arms. It was one of my most horrible experiences. We didn't feel good about what happened. We had gotten our butts kicked and lost one of our nicest men, Jimmy Chryster. Jimmy always had a knack of knowing what was coming up. He could describe the types of battles we were going to be in, and he had even predicted his own death.

13 November, a day to remember.

WO Larry Brown, Chu Lai 1967
(plexiglas cuts and a little blood on face)

CHAPTER TWENTY FOUR
RECONNAISSANCE AT LA NGA

The next couple of days found the maintenance crews working hard to repair the substantial combat damage inflicted upon us on 13 November. The squadron commander, Lieutenant Colonel Nevins, flew up from LZ Two Bits and assisted in getting priorities established to reconstitute the battle losses suffered at Dong Son. We started to receive replacement aircraft, and within a week, we were back to full strength.

Our operational pace slowed during this period of time, but it did not stop. We sent two Pink teams a day to LZ Porrazzo and conducted a reduced number of reconnaissance missions for the Third Brigade. Restricting ourselves to just what the brigade requested allowed us to provide reconnaissance that met their needs but did not produce any significant results.

In the majority of cases, the most significant results were obtained from missions we generated within the troop. I had a card index for each of these reconnaissance boxes and recorded all enemy activities reported within the box. Those activities may have been an aircraft firing report, an agent report, a FLIR (forward looking infrared) report, an MTI (moving-target indicator), or a host of other information that was reported in the division and brigade intelligence summaries. By faithfully recording this information to these cards, and also plotting the information on a map overlay, the enemy told us where they were operating. You would think that everyone in the S2 (intelligence) sections at squadron, brigade, and division would keep track of this information the same way. Well, they didn't. They kept their information compartmentalized and, as a result, very seldom had an accurate picture of where the enemy was currently operating in the AO.

Cavalry soldiers have a long and colorful history, but their primary historical orientation has been the enemy and their location on the battlefield. It was to that end that the troop created their own missions. Based on current information and information that we had previously recorded in those boxes, I would select what I considered that day's most likely location to find enemy soldiers. These boxes would be posted to the pilots' maps, and the scout pilots would devote an entire mission to searching just within the designated box.

Most people can understand how a scout, on horseback, could track an enemy unit or an individual across varying types of terrain but do not relate that capability to a scout mounted in a helicopter. The techniques used by both scouts are identical; the only difference is the mount.

On 22 November, Warrant Officer (WO) Larry Brown and his weapons aircraft, piloted by WO John Fieg, were assigned a reconnaissance box in the southern part of the AO. This box was adjacent to the contact area of 13 November and contained a small village with a stream running north to south on the west side of the village. As they entered the area, they maintained their airspeed while making their initial pass over the area. Receiving no fire, they slowed the aircraft and started a detailed reconnaissance of the area. As they approached the village from the south, Warrant Officer Brown talked to his observer on the intercom of the aircraft,

"Crosby, do you see any movement in this village?" Crosby responded, "Negative. I don't see a thing stirring."

"I don't either. That bothers me. There should be some people or pigs or something. Look, you can tell people are living here; everything is too neat. Keep your eyes open and stay alert. There is something wrong here, and I don't know what it is," responded Brown.

They continued their methodical search, going very slow and just inches above the ground. They moved away from the village and started a detailed search down the east side of the stream bank next to the village. Crosby said, "Come right. I have something in the streambed." The OH-13 turned to the right as Crosby directed Warrant Officer Brown to near the middle of the streambed.

"Do you see that leaf in the middle of the stream, sir?" Crosby asked.

"Yes, I do," responded Warrant Officer Brown. "I wonder why it's not floating downstream." Crosby looked closely at the leaf as Warrant Officer Brown brought the aircraft to a hover. "Hell, it's caught on a piece of commo wire!" said Crosby. Warrant Officer Brown looked closely and said, "It sure as the hell is. Let's see where it goes." Turning the aircraft to the right, they returned to the bank of the stream and found where the commo wire entered the stream.

Watching the scout perform these maneuvers, WO John Fieg got on the radio, "White One-Four, this is Red Two-Five, over."

"This is One-Four, over."

"This is Two-Five. What have you got, over?"

"This is One-Four. A piece of commo wire runs across this stream. We're going to follow it as far as we can, over."

"This is Two-Five. Roger, out."

Switching frequencies, he transmitted the report back to the operations center at LZ Porrazzo. As I listened to the spot report, I smiled when I heard that "superscout" Larry Brown had found a commo wire in a stream. I called the brigade S3, while my radio telephone operator (RTO) was talking to Warrant Officer Fieg, and relayed this spot report to him. He was incredulous as he repeated what I had just told him. He outrightly questioned the ability of any pilot to see a commo wire from the air. While we were talking on the radio, Warrant Officer Brown overheard a part of the conversation on the open mike of my RTO and wanted to know who it was questioning his scouting ability. I got on his radio frequency and laughingly told him some grunt that thought as fast as he moved. He grumbled some response and continued his reconnaissance.

Hovering up the stream bank, they saw that the wire had been buried in spots, but enough was above ground for them to follow it. They followed the wire up the stream bank into a series of spider holes. They thoroughly searched the area around the spider holes but didn't find any soldiers. Warrant Officer Brown said, "Let's follow it on the other side of the stream" as he turned the aircraft and returned to the stream.

Following the wire to the other side of the stream, they followed it to another set of spider holes. As they searched this area, Warrant Officer Brown, with that mysterious sixth sense all scout pilots have, felt the enemy presence. As he searched the ground in front of him, he thought, "*What's wrong? There is something wrong with this area.*" Suddenly, it clicked. "*What are banana leaves doing laid out on the ground?*" He said to Crosby, "Fire into those banana leaves on the ground."

As the machine gun tore the pile of banana leaves apart, a trench was revealed beneath the leaves. In the trench sat an eighty-two-millimeter mortar. He relayed this information to Warrant Officer Fieg and approached another pile of banana leaves. This time, he had Crosby drop a grenade on the leaves as they maneuvered out of the way. As the grenade exploded, there was a small secondary explosion. They returned to the area and discovered that a fifty-seven-millimeter Anti Aircraft gun was now uncovered. They continued searching the area and uncovered three more recoilless rifles, three ammunition caches, and a pile of soldier's packs and then discovered a bunker. As they hovered in front of the bunker, Crosby saw two NVA soldiers inside the bunker. He immediately fired at them as they started shooting at the scout aircraft. Crosby tossed a smoke grenade as Warrant Officer Fieg began his gun run. The bunker collapsed as three rockets hit it.

"One-Four, this is Two-Five, over."

"This is One-Four, over."

"This is Two-Five. We have to break station and return. I'm into my low-fuel light. Three has all the spot reports and has sent another team out, over."

"This is One-Four, wilco. We checked that bunker, and you got both of them, out."

Major Burrow and I were convinced that the presence of the NVA heavy-weapons company meant that there was a high probability it was near a regimental headquarters. These were probably elements of the unit we had fought on the thirteenth of November. We requested permission to insert our Blues, but the brigade did not want us to get in a fire fight this far south and denied our request. They had no intention of reorienting from their present missions of search and destroy.

This irritated the hell out of me since this was the same mentality that had prevented us from encircling the enemy on 13 November. We did the next best thing and requested air strikes. Then I sent our forward observer out with the team that was relieving Warrant Officers Brown and Fieg.

The team I sent out consisted of a new scout pilot and an experienced gunship crew. They passed Brown and Fieg in the air about halfway to the objective area. Once they got on station, the scout pilot, with very limited experience, could not find the enemy positions. Major Burrow, upon hearing this, went out to Brown and Crosby, questioning them closely. Warrant Officer Brown resented the implication that he hadn't seen what he'd said he'd seen. Major Burrow asked him, "Do you think you could find it again?"

Brown replied, "You damn right I can! Let's go."

He and Major Burrow took off and headed back to the AO. Upon arrival on station, Warrant Officer Brown and his observer, Sergeant Crosby, moved directly to the spot where the first fifty-seven-millimeter AA was located, and sure enough, it was still there.

"Six, this is One-Four, over."

"This is Six, over."

"Come on down and take a look. Here it is, and it looks suspiciously like a fifty-seven-millimeter AA, over."

"Roger. I'm on the way, out."

Even though the gunship was supposed to fly at altitude, Major Burrow was notorious for his low-level flying with a gunship. He always wanted to see what the scout was looking at. Warrant Officer Brown moved his aircraft out of the way and watched as Major Burrow approached the position. There was a sudden jerk of Major Burrow's aircraft as they saw the fifty-seven.

Warrant Officer Brown said to Sergeant Crosby, "Hah! See that? He remembers when one of those fifty-sevens blew up his aircraft on the thirteenth."

"One-Four, this is Six. Well, by God, let's get the artillery cranked up and those air strikes in here!"

The rest of the afternoon was spent putting in air strikes and artillery. As One-Four put in the first air strike, a five-hundred-pound bomb went off, and Brown watched as an entire tunnel system collapsed.

We had been working with this brigade for over a year and in this AO for the last two months. They knew that this one air cavalry troop had accounted for over 50 percent of enemy kills in the brigade AO, and they still couldn't believe what we were capable of.

That, in a nutshell, was what air cavalry pilots encountered every day. To this day, unless you were there, you just cannot comprehend how effective and lethal this type of organization was. Pound for pound, man for man, it was the most effective and efficient combat organization produced by the Vietnam War.

CHAPTER TWENTY FIVE
RETRIBUTION DAY

Captain Jack Turecek arrived at Chu Lai on 4 December 1967. We had been without an executive officer for the troop since Major Burrow assumed command on 10 November. As the operations officer for the troop, I had filled in on the supply part of those duties, and Major Burrow retained the administrative part of that function when he assumed command of the troop. The plan was to have Captain Erle Thomas assume the position as executive officer, and Captain Turecek would become the weapons (Red) platoon leader.

The following day, 5 December, was very typical for most of the day. We had two screening missions for units that were in contact with the enemy. These missions typically resulted in a firefight between our pilots and the enemy, with each trying to kill the other. Typically, the enemy lost, and this day was no exception with these two missions, resulting in eight enemies killed and no loss of any of our crew members.

An unusual mission was conducted in the afternoon when we put the Blues on the ground to provide security for an artillery survey team. We would fly to a known point on the ground called a survey control point (SCP). The survey party would set up their instruments over this SCP and record readings to a distant point that was to be the location of an artillery battery at some time in the future. We did this three times during the afternoon, all without incident.

As this very typical day was drawing to a close and the sun was preparing to set over the Que Son Valley, Major Burrow decided he would be the weapons ship for the last-light mission with Warrant Officer Brown as the scout pilot on the mission. Captain

Thomas decided this would be an excellent time to orient Captain Turecek on how we conducted last-light missions and also give him an overall orientation on the fire-support bases in the valley.

As they departed LZ Porrazzo, they were stacked at three different levels with Warrant Officer Brown at low level, Major Burrow at about two thousand feet agl (above ground level), and Captains Thomas and Turecek at about three thousand feet agl. Captains Thomas and Turecek would accompany the last-light team but did not expect to participate in any of the action the last-light team might stir up. This was strictly an orientation ride.

This team first flew to LZ Colt where they checked around the perimeter. Finding no evidence of the enemy, they turned toward the northwest and flew toward LZ Ross. There was high ground north of LZ Ross; in fact, at 3,107 meters, it was the highest piece of terrain overlooking the Que Son Valley. As Major Burrow (Six) and Warrant Officer Brown (One-Four) started their reconnaissance around LZ Ross, Captain Thomas (Red) decided to fly up to the top of this mountain.

"Six, this is Red, over."

"This is Six, over."

"This is Red. I'm going to take the new Red to the top of this hill mass to your north and give him an orientation on the AO."

"This is Six. Roger out."

As they cleared the top of the hill, Red flew north and turned the aircraft to the right, looking back to the south, and started to point out the fire-support bases in the Wallowa AO.

"Sir, I have four dudes in the open!" his door gunner said. "They're running for cover."

Looking out his door window, Captain Thomas scanned the area below him and saw the four soldiers running for the concealment that they hoped the trees would provide them. He noticed they were in full NVA gear. Bringing his rockets on line, he nosed the C-model Huey over into an attack position and started lining up his sight on the fleeing enemy.

"Jack," Captain Thomas said to Captain Tuereck, "get me a grid and send a spot report to Six."

Captain Turecek had been flying with his map in his lap during the entire mission. He looked at the map and called Major Burrow.

"Six, this is Red X-ray, over."

"This is Six, over."

"This is Red X-ray. We have four NVA in the open at Bravo Tango 015375. We are engaging, over."

"This is Six. Roger we are on the way, out."

Major Burrow looked at his map and called Warrant Officer Brown.

"One-Four, this is Six, over."

"This is One-Four, over."

"This is Six. Red has four NVA in the open and is engaging. Head up to the top of the hill and I'll see you on top, over."

"This is One-Four. Roger, out."

Looking to the north, Warrant Officer Brown could see Red as he started his gun run. He also saw Major Burrow start climbing and moving toward Red. Warrant Officer Brown pulled in all the power he had as he started to move toward the top of the hill. The OH-13 was woefully underpowered, and he cursed as he slowly followed Major Burrow up the hill.

"Okay, guys, here we go," Captain Thomas announced on the intercom as he started his gun run.

As they closed upon the enemy, Red selected two pairs of rockets while Captain Turecek got the minigun ready to go. As they attacked from above, Red lined up his sights and squeezed the trigger. Four rockets left the tube, and Red watched as they screamed toward the enemy, exploding on impact. Captain Turecek was hosing down the area with his minigun, watching as the stream of fire walked around and over the enemy soldiers.

Pulling back on the cyclic and adding power, Captain Thomas felt the aircraft mush through the bottom of the run then felt the blades biting clean air as the aircraft started climbing. As they were climbing out, his door gunner came up on intercom and announced, "Shit, we got another twenty or so just broke into the open." Nearing the apex of his climb out, Red smoothly moved his cyclic to the right front, slightly reduced his collective, and pushed right pedal. His aircraft seemed to fall over to the right and was now headed back toward the ground and the enemy, only this time attacking from south to north.

Adding collective, Red saw the enemy soldiers below. Pulling back on the cyclic, he brought the nose of the aircraft up and lined up on the running enemy. He reached down and selected three pairs and once again squeezed the trigger. Six rockets rippled from the gun tubes, eagerly flying toward the target. In seconds, they exploded in the middle of the running enemy. Captain Turecek was firing the minigun as both the crew chief and door gunner were firing their M-60s into the ranks of the fleeing enemy. The noise of the rockets firing, minigun and machine guns firing with the smell of cordite heavy in the air, brought a strange sense of familiarity to the crew as they engaged the enemy. To Captain Turecek, the action brought a surge of adrenaline, and a wandering thought passed through his mind, "*I guess what I've heard about the 1-9 is really true.*"

"Saber Six, this is Red X-ray, over."

"This is Six, over."

"This is Red X-ray. We have about twenty in the open and are engaging again, over."

"Roger, this is Six. I have you in sight and am getting in position to do a daisy-chain with you. Out."

As they neared the bottom of their gun run, Red pulled back on the cyclic and pulled up on his collective. As they started to climb to altitude, the enemy soldiers began shooting at them. The crew chief, Specialist Rush, stood with one foot on the skid, secured with the monkey strap around his middle, firing down the tail boom at the enemy. Captain Thomas looked over his left shoulder just as Specialist Rush was hit in the right shoulder and side and was thrown back into the cargo compartment. Some rounds hit the armored seat; Captain Thomas was sitting in, and shrapnel flew inside the cockpit and wounded him in the arm and leg.

"Jack, take the aircraft. I've been hit!"

"Roger, I have the aircraft."

The enemy thought that Captain Thomas and his crew were the only ones in the area. As he started to climb out after his gun run, the NVA jumped up and started shooting at him. They were facing to the north and did not see Major Burrow starting his gun run from the south.

Firing rockets and his minigun, he cut a swath through the running enemy. The enemy was taken completely by surprise by this attack from another gunship. Major Burrow noticed the NVA uniforms and, although it was nearing darkness, followed his instincts and called me back at LZ Porrazzo

"Three, this is Six, over."

"This is Three, over."

"This is Six. Launch Blue. We are in contact with an estimated platoon-size NVA force. We are in the vicinity of Bravo Tango 015375, over."

"This is Three. Wilco, over." Glancing at my watch, I noticed that it was 1730 and recalled thinking, "*It's a little late in the day to insert the Blues.*"

"Six, roger out."

Blue and Three-Five were called on the radio, and in minutes, the Blue Flight was airborne and en route to Six's location. We called the Third Brigade and received permission to insert the Blues.

While the Blues were en route, Warrant Officer Brown got to the top of the hill and was killing as many as he could. Once the Blues were on the ground, One-Four led them toward the last-known surviving group of NVA soldiers. As the point squad, led by Sergeant Carter, was moving across the field, they came under heavy fire from snipers in a bunker. Maneuvering his squad closer to the enemy, he threw a hand grenade into the bunker, momentarily silencing the fire. The squad rushed the bunker and killed the six NVA inside.

The task now was to search as many of the bodies as possible prior to being extracted from the contact site. One-Four flew around the battlefield, directing the Blues to the various bodies, and, in the process, discovered several more NVA, which he engaged and killed. The sun had retreated behind the hills to the west, and time was becoming critical.

As the Blues searched the bodies, it soon was apparent that this was no ordinary group of NVA soldiers as packs, map cases, binoculars, pistols, and pouches of documents were recovered. Working rapidly, the Blues searched as many bodies as possible, and as darkness descended upon the Que Son Valley, the Blues were extracted and flown back to our base camp at Chu Lai.

We had confirmed seventeen NVA killed, and as we sorted through the documents that evening, one of the more conspicuous items was a map case similar to the ones we used. As we examined it, we discovered it was one of ours! This was Warrant Officer John Flanagan's map case that had been left behind in his aircraft on 13 November. What John found amusing was that the NVA had corrected his locations for the various fire-support bases in the AO. And they had it correct! John still takes some ribbing about that.

The following morning, we turned over the documents and some weapons to the S2 of the Third Brigade. Within hours, the S2 called to tell us that we had apparently killed the regimental commander of the Third NVA Regiment, a political officer, and other staff officers from the Second NVA Division headquarters. We had also captured the plan of a future attack against the fire-support bases of our Third Brigade.

As we digested this, someone said, "Payback is a bitch." This was in reference to our encounter with this regimental commander and his soldiers the month before on 13 November.

Apparently, this command group had gathered on this hilltop to rehearse the upcoming attack on the fire-support bases. From this hilltop, you had a clear and commanding view of the entire valley and all of the fire-support bases. If Red had not decided to give an orientation ride to Captain Tureck on that fateful day, the enemy would have survived, and the Third Brigade fire-support bases of LZs Ross and Leslie would have been surprised and perhaps over run when the attack finally came on 3 January 1968.

As it was, armed with the plans for the attack, all fire-support bases were reinforced, and additional "beehive" ammunition was stocked on the fire-support bases. Late in the evening of 2 January and the early morning of 3 January, the Third NVA regiment and other elements of the Second NVA Division launched their attack upon LZ Ross and LZ Leslie. It was a massacre! Preplanned artillery and gunship fires and the direct fire of 105 howitzers using beehive ammunition decimated the enemy. As assault after assault was launched against the defenders of Ross and Leslie, they were beaten back by overwhelming fire. On the morning of 3 January, the defenders of Ross and Leslie checked the perimeter, and 289 NVA were lying in the wire. As we flew around the perimeters at first light, there were blood trails leading away from each fire-support base. It is unknown how many of the enemy died, but if it hadn't been for the last-light mission on 5 December, the results of this attack against our fire-support bases may have turned out considerably different.

CHAPTER TWENTY SIX
SABER SIX KICKS ASS AND TAKES NO NAMES

Midmorning, four days later, we received a call on our radio net from a Blue Max gunship (2-20 Aerial Rocket Artillery), asking for help. The 3-5 Infantry and a Third Brigade scout ship had fifty NVA in the open and couldn't contain them. Red (CPT Jack Turecek) and White One-Four (WO Larry Brown) were the next team in the slot and immediately responded.

Taking off from LZ Porrazzo, they headed north as fast as their aircraft would go. Of course, Red kept calling One-Four, telling him to get with it, and One-Four kept reminding Red that he had the throttle full open and the collective was up under his arm. As they neared the contact area, they could hear and see Blue Max making gun runs, and Red got on the radio and called Snoopy Flight (the Third Brigade scouts) to get a situation report.

As he started to receive this report, he spotted ten NVA moving along a streambed and immediately engaged this force. The enemy, all equipped with AK-47s, turned and fired back at him on full automatic. But by that time, his rockets were bursting within their ranks, and fire slacked off considerably; he executed a return to target and raked the streambed again with minigun and rockets. These two runs accounted for six NVA KIA.

"Red, this is One-Four, over."

"This is Red, over."

"I have five NVA in a streambed and am engaging at this time."

As One-Four pressed the attack upon the NVA, he and his aircraft became the immediate focal point for the NVA fire from the ground. As he flew closer to them, he could feel the impact of AK-47 rounds hitting his aircraft. A couple of rounds came through the canopy, spraying Plexiglas throughout the cockpit. His observer had already killed three of them, and One-Four had two others lined up in his sights as he squeezed the trigger. He watched as the bullets entered the body of what had been an NVA soldier, kicked left pedal, and lined up on the remaining NVA soldiers as he depressed the trigger. As bullets tore into the remaining NVA soldiers, a terrific volume of fire hit One-Four's aircraft from the left rear, and part of his instrument panel disappeared.

"Red, this is One-Four. Five NVA in full uniform, equipped with AK-47s engaged, five NVA KIA. The aircraft has taken a lot of hits and has lost the instrument panel. Get me pointed to the nearest LZ. I don't know how long this bird is going to fly."

"This is Red. Roger. Take up a heading of One Seven Zero. Are you okay?"

"Yeah, we're both okay, but they shot the shit out of this bird."

"Roger. Let's un-ass the area. Red out."

Just as Red and One-Four were departing, Saber Six (Major George Burrow) and White One-One (Lieutenant McMurray) arrived on station. Accompanying this team was White One-Two (Warrant Officer Inman) and Lieutenant Cox, the forward observer. A river ran through the contact area generally from north to south. The rifle company from 3-5 Infantry was on the northwest side of the river sweeping south. On the east side of the river were two platoons from another 3-5 Infantry Company, occupying blocking positions, and another platoon occupying a blocking position farther to the south on the west side of the river.

Arriving on station, Major Burrow contacted the company commander from 3-5 Infantry and located all of his soldiers on the ground. Moving out in front of the infantry toward the river, he soon detected a platoon-sized NVA force just south of where Red and One-Four had just killed eleven NVA.

Nosing the Charlie-model gunship over, he selected three pairs and dove on the enemy as he squeezed the trigger, sending nine rockets into their midst. Pulling up from the dive, he executed a return-to-target maneuver, lined up the enemy in his sight, and punched off another three pairs. That expended all of his rockets. His copilot (Warrant Officer Kreps) turned on the minigun and started engaging them. Since there were no rockets left, Major Burrow stayed at a low altitude as the door gunners and Warrant Officer Kreps engaged the enemy below. They made repeated low speed, low-level passes over this platoon. In the process, they became the target for intense ground-to-air fire. The aircraft was repeatedly hit by small-arms fire, and the hydraulic line for the minigun was hit. This was not good news. In any other type of Huey (A, B, or D models), if you lost hydraulics, you had a good chance of getting it back on the ground. The Charlie model was not that forgiving. If you lost your hydraulics, there was no chance moving the controls. They just froze up, and depending where you were when that happened, it was highly unlikely you would be able to safely land it.

Warrant Officer Kreps turned the minigun off, and they continued their low-level passes over the enemy until the door gunners had shot all of their ammunition. This initial engagement resulted in ten NVA KIA. Just as they ran out of ammunition, Red (Captain Turecek) returned to the contact area.

"Saber six, this is Red, over."

"This is Six, over."

"This is Red. One-Four is safely on the ground at Baldy, and I am back on station. What's the situation, over?"

"Red, your timing is impeccable. I am out of ammunition and need to go rearm. White One-One [Lieutenant McMurray] and you have it. I will be back as soon as I rearm."

With that, he climbed to altitude and flew to LZ Baldy where he rearmed, refueled, and returned to the battle area. Upon his return, he flew next to the river, flying from south to north along the east side of the river. His door gunner spotted six enemies moving next to the river and immediately engaged them with his door gun. Major Burrow came around to the right and lined up on the enemy. He made his gun run from south to north. As he climbed out after his rocket run, he observed more enemies farther north along the river.

Mentally, he noted their location as he executed a return to target and, for the second time that day, expended all of his rockets. Staying low level after his second gun run, he flew to where he had spotted the other group, and his door gunners immediately engaged them. In these two engagements, he had killed another twelve NVA. Continuing up the river, he spotted another large group of NVA in the open, in a rice paddy next to the river. Having expended his entire load of rockets and door-gun ammunition, he decided to activate his minigun even though he knew it had a hydraulic leak.

He cut a swath through the enemy forces with the minigun. Starting his second pass with the minigun, the controls started to get stiff, and then the minigun jammed. He immediately turned off the minigun system. Having plenty of fuel, but being out of ammunition, he directed the scout over to an empty field so he could get door-gun ammunition for his door gunners. As soon as he had the ammunition on board, he returned to the battlefield. Having no rockets, he hovered across the field, doing pedal turns as his door gunners killed the enemy. With adrenaline pumping through his veins, he appeared to be everywhere on the heavily contested battlefield. His aircraft became the prime target for intense automatic—and semiautomatic-weapons fire. He made repeated passes through a virtual wall of fire and completely disorganized the enemy. He struck fear in their hearts as it appeared that nothing could stop him. Running out of ammunition again and low on fuel, Major Burrow and his crew left the battlefield and left behind forty-one of the enemy dead on that battlefield.

As the afternoon wore on, Red and One-Four were back in the action with a new aircraft as they shifted their attention to the westside of the river. As One-Four slowly searched the area, he came upon another group of NVA and immediately engaged them. While One-Four was engaging two enemy soldiers, Red saw another two attempting to evade. He nosed the aircraft over and punched off two pairs of rockets. This action resulted in another four enemies KIA.

The day's action, in supporting 3-5 Infantry, resulted in Bravo Troop accounting for fifty-six enemies KIA in a single engagement. Major Burrow and his crew established a record kill for a single engagement with one helicopter, and Major Burrow received the Distinguished Service Cross for his actions in this battle.

CHAPTER TWENTY SEVEN
THE SECOND BATTLE
OF PHU 'O' CHAU

Just about three months earlier, we had our first big battle around the village of Phu 'O' Chau, and today, December 14, we were returning. The Fifth Battalion of the Seventh Regiment (5-7) conducted an air assault into an area near Phu 'O' Chau, and we were conducting a screen to the south of Phu 'O' Chau. Due to battle damage, the troop was short on scout aircraft and had borrowed an H-13 from the Third Brigade scouts (Snoopy Flight). Red (Captain Turecek) and Warrant Officer Moore were the first team on station. On this first mission, we had two gunships flying together. As the air assault was in progress, Red saw two personnel in black PJs, attempting to hide something under their shirts. Dropping down from altitude, he made a low level, low-speed pass over them. As he turned around and started his second pass over them, they started to run from him, and he saw what they were trying to conceal. Under their loose-fitting shirts were NVA packs. Quickly lining up on them, he selected one pair and squeezed the trigger. Two rockets left the tube, flying toward their target. Since this was a low-level rocket run, he broke hard right, but even then, he flew through some of the shrapnel from the rockets. He continued the right turn and flew to the remains of the two soldiers he had just killed. Verifying they were dead, he climbed back to altitude while Warrant Officer Moore gave the spot report to troop operations.

As they continued their reconnaissance, Warrant Officer Moore saw two NVA with packs and weapons, trying to hide from them.

Nosing the aircraft over, he started his gun run on the two soldiers. They watched as the gunship started its dive upon them. They had been under attack by helicopters before and knew if they stayed where they were, they would probably be killed. The aircraft was diving right at them; they broke from their position and ran toward the nearest hooch, hoping there would be a tunnel in the hooch. All they had to do was reach the hooch.

Warrant Officer Moore selected two pairs and watched as they started to run for the cover of the nearest hooch. Pushing a little more right pedal, he lined up his aiming point on the fleeing soldiers and squeezed the trigger. Just as the rockets exploded, one of the soldiers dove into the hooch. The other one didn't make it and lay dead about three meters from the entrance to the hooch. Pulling up from the gun run, Warrant Officer Moore climbed to altitude, lined up on the hooch, selected two more pairs, and blew the hooch away. At the bottom of the gun run, he pulled in power, leveled off, remained low level, turned right, and circled the hooch. He couldn't confirm that he had killed this last soldier since the hooch had collapsed and was now burning vigorously. He climbed to altitude, and he and Red continued the screen with no further contact on their fuel load.

As they departed station, Lieutenant Rudy von Watzdorf, in a scout bird, and WO John Fieg in a gunship arrived on station. As Red and Warrant Officer Moore departed, they briefed the incoming team on where they had last seen the enemy. Lieutenant von Watzdorf flew to the burning hooch and, using that as his start point, conducted a high-speed reconnaissance of the area within two thousand meters of the hooch. Detecting no enemy and receiving no fire, he slowed down and started his detailed reconnaissance of the area.

The team had been working the area for about thirty minutes when Major Burrow arrived on station and checked in with the team. He was en route to LZ Porrazzo from a meeting at brigade. He was above the team, observing them work the area, when his crew chief alerted him that he had observed some movement about five hundred meters north of where the team was working. Turning the aircraft in that direction, Major Burrow said, "Let's check it out." As they approached the area, Major Burrow's copilot, Warrant Officer Kreps, said, "There they are! Two NVA with packs and weapons." As they started their gun run, Warrant Officer Kreps called the team on station, letting them know what they had observed and that they were going to attack.

The NVA soldiers had heard the aircraft to their south engage their comrades and knew from past experience that they needed to put some distance between themselves and those aircraft. They came to the edge of a rice paddy and knew that safety lay in the bunkers and tunnels on the other side of the paddy. As they started across, they heard a helicopter getting closer to them. One of them turned and saw to his horror that a gunship had just started a gun run, with them as the target. Knowing he was too far from the safety of the bunkers, he placed his AK-47 on automatic and turned to engage the aircraft that was bearing down on them. Adrenaline surged through him as he aimed at the helicopter and pulled the trigger. He saw smoke erupt from the rear of the rocket tubes and knew they were firing at him. He saw the first rocket impact about ten feet in front of him. That was his last thought as his body was blown apart by another rocket that landed beside him. He died in an instant, not knowing that the devastatingly accurate rocket fire had also killed his comrade. Warrant Officer Kreps called troop operations, informing them that another two NVA had just been killed in action.

Major Burrow circled the area, looking for more NVA, but none showed themselves. He soon departed station and returned to LZ Porrazzo. At 1100 hours, WO John Fieg received a call from the 5-7 Rifle Company, alerting them that they were in contact with an unknown-size enemy force, and requested some assistance in locating all elements of this force. The team moved toward the company with Lieutenant von Watzdorf leading the way in his H-13.

As they arrived over the contact area, Lieutenant von Watzdorf contacted the company commander and confirmed the locations of all friendlies. He immediately saw where the heaviest fighting was taking place as smoke was hanging over the contact area. He approached from behind the friendly forces and informed the company commander that he was going to screen their west flank. He turned left toward the west and slowly moved down the line until they had cleared the contact area. He turned right, picked up speed, and made several high-speed passes over the west flank and moved forward of the friendly positions and started working his way toward the enemies location.

His observer yelled, "Come right!" as he started to engage an enemy platoon directly below them with his M-60 machine gun. The enemy immediately returned fire, and they both could hear and feel bullets hitting their aircraft. A round went through their windscreen, and razor-sharp shards of Plexiglas sprayed both of them. The observer immediately dropped a smoke grenade as Lieutenant von Watzdorf broke to the right and moved back toward the friendlies while calling to his gunship that they were taking fire.

WO John Fieg saw the tail of the H-13 come up as it executed a sharp right turn. He immediately selected two pairs as he watched the scout engage the enemy force below. He saw the smoke grenade explode as the H-13 straightened out and headed away from the contact area. He simultaneously heard Lieutenant von Watzdorf call that he was taking fire. Mr. Fieg had already started his gun run and squeezed the trigger as soon as the scout was clear. The enemy now concentrated on the attacking gunship as all fire was focused on this menace from the sky. As the four rockets exploded, all ground fire ceased. The crew chief and door gunner kept fire on the enemy position as the gunship climbed back to altitude and executed a return to target. He placed four more rockets in the area and, as he was pulling out his crew chief, informed him that they killed at least four of them.

Warrant Officer Fieg called Lieutenant von Watzdorf to tell him to return to the area. Lieutenant von Watzdorf replied that he had lost his hydraulics and probably had other damage to the aircraft. Warrant Officer Fieg told him to take up a 180-degree heading, and the team started back to LZ Porrazzo. Major Burrow,

who had been following all of this radio traffic in the operations
bunker, got up and left for the contact area. We had no scout
aircraft available at Porrazzo, so Captain Burnham, in his UH-1D
lift aircraft, went with him to act as his chase bird.

Arriving on station, Major Burrow contacted the company
commander from 5-7 Infantry and let him know he was on station.
As he was getting orientated, he saw an NVA platoon in front of 5-
7 Infantry. He selected two pairs, nosed the aircraft over and
punched off the rockets at the nearest point of the enemy, and
fired another two pairs into the middle of a four-man group. He
saw seven of them go down, and since he didn't have a scout aircraft
with him, he leveled off at the bottom of the gun run and flew
toward the edge of the rice paddy in front of him. He saw three
more running for the bunkers at the edge of the rice paddy and
cut them down with his nose-mounted minigun. They flew over
all of the bodies, making sure they were dead. Still low level, he
turned south and started toward one of the friendly platoons that
were being engaged by an unknown-size enemy force in some
prepared positions in the hedgerows next to a rice paddy. He could
see the enemy along the edge of the rice paddy and decided that
the easiest way to get them was to fly the length of the hedgerow
and fire it up with his minigun.

The NVA platoon leader in the hedgerow heard and then saw
Major Burrow's aircraft start his gun run down the hedgerow and
started yelling at his men, "Shoot the helicopter, shoot the
helicopter." All guns turned toward the helicopter, and they opened
fire on the biggest gunship target they ever had to shoot at.

Major Burrow and his crew started their minigun run, and
suddenly, they were the target for all the NVA soldiers in this
hedgerow. As they pressed the attack upon the enemy, they could
feel and hear rounds hitting their aircraft. Suddenly, the minigun
quit firing! Immediately seeing and hearing this, the NVA stood
up in their prepared positions and took aimed shots at the helicopter
just a couple of feet above them.

With the minigun jammed, it was time to get the hell out of
there. This was not the time to attempt a climb to altitude. They

turned to the right; and as they turned, a heavy volume of fire hit the aircraft, and Plexiglas shards were flying through the cockpit area. Major Burrow said, "Shit, I've been hit." His face was peppered with Plexiglas cuts, and he had a burning sensation in his right eye. They flew away from the contact area low level until they were out of small-arms range. Major Burrow knew they had taken a lot of hits and decided they'd better check the aircraft over before they attempted to fly all the way back to Porrazzo.

He called Captain Burnham and told him to keep a sharp eye out while they were on the ground. He landed the aircraft; and Warrant Officer Kreps, the crew chief, and Major Burrow started checking the aircraft over from nose to tail. Nothing vital had been hit, so they started it up and flew back to Porrazzo. Major Burrow was treated for the facial cuts but did not tell anyone that a piece of Plexiglas was in his right eye. He knew if that was reported, he would be grounded and probably evacuated to Japan to have eye surgery performed. He would, of course, have to turn over command to someone else, and he wasn't quite ready to let that happen.

We continued to have sporadic contact the rest of the afternoon, and at 1600 hours, both Captain Turecek's and Warrant Officer Moore's aircraft were both shot up. Captain Turecek's copilot was wounded and losing a lot of blood, so the team departed station and flew to LZ Baldy.

At 1611 hours, Warrant Officer Brown (One-Four), in the scout aircraft, and Warrant Officer Zahn (Two-Eight), flying the gunship, flew to the area of contact and continued the screen for the 5-7 Infantry. At 1630 hours, Specialist Buchanan, Warrant Officer Brown's observer, observed two NVA hiding in a hedgerow. He fired into the hedgerow; they saw one of the NVA soldiers collapse, and then the hedgerow erupted into a wall of return fire from twenty feet away. Blood spurted from Specialist Buchanan's right eye as his head slammed backward. The machine gun stopped firing as he lost his grip on it, and he slumped forward against his shoulder harness. Plexiglas shards were flying everywhere, and the instrument panel disintegrated with pieces of the panel imbedded in Warrant Officer Brown's right leg and hand.

Turning hard left, he transmitted his radio call to Two-Eight, "I'm taking fire! I have been hit!" Two-Eight saw the tracer fire reaching toward One-Four from the hedgerow, nosed his hog-configured gunship into a dive and launched four pairs of rockets into the hedgerow, and said, "Roger I'm rolling in hot."

Blood was being picked up by the rotor wash from Buchanan's head injury, and a red haze was forming on One—Fours' visor. He reached up with his left hand to raise the visor, but the visor was stuck. His left hand went back to the collective as he pulled up on it.

"Two-Eight, this is One-Four, over."

"This is Two-Eight, over."

"This is One-Four. I'm in deep shit. I think Buchanan is a line one [code for dead], I can't get my visor up, and blood is coating it. I can only see under the edge of it, and if that's not enough, I have a stuck tail rotor. Get me pointed in the right direction for Baldy, over."

"Roger. Come right, slight pause, hold what you have."

"Am I high enough to clear the trees?"

"Roger. You're fine. I'm going to drop down and fly next to you. Hang on, buddy!"

If someone had overheard this conversation, he would have heard two very calm voices talking back and forth. They were both very much aware of how potentially disastrous this situation was, adrenaline was pumping through their veins, and yet, they maintained a firm grip on their emotions.

One-Four's aircraft was out of trim with the nose of the aircraft far to the right of the flight path. As they neared LZ Baldy, Two-Eight and One-Four continued talking to each other,

"You're looking good, One-Four."

"How far from Baldy are we?"

"We're about four minutes out. Try your pedals again."

"I have; there's no response."

"Think about what you have to do. Shallow approach; keep your airspeed up; just before touchdown, roll off a little throttle; let it straighten up; when straight, down on the collective; and let it slide to a stop."

"Roger. I've been going over the procedure in my head. Thanks."

"One-Four, we have clearance straight in. Lose some altitude [*pause*]. That's good hold what you have. Keep your airspeed up [*pause*]. Come left [*pause*]. A little more [*pause*]. Good, hold what you have. Lose a little more altitude [*pause*]. Keep your airspeed up. You're over the runway, can you see it?"

"Barely."

"I'm with you, buddy. You're about a foot off the runway. Roll off some throttle [pause]. You're straight with the runway. Lower your collective."

LZ Baldy was a dirt runway covered with the ubiquitous PermaPrime. As he lowered the collective, the skids touched down and dug furrows into the runway as the H-13 slid to a stop. Larry slumped back against the bulkhead. His fatigues were soaked with blood, and sweat was dripping from his nose and chin. He took a deep breath and rolled off the throttle and felt someone frantically trying to unbuckle his seat belt and shoulder harness. He couldn't see the person doing this, so he pulled off his flight helmet and looked into the face of Buchanan.

Buchanan had a bleached-out look due to the loss of so much blood. Blood was still flowing from the hole in his head that used to contain his right eye. He was grabbing at One-Four and was saying, "Come on, sir, get out of the aircraft. I can't let you die on me." He stumbled backward and grabbed One-Four's outstretched hand and said again, "Come on, sir, get out of the aircraft!" Warrant Officer Brown swung his legs outside and stood up under the rotor blades, which were coasting to a stop. Buchanan collapsed in his arms and passed out. They were both taken off the runway to the aid station near the runway. Warrant Officer Brown was patched up and returned to the troop. Buchanan was given emergency first aid and flown to the MASH at Chu Lai.

We called the Third Brigade "Snoopy Flight" at LZ Baldy and informed them that the H-13 we had borrowed from them that morning was on the airstrip at Baldy and had twenty-two bullet holes in it. Needless to say, they were not happy campers.

That evening, we went to the hospital to visit Buchanan. His head was wrapped in bandages, and blood was still soaking through them. As we were there talking with him, I got a little queasy and had to sit down. As we prepared to leave, he reached up and grabbed Mr. Brown by the arm and told him to make sure he sent his cav hat to him. I wonder if he ever got it.

We had killed thirty-one NVA during this day's operation, with several aircraft shot up and four of our people wounded.

Another day in the AO slowly wound to a close.

CHAPTER TWENTY EIGHT
LEAVING BRAVO TROOP

December 24, 1967, was a normal day at LZ Porrazzo—several contacts with elements of the Third NVA Regiment, several aircraft firings, one aircraft hit, several NVA KIA—and it was time to leave Porrazzo and return to our base camp at Chu Lai. We had been short on lift aircraft this day due to scheduled and unscheduled maintenance on the UH-1Ds. My aircraft was one that was in for maintenance, so in a rare occurrence, I was riding to and from Porrazzo as a passenger.

For some reason, we did not leave Porrazzo with the rest of the troop. As we took off, the sun had already set, and it started to get dark as we followed the main road, QL1, back to Chu Lai. Sitting in the back, facing the open cargo door, my mind wandered as I looked outside and watched the terrain pass below us. I had an overwhelming urge to unbuckle and jump out, just as we had done so many times back at Fort Campbell. Of course, I didn't, but the old airborne urge was still alive and well. I settled back in the seat and, on intercom, asked the pilot to tune in to the AFN station. It was Christmas Eve, and they played one Christmas carol after another without a break.

As darkness gathered a firm grip over the terrain below, I thought of my family and, particularly, my children. I also thought of all those Vietnamese children who no longer had a father. As we flew down QL1, "Silent Night" was playing when I saw this single building with a string of colored lights strung across the front of it. I was surprised and immediately jumped to the conclusion that here was a Christian family living in a sea of Buddhists. I had nothing to justify such a thought, and for all I knew, the colored lights may have been for some party held by the occupants. But, it was Christmas Eve; the music and those colored lights put me in a melancholy mood. For the rest of the flight back to Chu Lai, I closed my eyes and visualized myself at home, listening to these same Christmas carols, watching my kids as the anticipation of Christmas morning and the opening of presents drew nearer.

Every year since then, when we start singing "Silent Night" at the Christmas-eve candlelight service my wife and I attend, I am mentally in that helicopter, flying over that Vietnamese building with the colored lights. And regardless of where we are—be it Obendorf, Austria, or the First Presbyterian Church in Killeen, Texas—I am grateful that I survived, that so many of my friends survived, and that all the killing, Vietnamese and American, has stopped.

On December 28, 1967, Lieutenant Colonel Robert Nevins passed the colors and command of the squadron to Lieutenant Colonel Richard Diller. Bravo Troop in Chu Lai noted this change of command but did not pause as we continued our pursuit of the Third NVA Regiment in and around the Que Son Valley. Several days later, I left for R&R in Hawaii. I was to meet my wife there, and we would spend the week together. It was a trip I looked forward to with mixed feelings. On the one hand, there was the possibility that this separation may have improved our relationship, but on the other hand, a more realistic look at where we had been and where it appeared we were going didn't raise much hope that this would be a joyful reunion.

We did the normal tourist things one does when in Hawaii, but at the end of the week, I was ready to return to Vietnam. It was a strained week. Her ever-shifting personality had me on edge as I waited for the first eruption of her temper. I did not have long to wait. At dinner that first evening, she lost her temper over some inconsequential thing, which I long ago repressed. The entire week was unsatisfactory, and she had no interest in what I had just left or cared. From her point of view, I had it easy compared to her responsibility of working and caring for the children. I heaved a sigh of relief as I put her on the plane that took her back to the States.

While I was on R&R, the Third NVA Regiment conducted its assault against the Third Brigade fire-support bases on 3 January 1968. The day before, the troop had located the advance elements of this attacking force at last-light and, in the fierce fighting that followed, killed thirty of the enemy. As I mentioned earlier, the fight on December 5, when we killed the Third NVA regimental commander, resulted in our capturing the battle plans for the winter and spring offensive for the Second NVA Division. It was the possession of these plans that allowed the brigade to prepare for the attack. Notwithstanding this advance preparation, at fire-support base Ross, the enemy breached the wire but was ejected by fierce hand-to-hand fighting. At fire-support base Colt, the enemy attempted a human wave assault against the perimeter. The 105-artillery pieces of the base lowered their barrels, loaded beehive ammunition, and repeatedly fired into the attacking mass of soldiers. The attack was stopped, and the remaining enemy retreated into the night, taking as many of their dead and wounded with them as was possible. At daylight, several hundred bodies were hanging in the wire, and the scouts of Bravo Troop followed blood trails into the surrounding jungle. There was sporadic contact, but the major force had disappeared.

I returned from R&R the following week, and on 17 January, we were alerted to prepare for a move farther north. On the same day, squadron headquarters left LZ English and flew into LZ El Paso, which was located to the west of the provincial capitol of Hue. This ended Operation Pershing for the squadron and was the beginning of Operation Jeb Stuart. On 25 January, Bravo Troop flew north to our new base at LZ Evans, north of Hue along the road known as QL1. This ended our participation in Operation Wallowa. As our last ship lifted off the pad at Chu Lai, I subsequently learned that they flew low level over the Americal Division headquarters and dropped CS grenades as their farewell to the Americal.

On 26 January, the squadron headquarters and Delta Troop moved from LZ El Paso to LZ Evans. The squadron headquarters was about a mile from Bravo Troop's location. On 30 January, Lieutenant Colonel Diller informed me that I was being transferred to the squadron staff to assume duties as the squadron supply officer (S4). This was a job I did not want, and as hard as it was to leave the troop, this assignment made it just that much harder.

During the nearly year-long Operation Pershing, the squadron had killed one-third of the NVA killed by the entire First Cavalry Division; 1,727 enemies were killed, 602 of the enemy were captured, and the squadron initiated 82 percent of all contacts made by the division. These figures do not include the 918 enemies killed or the 186 captured by Bravo Troop in Operation Wallowa (1 October 1967-25 January 1968). At the time, I didn't realize just how unique and special the 140 men of this troop were. We were a band of brothers that time and circumstance had brought together in this place, in this war, and fought a type of warfare that was unequaled by any other company-size unit in Vietnam. During our three plus months in Operation Wallowa, we had three of our comrades killed (two in an accident and one from contact with the enemy) and had fifty wounded. Unlike so many other units that had success on the battlefield, often with horrible losses, this troop had unparalleled success on a consistent basis with the absolute minimum of losses.

The following morning, 31 January 1968, I tossed my belongings in a jeep before the first-light team took off and drove the mile to squadron headquarters. I was going to a relatively safe job at squadron headquarters and was leaving behind the bravest, most disciplined, and toughest band of warriors I would ever know. "*God,*" I thought, "*I'm going to become a rear echelon puke.*"

CHAPTER TWENTY NINE
TET OFFENSIVE 1968

As I drove toward squadron headquarters, I heard the first-light team depart the Bravo Troop area. It was a gray morning with a ceiling of about one hundred to two hundred feet, and it was miserable weather for an air cavalry troop to operate in. Low-lying scud prevented the gunships from operating at their customary 1,500-foot level. As I approached the squadron-headquarters area, I saw three aircraft take off and fly generally to the south toward Hue.

We pulled up to the operations bunker, and I went inside, trying to find out where I was going to work and bunk down. The radios were full of traffic, and it was obvious that something was up. I asked one of the RTOs what was going on. He replied, "Bravo Troop just reported that there is a large NVA force in the vicinity of Hue Phu Bai. They are scrambling all the gunships they can get airborne to engage them." I asked him where I could find the squadron commander or the S3. He informed me that they both were airborne en route to Hue. I could sense that this was going to be a long day; so I went to the jeep, pulled out my gear, and set it inside the operations bunker. I told the driver to return to the troop as I moved inside the operations bunker.

As I listened to the spot reports coming in, it was apparent they had found a large enemy force. I really felt that I was out of it completely. I could visualize what it was like; but sitting in this bunker, listening to a spot report sent by one of the radio telephone operators (RTO) in the troop, lacked all of the urgency one would receive at the troop command post. I already missed being with the troop.

While listening to the reports come in, Blackhawk 2 called to let the squadron know he had been seriously wounded and was being medevaced out. As he put it, "I have a million-dollar wound, and I'm going back to the States." He had been shot over Hue and had landed at the special-forces compound in Hue. There was no sorrow in his voice; in fact, he was quite happy about the whole situation. As soon as I heard that, I perked up. Since he had been the S2 (intelligence officer), there was hope for me yet. When Lieutenant Colonel Diller arrived back at the squadron command post (CP), I volunteered to fill the position, and he agreed. Inside, I was mentally saying, "*All right!*" That put me back in operations where I felt I belonged and got me out of the supply position. I couldn't have been happier.

When I asked where I was going to bunk, they pointed to a container express (CONEX)—a metal box about seven feet high, seven feet wide, and about ten feet long, which was normally used to ship equipment in. I hauled my gear over to the container and put it inside. It didn't look like anyone else was in there, so I hustled back to the operations bunker to start my new job. Sergeant first class Mills was the intelligence NCO for the squadron, and he immediately took me under his wing and started to teach me my job.

The first thing he did was get me introduced to the Tactical Operations Center (TOC) crew. Major Bill Sorenson was the S3 (operations officer) of the squadron, and I soon learned the names and positions of the other personnel in the TOC. We had two map boards in the TOC. One was for operations, and the other was for intelligence. I was given an overview of the Jeb Stuart AO. For the past four months, I had been concerned only with the Third Brigade AO, but now I had to reorient my thinking. The 1-9 Cavalry Squadron was the reconnaissance squadron for the entire division. We were the eyes and ears for the First Cavalry Division commander, Major General John Tolson. We were kept under division control but worked in conjunction with each of the three brigades in the division. Alpha Troop worked with the First Brigade, Bravo Troop worked with the Third Brigade, and Charlie Troop worked with the Second Brigade. Delta Troop was a ground cavalry troop mounted in jeeps and three quarter-ton trucks that performed ground-convoy escort and route reconnaissance. At times, they would become the squadron reserve to be air assaulted in to support one of the rifle platoons if the brigade could not reinforce them.

While looking at the maps, I overheard on the radio that one of the gunships from Bravo Troop had been shot down. The ceiling was seventy-five to 150 feet with intermittent rain showers. The weather was such a factor that some OH-13 pilots turned back because of a lack of instrumentation in the aircraft. The C-model gunships were flying low level, in and out of the clouds as they approached Hue. The low ceiling coupled with the rain made the act of flying extremely dangerous and attempting to engage the enemy from this low altitude questionable for the gunships.

Warrant Officer Maehrelein, from Bravo Troop, had been sent to Hue Phu Bai on a resupply run in his H-model Huey. He was confident (as only the young can be) as he climbed up into the low ceiling and broke out on top at about eight thousand feet. Flying with him that day was a new pilot, who was sitting in the right seat, and his regular crew of Specialist Duncan, the door gunner, and his crew chief. As the needle swung on his instruments, he initiated his NDB (nondirectional beacon) approach into Phu Bai and started a spiral descent into the clouds. As they were descending into the clouds, Warrant Officer Maehrelein clearly remembered that he was most concerned about the guy wires around the antennas near Phu Bai. This was a hairy approach, and just as he broke out of the clouds about one hundred feet from the runway, his radio came alive with "Mayday, Mayday. I've been hit, and I'm going down!" He recognized the voice of Lieutenant Babcock and knew he couldn't be too far away. He executed a 360-degree turn in an effort to see where he could have gone down. He saw another Huey in the distance and flew toward it. While flying toward this Huey, he started over flying large groups of enemy soldiers. They started shooting at him, and he pulled up into the low-lying clouds and then back out. He did this four or five times and then saw smoke rising vertically in the distance.

As he flew toward the smoke, he was jinking left and right to throw off the aim of the enemy below him. The fire directed toward him became more intense, and he once again flew into the clouds. He went through a layer of low-lying scud and was in a space between the clouds and could see the smoke rising ahead. He flew to the smoke and lowered his collective. As he broke out of the cloud layer below him, he became the target for approximately eighty enemy soldiers. He kept his airspeed up to eighty or ninety knots as he took in the scene below and ahead of him.

The enemy were in two groups of approximately forty soldiers per group. He saw the group below him with two of the crew members and the group ahead with the other two crew members. His door gunner started shooting, and most of the enemy in the group below him jumped into a trench near their location, leaving the two crew members standing by themselves. He executed a hard left turn while lowering the collective, shooting an approach to the crew members. They flew parallel to the ditch as Specialist Duncan fired down the length of the trench, killing and wounding an unknown number of them. On touchdown, Lieutenant Babcock and the other crew member leaped into the aircraft.

He saw the other group ahead of him start to run and scatter but not before they shot and killed the other two crew members. They were lying in the rice paddy ahead of him, and he knew what he had to do. His aircraft had become the target for every NVA and PF soldier around them. He picked the Huey up to a hover and hovered over to the bodies and landed next to them. Specialist Duncan jumped out of the Huey and dragged the bodies onto the aircraft while the pilot on the right side fired his .38-caliber pistol at the enemy. As soon as the bodies were on board, Maehrelein executed a maximum-performance takeoff into the clouds seventy feet above him and flew to Phu Bai to drop off the bodies. He received an impact Silver Star for his actions, but I always have felt he should have received the congressional Medal of Honor for his unflinching courage above and beyond the call of duty. He exemplified the unwritten code of the 1-9 Cavalry of never leaving anyone behind, dead or alive.

On last-light reconnaissance, Bravo Troop sighted an NVA company moving toward Hue and immediately engaged the enemy. This engagement resulted in fifty-four enemies being killed and signaled the beginning of the Battle of Hue.

I drew a sketch of the operating area to put most of the key areas firmly in my mind. It was important that all who were involved in directing operations have a clear mental picture of where the major areas of interest were located and how any current action would relate or have an impact on any adjacent areas. As a staff officer, I always felt you needed to memorize key areas in the AO so that you could mentally keep up with any battles and make intelligent decisions and recommendations to the commander.

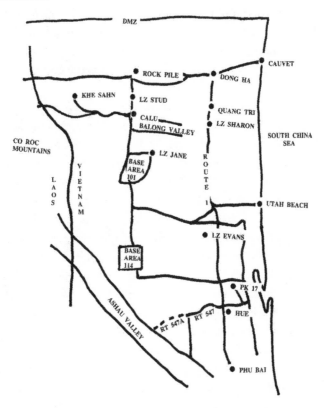

(SKETCH 1): Sketch of Jeb Stuart Area of Operations

Throughout the month of February, B Troop continued support for the Third Brigade in the much-publicized battle in and around the city of Hue. On 2 February, the troop was supporting the Third Brigade in the vicinity of Hue. While providing an aerial screen for the ground units, the troop commander (MAJ George Burrow) became the target for intense ground-to-air fire. His aircraft was hit, and they were forced to make an emergency landing. But this time, upon contact with the ground, the C-model gunship rolled over. Miraculously, the crew crawled out of the aircraft but was immediately engaged with small-arms fire. The scout ship engaged the enemy positions, placing a devastating amount of fire upon the enemy. This suppressive fire allowed the crew to be extracted and resulted in fifteen NVA being killed. This was the thirteenth time Major Burrow had been shot down. When the division commander (Major General Tolson) learned of this, he said, "That's pushing your luck too far" and replaced him as troop commander with MAJ Jimmy Weeks, who was the current XO for the troop.

And so, for Major George Burrow, the war was over. He revealed to the medics the next day that he had been flying for the last two months with a piece of Plexiglas in his right eye. When this was confirmed, he was immediately flown out of country so his eye could be operated on. This warrior had forever impacted my life and those of the men under his command. He was, and still is, larger than life and shall forever remain a shining example of what it means to "lead" on the battlefield. While every man in Bravo Troop was a true warrior and hero, MAJ George Burrow, WO Larry Brown, and WO Tom Maehrelein are three of my personal heroes.

The departure of Major Burrow—followed by Warrant Officers Brown, Pratt, Flanagan, Zahn, and Maehrelein—cemented my severance from Bravo Troop, and I turned complete attention to my new duties. There was much to do.

As the Tet offensive progressed throughout the I Corps area, we continued to be plagued with miserable flying weather. However, we kept flying. In the first half of February, we were stretched thin with only two air cavalry troops and one ground cavalry troop to support four brigades: two from the First Cavalry Division and two from the 101st Airborne Division. The 101st Airborne Division was located to our south in the hills to the west of Hue. The divisional cavalry squadron—the Second Squadron (Airborne), Seventeenth (Air) Cavalry—was with them, which was interesting to me since that was the unit I was in prior to going to flight school.

About the third of February, I was posting the map in the TOC when one of the RTOs came to get me and said there was someone on the radio that wanted to speak to me. I made the radio call and heard in response, "Damn a bear, how in the hell are you doing?" It turned out to be Sergeant first class Brandon from 2-17 Cavalry. I about fell over. He had been my radar platoon sergeant when I was the troop commander for headquarters troop in the 2-17. We talked for a while, and he informed me he had learned from one of the guys in Bravo Troop that I was the S2 and got the squadron frequency from him that day. After we got off the radio, I couldn't help but reflect that while it was a very large army, it was also a very small army. I never heard from him again, and to this day, I wonder if he survived his tour in Vietnam. This was a very close brotherhood.

The NVA had cut the road between Da Nang and an outpost called PK 17 north of Hue. We could not receive supplies from the south, and the seaport to the north at Dong Ha became critical in the division resupply effort. For a short period of time, we had to rely on aerial resupply for food and ammunition. Aerial resupply with Air Force C-130s was very iffy because of the marginal weather. So the no.1 priority for the squadron was to keep the road open between PK 17 and Dong Ha. Delta Troop was given this mission with Bravo and Charlie troops on call to assist.

Delta Troop mounted in their jeeps, and three quarter-ton trucks patrolled the road twice a day. Before any convoys could travel the road, "Dusty Delta" had to clear the road and then escort a convoy to Dong Ha and another one back from Dong Ha. This was dangerous work at the height of the Tet offensive. They could clear the road as they went, but there was no assurance it would remain clear for their return trip. Land mines and ambushes were a constant danger and required constant vigilance. To make matters worse, the NVA had started to blow up bridges during the night.

One of my primary duties as the S2 was to gather as much information about the enemy as possible and come up with an educated estimate of where they were and what they were going to do next. There was an overwhelming amount of information available, and the trick was to get it organized in such a manner that it became useful intelligence. I was inundated with daily intelligence summaries (INTSUM) from division, agent reports, aircraft firings, side-looking airborne radar (SLAR) reports, forward-looking infrared radar (FLIR) reports, contact reports throughout the division, and, of course, the spot reports from our own troops. The division INTSUMS were prepared by intelligence branch personnel and followed a format that discussed enemy intentions, unit identification from prisoners, and reports from higher headquarters. From my foxhole, the only useful pieces of information were the agent reports.

Sergeant first class Mills and I organized the AO into ten-thousand-square-meter blocks and numbered each of these blocks on the map. We then prepared an index card for each numbered block and recorded any incident that occurred in that block on the index card. We also prepared an acetate overlay for squadron spot reports, another overlay for aircraft firings, another one for agent reports, another one for SLAR and FLIR reports, and another one for all division contact reports. At the end of each day, we would put all five of these overlays on the map, and sure enough, the enemy told us where they were located. It now became a simple matter for me to recommend where we should concentrate our reconnaissance efforts.

After the second bridge had been blown on Route 1, I was sitting in front of the map, studying the overlays and reviewing previous spot reports for the past couple of days to determine if there was any indicator that would signal us which bridge they were going to target. I was concentrating on the bridges that had been blown and discovered in each case that the night before each bridge had been blown, there was an FLIR report in the vicinity of the bridge. I got excited about this information and decided I needed to share this with the division G2. It was around 0100 hours when I got in my jeep and drove to division headquarters and woke up the G2. We went to the G2 section in the division TOC, and I asked where they posted their current information. To my dismay, I discovered that the G2 section was compartmentalized into various intelligence-gathering cells, but there was no one place where it was displayed on a map. We got in my jeep and drove back to squadron headquarters where I showed him how we displayed and analyzed information with emphasis on the bridges. Thereafter, whenever we had an FLIR report in the vicinity of a bridge, a platoon of infantry was deployed to secure the bridge. We never had another bridge blown as long as we were in I Corps.

While we were removed from the daily combat each troop was involved in, we received our share of mortar and rocket attacks. On 11 February 1968, the squadron area became the target for a mortar attack. The foul weather had contributed to the very intense cold I had developed. To alleviate some of the symptoms, I was taking some codeine-laced cough syrup, which the GIs affectionately referred to as GI gin. It was around 2000 hours when Major Sorenson left the TOC to go to the latrine. He hadn't been gone more than two minutes when the first mortar rounds impacted around us. All of us in the TOC fell to the floor and got as close to the sandbags surrounding our tent as possible. There was a brief pause, and another series of mortar rounds fell in our vicinity. During the next pause, the tent flap was thrown aside as Major Sorenson, pants around his knees with one hand trying to hold them up, dove into the tent and scurried next to the sandbags. Those of us who saw this started to laugh, which set me off on another coughing spree. Captain Doug Woods, an assistant S3, described how in the next pause in the firing he sees my hand come up and start feeling around on top of my desk looking for the cough syrup, finding it, and then disappearing behind the desk, cough syrup in hand. He started laughing as he witnessed this and continued chuckling throughout the mortar attack. After the mortar attack was finished, none of the TOC crew had been hit, although our tent was ripped in many places.

The Delta Troop area was in the vicinity of the TOC, and we soon heard calls for medics. Several of us left the TOC and hurried to the Delta Troop area and assisted in treating those that had been wounded. Eleven of the Delta Troop soldiers had been wounded by the shrapnel, and three had been killed. Once again, humor and horror were companions in this deadly attack.

It was apparent from the indicators; there was a great deal of enemy movement in the Ba Long River Valley. On 18 February, Charlie Troop was given the mission of conducting reconnaissance the next day along the Song Tach Han River. Heavily traveled trails were observed moving into base area 101. It was apparent that the enemy was moving a force into the base area in an effort to bolster the units in contact around Quang Tri. Unable to place troops on the ground, the division responded by placing arc lights (B-52 strikes) and numerous air strikes into the enemy assembly area. It will never be known how many enemies were killed; but the enemy never received reinforcements around Quang Tri, and as a result, the enemy was repulsed from the vicinity of Quang Tri.

Slowly, the Tet Offensive came to a close. In every battle with American forces, the NVA were soundly defeated. In every sense of the word, we were victorious and had soundly trounced them on the battlefield. The squadron alone had killed over 550 NVA during the month of February. Imagine our surprise when we read press reports that indicated we had been badly mauled, and this was a setback for American forces! What rubbish, what tripe! And yet, that was and still is the prevailing view held by the journalists who covered the Tet Offensive.

At the beginning of March, we had four American divisions in I Corps, and had the American political will been made of steel, we would have been ordered to turn north and end this war. Instead of steel, we had pudding, and the war dragged on for another four years. This was a decisive point in the war, and the political leadership let it slip through its grasp. We had pounded the North

Vietnam Army into the ground, and this was the time to finish them off.

There is no doubt that the images of the American embassy being attacked by the NVA or the provincial capitols being attacked throughout South Vietnam and the daily headlines screaming about the immanent collapse of Khe Sahn all contributed to this helpless, defeatist feeling that was generated by the press, which soon gripped the Johnson administration.

The Tet Offensive was a turning point that should have seen us march north and bring the war to an end. Instead, it marked the beginning of the abandonment of the American forces by their elected leadership, some of their own military leadership, and, most of all, by the American people. There was no will to win, and if you lose that, you cannot win.

CHAPTER THIRTY
RELIEF OF KHE SAHN AND
INTO THE A SHAU VALLEY

For months, the media (print and TV) had been forecasting that the Khe Sahn Combat Base (KCB) held by the marines was about to be overrun. This was going to be another Dienbienphu similar to the French defeat in 1954. The marines had reported that the KCB was surrounded by up to three North Vietnamese divisions. As the Tet Offensive progressed, army intelligence was reporting that elements from two of the divisions that were supposed to be surrounding the KCB were, in fact, engaged in fighting in and around Hue. While it turned out that army intelligence had a more accurate picture of what was actually deployed around the KCB, it had little impact on future events for us.

On 15 March, we received a First Cavalry Division operations plan (OPLAN) for Operation Pegasus, the relief of the KCB. The squadron's primary mission was to prepare the battlefield for the division. Beginning on 25 March, we were to detect and assure the destruction of antiaircraft and automatic-weapons positions, detect and destroy troop concentrations, select and prepare the brigade LZs, select the air corridors into the LZs, and neutralize the enemy that could influence those corridors. The division gave us six days to accomplish these missions, and I recall thinking at the time, "*This is a great cavalry mission!*"

Around the twentieth of the month, Lieutenant Colonel Diller, I, and either the division G2 or the G3—I can't remember which—flew up to KCB to get a briefing on the situation. As we landed on the airstrip and started to shut down the Huey, a marine came running up, telling us we couldn't park the aircraft there. They were convinced it was going to draw artillery fire from the Co Roc Mountains to the west. Rather than get into a discussion over this point, Lieutenant Colonel Diller sent the aircraft back to LZ Stud with instructions for him to return in a couple of hours. As I recall, the marine escorting us back to the TOC was in a crouched position as he ran across the airstrip back to the TOC. It was obvious that he expected artillery to start falling momentarily. We hustled along behind him until we were inside the TOC.

Once inside the TOC, we moved down to another level and were ushered into a briefing room. Here, we received a briefing from the commander, S3, and S2 of the brigade-sized element that was defending the KCB. A couple of significant things stand out in my mind as a result of that briefing. First and foremost was the fact that they hadn't sent patrols off the base for two weeks, and secondly was the absolute belief and fear that the NVA were tunneling in under the KCB and were going to blow it up from below. This was hard for me to understand, and I could find no rationale for not patrolling around the base. In later years, I heard General Westmoreland explain that he had told the commander at KCB to keep his patrols close in. If you don't know what is going on outside the wire, then I can see why you might fear that the enemy was tunneling in under the wire to blow you up. I questioned them about the size and identification of the force they felt was surrounding them. They still felt they were surrounded by the same three divisions that were reported prior to the Tet Offensive.

Following this meeting, we flew back to LZ Evans and started our preparation for Operation Pegasus. I made a sketch of the area following this operation, which generally shows all of the major LZs in relation to the KCB.

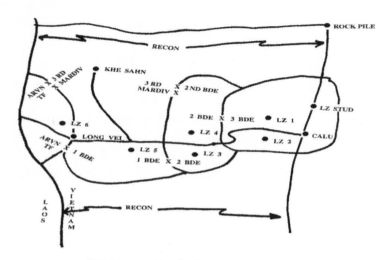

(SKETCH 2) Sketch of the relief of Khe Sahn.

This was to be a phased operation with the Third Brigade air assaulting into LZs 1 and 2, followed by the Second Brigade into LZs 3 and 4, the First Brigade into LZ 5, and the ARVN TF going into LZ 6. We would air assault one brigade at a time into their respective LZs while, at the same time, have a ground element proceed from Calu as the division cleared the road between Calu and Long Vei. This was a very straightforward and simple plan. There were a lot of moving pieces that would all be in motion at the same time, but we had done this so much everyone knew what everyone else was supposed to do and when they would do it. If the division had tried this type of operation their first year in Vietnam, it may not have been as successful, but there was no question that the First Cavalry Division was the unit to get this job accomplished.

On 24 March, I was sent forward with a small contingent from the S2 and S3 shop to set up a forward CP at LZ Stud. This would improve communications with the teams in the AO and have us in a position to react to unexpected events. We set up in an open field and erected a general-purpose (GP) small tent. Inside, we set up some field tables and placed a couple of radios on them and then erected two RC-292 antennas. We placed a couple of chairs inside, made our commo checks, and were in business.

I must admit I was a little nervous with no wire and only a platoon providing security for the jump CP. We seemed awfully vulnerable, and while this was not the first time I had spent outside the wire, I was just a bit more aware of what was going on around me. Late that night, I wrapped up in a poncho liner, lay down on the ground, and went to sleep. I awoke a couple of hours later to the ground shaking and the overwhelming sound of a low rumble underneath me. As I awoke, my first thought was that we were having an earthquake; but as I fully woke up, I associated the rumble with explosions, and it finally dawned on me that we were hearing and feeling the results of an "arc light" mission going in within several thousand meters from us. While I had conducted bomb damage assessment (BDA) of arc-light missions (B-52 bombing runs with five-hundred—and 750-pound bombs) in the past, they were usually after the fact. On the few BDA missions that were live, I had held several miles away, watching the bombs go in. This was quite different. Feeling the ground tremble from the impact of those bombs several thousand meters away was awesome and I once again wondered how anyone could live through that, and yet, some did. I recalled on some BDAs going into the area immediately after the strike was completed and finding NVA soldiers walking around with blood running from their eyes and ears in a dazed condition. The destruction wrought by these air strikes is hard to describe. It was total destruction with nothing left standing in the strike zone.

As the S2 for the squadron, one of my jobs during this period of Operation Pegasus was to recommend six arc-light boxes to division on a daily basis. For six nights, we put in six arc-light missions around the KCB. It was an awesome display of power and, I am sure, very costly and demoralizing for the NVA forces these strikes fell upon. I am also sure that not all of the strikes fell on NVA forces, and in some cases, all we blew up was jungle, but I can assure you that just being in the vicinity of one of these strikes was a bone-shaking and nerve-rattling experience.

While each of the troops was comfortable working very closely with the air force and the division forward air controllers (FAC), Operation Pegasus took us to new heights in putting in air strikes.

All of our pilots had the frequency of the division FACs, and the FACs had each of our troop frequencies. Starting on 24 March, we were putting in an average of one air strike an hour somewhere in the AO. On 29 March, this was stepped up to one air strike every half hour; and on D day, 31 March 1968, we were employing one air strike every fifteen minutes throughout the division AO. It was an unprecedented use of air power in support of ground tactical operations.

If one of our scouts received fire from an area, we were able to call the FAC and put in an air strike to eliminate all ground resistance from that point. Conversely, if an air-force flight was unable to put in a strike in North Vietnam, they would call our FACs to determine if we had a target before they flew to the dump zone to jettison their load of bombs. This was an example of joint warfare and cooperation between the services I had not seen before. It amounted to an air cap that was used to the maximum.

In addition to the tactical air, we also used another type of air support, in the form of daisy cutters that were used to blow LZs in the middle of the jungle. These were one-thousand-pound bombs or greater and were flown by C-130 aircraft. When these went off, there was nothing left standing, which was exactly what we wanted. The squadron selected all of the LZs for the brigades, and in that process, we looked for terrain to use as LZs, which was also commanding terrain that would give us control over the surrounding area. Many of the LZs we selected were in the middle of heavy-growth jungle, and these "daisy cutters" were exactly what we needed to create a suitable LZ for the brigades.

While in the process of preparing the battlefield for Operation Pegasus, we still had the mission of providing support for the rest of the division who were not yet involved in this preparation phase of the operation. They were still operating in the Jeb Stuart AO and required our eyes to protect and guide them in their daily operations.

There were always brigade commanders who demanded that the air cavalry troops be attached to their respective brigades. Thank God, we had a division commander and squadron commander who understood that this would fragment the division-reconnaissance effort, and they did not buckle to that type of pressure.

With the squadron under division control, the squadron commander was able to tailor the squadron to meet the needs of each troop and often would require the assets from one troop to support the efforts of another troop without having to get permission from anyone else.

On D-1, 30 March 1968, a Charlie Troop scout encountered what he considered a possible enemy battalion-size element in the Second Brigade AO. He called for air strikes and artillery and systematically pounded the position until all fire from that area ceased.

D day arrived, and the Third Brigade began their air assaults into LZ's One and Two. Each air assault was preceded by an artillery barrage and supporting fire from the 2-20 Aerial Rocket Artillery (Blue Max). Our teams screened around the flanks of the objective as each lift went in. It was a sight to behold! Artillery was pounding each LZ, and in the distance, you could see ten to fifteen Hueys in spaced flights as they approached the LZ. As the first lift started a long final into the LZ, a smoke round hit in the middle of the LZ, signaling that the last round of artillery had impacted. On they came, lift after lift, until there were enough men on the ground to secure the LZ. This was followed by five Chinooks, each sling loading in a 105 howitzer and the initial load of ammunition for each artillery piece. What a sight, and what an airmobile operation. This was textbook stuff, and it couldn't be better. This was what the Howze Board had visualized just a few short years before, and here we had the First Team performing and proving the value of that vision and the concept. God, it was great to be a soldier participating in this operation! We were kicking ass and taking no names!

As this first airmobile operation started, the ground forces at Calu started their movement toward the west up route 9 toward Khe Sahn. In the days that followed, these magnificent airmobile operations were repeated into the Second and First Brigade areas followed by the insertion of the ARVN Task Force into LZ 6, north of the Long Vei special-forces camp. We had whipped the NVA during Tet, and this operation was punctuating that point.

On April 4, Alpha Troop found a Chinese 155-towed artillery piece and a small-arms cache, which they promptly destroyed. The next day, they encountered an NVA company and engaged. It started out with the scout observing and killing three enemies and following their trail where he ran into another fifteen and killed them. In the process, they saw movement on the periphery of the contact area and called for another hunter-killer team. When this team arrived on station, they found another thirty-five NVA and immediately engaged them, killing all of them.

On April 10, a scout from Alpha Troop observed a Chinese Communist (Chicom) truck, and the Cobra engaged the truck. A huge secondary explosion occurred as the truck exploded. Waiting until the explosions stopped, the scout was finally cleared back into the area. As he flew around this area, he saw something unusual. There were unmistakable signs of a tracked vehicle. Flying low and slow, the scout followed the tracks back to a PT-76—armored reconnaissance vehicle. He was engaged by the vehicle and the dismounted NVA soldiers around it. The Cobra rolled in, engaging the vehicle while, at the same time, calling for air strikes and artillery. At the end of the engagement, one PT-76 was destroyed, and fifteen enemy soldiers were killed. Another hunter-killer team continued following the tracks of other vehicles all the way to the Laotian border. Of course, the rules of engagement did not allow us to continue across the border. What a hell of a way to fight a war!

While this fight was in progress, another Alpha Troop team was conducting a BDA of an arc-light mission and found approximately one hundred NVA soldiers in bunkers and wandering around in the open. They immediately engaged them but received a heavy volume of fire in return. They disengaged and called in artillery fire using airburst ammunition and pounded them until they ran out of daylight. Several secondary explosions were observed, and they confirmed that at least thirty NVA had been killed.

Our preparation of the battlefield was a success! Not one aircraft was lost during any of the insertions. Seven days after, we put soldiers in the first LZ; the ground force from Calu walked in the front gate of Khe Sanh. Resistance and contact had been light and certainly not the ferocity and organized resistance one would expect from three NVA divisions. To this day, I believe two of the divisions that were reported in and around Khe Sanh had been fighting around Hue and retreated across the border with the rest of the NVA after we kicked their ass out of the country.

Khe Sahn was crawling with rats and, within two days, had picked up the unofficial name of LZ Rat by the soldiers of the First Team. On April 14, 1968, the First Team began a phased redeployment out of the Pegasus AO back to LZ Evans, leaving behind the Second Brigade and elements of Alpha Troop to keep pressure on the remaining elements of NVA forces. Operation Pegasus was a classic airmobile operation that was conducted with precision and a clear objective. From the squadron's perspective, it was a classic cavalry mission that illustrated once again the role of cavalry in division operations. Find, fix, and report enemy locations, conduct offensive operations when required or called upon, and, above all, keep the division commander from being surprised by unknown enemy-troop movements. And that we had accomplished! In twenty days of combat operations, the First Team had broken the so-called siege of Khe Sahn and was moving on to a much more daunting operation.

It was interesting to me that the efficiency of the relief of Khe Sanh was not newsworthy. The siege of this base and the forecasted disaster this would impose upon our efforts in Vietnam were not fulfilled and, in some media circles, must have been a huge disappointment.

As we moved back to LZ Evans on April 14, we began our countdown (D-5) into Operation Delaware Ban-Son, which was the name of the raid the First Team was preparing to conduct into the A Shau Valley to our south. Intelligence reports indicated that the valley was a haven and supply area for the NVA. The division mission was to disrupt the enemy supply network that existed throughout the valley and to destroy the infrastructure. Once again, the squadron mission was to prepare the battlefield as we had for the relief of Khe Sahn. Alpha Troop was given the mission to continue supporting the division elements that were still in the vicinity of Khe Sanh and to respond to enemy activity in the Jeb Stuart AO. Bravo and Charlie troops started their reconnaissance efforts in the valley, and Delta Troop was once again prepared to act as a reinforcing element for either of the air cavalry troops.

It was soon apparent that this was going to be more difficult than the Khe Sanh operation. For the first time, we encountered a solid air-defense network with mutually supporting 37 AA weapons and some missiles. For the five days prior to the brigade's air assaults, scout teams of B Troop and C Troop conducted extensive reconnaissance missions in the valley. Landing zones were selected and prepared by tactical air utilizing "daisy cutters." During this time, 308 air strikes were employed by the squadron to destroy enemy antiaircraft positions and automatic-weapons positions. The reconnaissance spot reports received by squadron indicated that a well-established road and supply system had been developed in the valley. This was, in turn, confirmed by indications of many vehicle sightings and well-constructed and used roads.

On D-5 (14 April), a scout team from C Troop, flying a reconnaissance mission around Aloui, received heavy antiaircraft fire. The enemy position was engaged with troop weapons and air strikes. After the enemy guns were silenced, the scout team returned to the area to determine the damage inflicted. The enemy was destroyed and had sustained an unknown number of casualties. The enemy position consisted of three thirty-seven-millimeter cannons positioned in a triangle composed of reinforced earthwork, with numerous bunkers and fighting positions along the perimeter of the triangle. The enemy was not trying to evade the squadron's reconnaissance effort but was instead responding to this intrusion with heavy antiaircraft and automatic-weapons fire. Throughout the entire AO, targets that were engaged resulted in numerous secondary explosions.

On D day (19 April), Third Brigade was inserted into LZs Pepper and Cecil. Second Brigade air assaulted into LZ Stallion, which was located on the Aloui airstrip. During the landings of the brigades, enemy fire was heavy, and numerous ships were hit with several losses. The squadron conducted extensive reconnaissance missions in and around the LZs, finding and destroying the enemy positions.

A communications problem existed with the units located in the valley and the supporting elements on the other side of the eastern ridge. To alleviate this problem, a DISCOM (division support command) relay station was installed on Signal Hill, Hill 1487. To initiate this, the First Platoon of D Troop was air assaulted on the Hill on 21 April to provide security for the relay station. Although the platoon had several enemy-probing actions throughout their stay on the Hill, it was never seriously threatened.

The enemy had an armored capability, as verified by C Troop. A report was received from LZ Cecil that noises of engines being started were heard to the southwest of the LZ. C Troop sent a scout team out to investigate the noise and was rewarded by one of the most significant finds of the operation. A kilometer to the southwest of LZ Cecil, a truck stop was uncovered when the scout ship received heavy automatic-weapons fire. The team was not able to engage with their troop weapons due to the intense .30-caliber weapons fire. Air strikes were called for, and the area was engaged with artillery. One Chicom truck was hit, resulting in several secondary explosions, and five PT-76 tanks were observed withdrawing from the area. The tanks were engaged, resulting in one tank destroyed. The remainder of the enemy tanks withdrew across the Laotian border.

The twenty-fifth of April was a good day for the squadron. B Troop, at YC 388987, spotted two 2 ½-ton trucks, two three-fourth-ton trucks, one one-fourth-ton truck, and five, five by ten foot hooches. A reconnaissance team landed near the trucks and found radio equipment in one of the 2 ½-ton trucks. C Troop, at YD 359012, found a truck park containing over fifty flatbed trucks, two of the flatbeds having thirty-seven-millimeter antiaircraft weapons mounted on them. On both of these different sightings, the enemy positions were engaged, resulting in the equipment being either destroyed or captured.

Since the possibility of the enemy using armor against friendly units existed, antitank protection was stressed. With this in mind, six 106 recoilless rifles from D Troop were transported with one-fourth-ton carriers by CH-47s (Chinooks) to the vicinity of Ta Bat airstrip, near YC 4295, to give the Third ARVN Regiment, working the southern portion of the A Shau Valley, antitank protection. This antitank capability supported the Third ARVN Regiment until the close of the operation. Toward the conclusion of Operation Delaware Lam-Son 216, the squadron conducted deception-and-denial operations in the southern and northwestern portions of the A Shau Valley. This allowed the division to extract out of the A Shau Valley with minimum delay. Also during this time, the squadron's successes multiplied as enemy targets such as ammunition-and-supply storage areas, bunkers, trucks, gun emplacements, and personnel were engaged and destroyed or captured.

On 11 May, B Troop covered the extraction of the Third Brigade from LZ Tiger. Then on 12 and 13 May, C Troop supported the withdrawal of the remaining units as Operation Delaware Lam-Son 216 came to a close. Overall, the raid was a success, and once again, the 1-9 Cavalry had proven its battle worthiness.

The day finally arrived when I received orders informing me that my tour of duty was about to finish, and I was to leave Vietnam on 24 May 1968. My replacement was selected, and I spent about a week giving him my perspective on how to do the job (I don't remember who it was that replaced me). On 19 May, I boarded a Huey and flew back to An Khe. When we arrived at An Khe, we learned that LZ Evans had been hammered with a 122 rocket attack right after we left, and in the process, a big part of the ammunition dump at Evans had blown up. It was hard to believe that my first tour in Vietnam was coming to an end.

CHAPTER THIRTY ONE
GOING HOME

That evening, those of us that were going home sat at the Ninth Cav Officers Club (the Shenandoah) at An Khe. We had steaks and a couple of beers and marveled that we had lived through the previous year. In my case, I knew it was only through the grace of God that I was sitting there that evening. I felt then, as I do now, that God had something in mind for me. I still don't know what that is, but I am convinced that I will not die until that purpose has been fulfilled.

The next few days were spent outprocessing from the troop and the division. The jungle had started to reclaim the hillside where the boat people (the ones who brought the squadron to Vietnam) had built those hooches just a few short years before. They were falling apart, and the sight of those ruined hooches had a melancholy impact on me. They represented what had been but was no more. While there was activity in the squadron rear area, the sight of those dilapidated hooches imparted a sense of foreboding and a lack of fulfillment, which I had difficulty shaking while I remained at An Khe.

On the twenty-second, I flew down to Tan Sa Nut in a Caribou and, on the morning of the twenty-fourth, boarded another Tiger Airways plane and was finally on the way home. We taxied to the runway, and holding short of the active, we all watched as a pair of F4-Cs rolled down the runway and lifted into the sky. I wondered if they were flying up north or if possibly they were flying out to support a unit in contact. We rolled onto the runway and, within minutes, were airborne. As we climbed out of small arms and B-40 range, I started to relax. Soon we were well beyond antiaircraft firing range, and I slumped back into my seat and drifted off to sleep.

We flew to McChord Air Force Base near Tacoma, Washington. As we started to descend through the clouds, I started tensing up, and as we broke out of the clouds over Puget Sound, I discovered I was on the edge of my seat, expecting to take fire from below. How foolish I felt as I looked nervously around me. No one appeared to notice how uptight I was. I pulled a Lucky from the pack of cigarettes, lit it, inhaled deeply, and settled back into the seat as the announcement was made that we were north of Tacoma and would soon be landing at McChord.

As I looked down on Puget Sound, I tried to get oriented as to where we were. Having been raised in Bremerton, I was familiar with this part of Puget Sound and recalled how in the early fifties we had to take a ferry to get to Tacoma since the Tacoma Narrows Bridge had not been rebuilt yet. Of course, we could have driven down to Olympia and come around that way, but we usually took the ferry across the narrows to Tacoma.

As I looked below, the departure of my brother Ray as he shipped out for the Korean War suddenly popped into my mind. He was a soldier in the Second Infantry Division and was stationed at Fort Lewis when his unit was shipped to Korea. I recalled the last few days before he departed and how hectic they were for my parents and what a sad day it was for all of us—but especially for Mother—the day his ship departed for Korea. In today's world, it is difficult to remember that, for that war, we still shipped our soldiers to war in troop ships, not aircraft.

As we heard and felt the landing gear drop into position, the stewardess announced that it was time to bring our seats to an upright position and extinguish all cigarettes. I stubbed out my cigarette, brought my seat upright, and cinched my seat belt tighter as we started our straight-in approach to McChord. As the wheels touched the tarmac, there was a loud cheer that reverberated through the aircraft as we rolled off the runway and taxied toward the terminal. Home, safely home at last.

My family had been living in Bremerton while I was in Vietnam. My wife at that time had a job, and she and the children had settled into the community at Bremerton. It was wonderful to see, hug, and be with the kids again, but my reunion with her was less than joyful. Much of this part of my life I have repressed, but one memorable incident occurred while we were driving across Montana en route to Fort Knox, Kentucky. It was dark, everyone else in the car was asleep, and I was listening to some music on the radio. Suddenly, a red light flashed on the dashboard, and adrenaline surged through my body as I instantly checked my instruments and started looking for a place to land. Just as quickly, I realized that the low-fuel light had come on, and I smiled as I thought, "*Man, are you overtrained!*"

In the years that have followed my first departure from Vietnam, I often think back to the suddenness of the departure and the fact that I was not emotionally ready to leave that life-threatening combat zone and return to civilization in just a matter of hours. There was no time to throttle back into a more subdued fashion of personal behavior. I was definitely in the fight or flight mode, and by that, I mean I was mentally and physically alert and ready for whatever danger that came my way. As the months passed, I slowly eased back into being a more relaxed and civilized soldier in a noncombat zone.

Within two years, I was back in Vietnam and was fortunate enough to again be assigned to the 1-9 cavalry in the First Cavalry Division to form and command a provisional air cavalry troop: Echo Troop. This was the Vietnam War's version of Pappy Boyington's Black Sheep and is another story altogether. After this second tour, I attended the Army Command and General Staff College, attended Benedictine College for a year and obtained my bachelor's degree, served a couple of years on the Army General Staff in Washington DC, and finished up my active-duty career as the squadron commander of the 1-17 Air Cavalry Squadron of the Eighty-second Airborne Division and retired from the United States Army on 31 July 1978 at Fort Bragg, North Carolina.

In the years that have passed since that first year in Vietnam, I have tried to reconcile all that killing and loss of life with some noble cause. We did not free a nation from the oppression and yoke of Communism. We were unable to prevent the atrocities that occurred in Cambodia after our departure, and to this day, Vietnam veterans are still reviled by many in our own country. What was our noble cause? Trying to compare the outcome of the Vietnam War to any other recent American war is pointless. There simply is no comparison. The veterans of World War II had achieved unconditional victory; the Korean War veterans, while ignored during and after the war, were able to at least fight their war to a draw.

In December of 1961, three thousand United States military advisors and support personnel arrived in Vietnam and started the American commitment to Vietnam. In the early-morning hours of April 30, 1975, the last marine guards boarded a helicopter on top of the United States Embassy in Saigon and flew to their waiting ship, thus ending the American commitment and pledged support to the Vietnamese people. Over three million men and women served in our armed forces in Vietnam; 58,000 of our service personnel were killed in Vietnam, over one thousand were reported missing in action, and 150,000 were seriously wounded. Nearly a million North Vietnamese and Vietcong soldiers and nearly 250,000 South Vietnamese soldiers died in that war. This does not count the thousands of civilians that were killed by the North Vietnamese, South Vietnamese, the Americans, and our allies that fought with us.

The American soldiers and the Vietnamese people we had pledged to defend were abandoned, cast aside by a political and media process that had judged the American commitment not worthy of continued effort. I sat in my family room in Alexandria, Virginia, on April 30, 1975, watching this nationally televised "final scene" play out with tears streaming down my face. I listened as Walter Cronkite and Harry Reasoner (network news anchors with high ratings at that time) explain why "we should never have gotten involved," "this was the best solution," and praising the efforts of all those reporters that had gone to Vietnam, etc. While I knew this end was the one that had been scripted in the White House and the Pentagon, as I watched it, I felt betrayed and unfulfilled.

CHAPTER THIRTY TWO
COMING TO GRIPS WITH IT

After I retired, my former wife and I divorced, and I remarried. Ten years after I retired, twenty years after my first tour in Vietnam, I was working for the United States Army Battle Command Training Program at Leavenworth, Kansas. One day in 1988, John Flanagan, who was working on another government program, showed up at Leavenworth, and we went for lunch. We had a great reunion at lunch and remarked that it truly was a celebration of life. As we talked, we marveled that we had lived through all of that and, when we parted, gave each other a hug.

Larry Brown and I had kept in touch over the years and, in fact, had one hell of a get-together at Eglin Air Force Base in Florida. This was during a joint exercise while I was the Seventeenth Cavalry Squadron commander, and Larry was a major in the Oregon National Guard. I had returned from the nightly briefing at division headquarters and was told, "Saber Fourteen is over at the Officers Club." I couldn't believe it! I jumped in my jeep and had my driver take me to the club. My driver was not prepared for what he saw a couple of hours later when Larry and I staggered out of the club, singing all these Vietnam-era songs all the way back to the squadron area. At any rate, John was the first guy from the troop, other than Larry, that I had seen since 1968.

I took another job to manage a virtual simulation site for the army in Germany. In 1990, my wife and I were living in Butzbach, Germany. On 13 November, I decided I would call as many people from Bravo Troop as I could locate to remind everyone how fortunate we were to have survived this day in 1967 and still be alive. I called Larry Brown first and got several telephone numbers of some of the guys from him and started down the list. I called George Burrow next. His wife, Ruth, the only German I know who has a Texas accent, answered the phone, and after we chatted, she gave me his office phone number. When I identified myself and told him I was calling from Germany (he worked in San Antonio, Texas), George asked me why I was calling. I replied, "It's the thirteenth of November, a day to remember." There was a pause, and he said, "What the hell does that mean?" I responded, "Don't you remember this day in 1967 when we all got shot down, and you spent the night on the ground in a rice paddy?" "Bert," he said, "you son of a bitch! You're calling me from Germany to remind me of the worst day and night in my life?" I started laughing; and before I knew it, the intervening years vanished, and it was as if we were sitting in the operations tent again, and that old familiar banter was started. It was a very warm and wonderful feeling to talk with him again. I spent several more hours on the phone that day, calling about fifteen other members of the troop, and have tried to do the same thing every year since then. It is a wonderfully warm and satisfying feeling to touch one another's life once again even if it is only for a few minutes.

Steve and John Burrow, sons of George and Ruth, work for the Directorate of Public Works at Fort Hood, Texas. When Eileen and I returned from Germany, I became the site manager of the Close Combat Tactical Trainer at Fort Hood. Steve and I have talked frequently over the years, and when I first told him the story of his dad's response to the first time I called him on 13 November 1990, Steve said, "What do you mean he said it was the worst day of his life? That's the day I was born!"

After John Flanagan and I had met each other at Leavenworth, we kept in touch, and John tried to get me to join the Vietnam Helicopter Pilots Association (VHPA). I resisted his efforts because I had this vision of a bunch of disgruntled veterans walking around in field jackets, talking about how Vietnam had screwed them up. John kept after me; and soon I had Larry, Bob Zahn, Lou Rochat, and others encouraging me to join and attend one of the conventions that are always held over the Fourth of July weekend. We were still in Germany in 1994 when they finally convinced Eileen and me to come back and attend the VHPA convention being held that year in Philadelphia, Pennsylvania. As we boarded the plane in Frankfurt, I was carrying my cav hat in hand.

When we arrived at the hotel, one of the first things I saw outside of the hotel was a UH-1C helicopter sitting on a trailer. It belonged to the North Carolina chapter of the VHPA, and they had brought it all the way from North Carolina for this reunion. I placed my cav hat on my head as we entered the lobby. The level of noise from the hundreds of people in the lobby was making it hard to hear as we registered. As we moved through the crowd, I saw another cav hat, which happened to be sitting on top of Larry Brown's head. He was wearing a jumpsuit that had a variety of patches sewn on it with neat things like "Guided tours of the An Lo Valley," coolie hats (with each hat representing five kills), a map of Vietnam with all the places he had fought embroidered on the suit, etc. I also learned he had a different jumpsuit for each day of the convention, all in different colors with different patches and different sayings for each jumpsuit. He was a thing of beauty!

The lobby was packed with pilots, their wives, and some older children. The bar was going full blast, and people were gathered in groups, either sitting down or standing. Occasionally, you would hear a whoop as someone recognized a person they hadn't seen since Vietnam. I uttered a few of them myself during the reunion as Jim Pratt, Bob Zahn, Steve Ellis, Tom Maehrelein, Bob Lackey, Barry MacAlpine, Mike Covey, John Flanagan, Lou Rochat, Al Demilo, Joe Armeline, and even Charlie Rayl, my old flight-school buddy, reappeared from the past. The lobby was packed, banners were hung from the second—and third-story railings, and for good measure, there was an OH-6 helicopter in the lobby. Joyous pandemonium is the best way to describe the feeling that surrounded us as we made our way to our room.

Our luggage had not arrived, and we were going to take a short nap; but I was keyed up, so we splashed some water on our faces and prepared to go back downstairs to find my old comrades.

Eileen was tired, and I knew she was nervous at the prospect of meeting all of these people from my past; but she stuck her chin out, squared her shoulders, and said, "Let's go!"

We plunged into the crowd and soon found the Bravo and Echo troop comrades gathered around a coffee table near the bar. As we talked, the years melted away, and we, once again, were reliving all of those harrowing and hazardous missions. It was as if we had just returned from some of those missions. It was a wonderful feeling, being with these faithful, brave, and aging warriors. While I was one of the oldest, I wasn't *the* oldest, and there was plenty of gray hair in that lobby. We laughed, cried a little bit, drank a lot of beer and bourbon, and went out for dinner. I was overwhelmed.

Sitting in a nearby restaurant, we laughed, ate the meal, told more stories, and drank a lot more. As I gazed around our group, I had this overwhelming feeling of fulfillment wash over me. This was the first time since Vietnam that I had felt so close to these men and those memories. And why wouldn't I? These were the guys that had put it all on the line every day in Vietnam. They were the ones who would have given their life for me, or I would have given my life for them. There was no pretense, there couldn't be. We had relied on one another in the absolute toughest of times and had never been disappointed. I looked at Tom Maehrelein and remembered what he had done near Hue in order to never leave anyone behind and how badly he was wounded later; Bob Zahn and how his shooting had saved so many of us; Larry and Carol and their wedding in Vietnam and how Larry could always find the enemy; Steve Ellis who was wounded so badly when he was shot down and how Lou Rochat and his back seater sat a Cobra down next to him. (Lou jumped out, pulled Steve out of the OH-6, carried and dragged him to the Cobra, put him in the front seat of the Cobra, and then flew the OH-6 out.); how Lou lost his leg a month later; how Barry McAlpine and Bob Lackey toughed it out on the ground in the Blues; and how John Flanagan, Mike Covey, and Jim Pratt flew into the jaws of hell to get them and the rest of the Blues out of deep shit.

Anyone passing by our tables would have thought, "*Here's a bunch of people who work together and are out for a night on the town,*" never realizing that the men sitting there were true warriors, that every one of them was an honest-to-God hero, and that everyone there had killed a substantial number of the enemy in Vietnam and had a substantial number of the enemy try to kill them. Here was a group of survivors with a shared background, and that background had forged a link between us that was stronger than any family tie. In that group was a wine broker, airline pilot, general contractor, chiropractor, accountant, two simulation managers, helicopter-company manager, photographer, and two guys that loved to sail. We were as far from the television depiction of a Vietnam veteran as you could get.

We made it back to the hotel, and the lobby was rocking. The bars could not keep up. The cash-register tapes had piled up behind the registers and were cascading down to the floor. You could tell that everything was on track, the stories were getting more animated, the voices were louder, the cigarette smoke was heavier, and we were having a hell of a good time. We made our way to the second floor where there was a DJ playing a lot of good music from the sixties and seventies, and it was louder up there than it was downstairs. The music was cranked, the drinks were flowing, and Eileen and I were dancing every dance. One record stopped, and this familiar heavy beat started coming from the DJ, and the words began, "In this dirty old part of the city, where the sun refuse to shine, people tell me there ain't no use in trying." The beat got heavier as people start singing, "Now my girl you're so young and pretty, and one thing I know is true, you'll be dead before your time is due, I know." The music raises an octave, and the beat gets heavier. "Watch my daddy in bed he's dying, watch his hair it's turning gray, he's been working and slaving his life away, oh yes. I know, yea, yea, yea." The chorus has everyone singing at the top of their voice, "We've gotta get out of this place, if it's the last thing we ever do, we gotta get out of this place, girl there's a better life for me and you!"

Larry and Mike Covey were on top of one of the tables, arms around each other's shoulder, a beer in the free hand, singing the chorus at the top of their lungs. That song, "We've Got to Get Out of This Place," was the unofficial anthem of the Vietnam War. It had to be played at least four more times that evening, and on each occasion, we stopped dancing and sang that song at the top of our voices. By three o clock in the morning, I was done for, and Eileen and I struggled back to our room. We got up at around nine o'clock and went downstairs for breakfast where the bar was already open. I was hoarse from the singing the night before. We had breakfast, said good morning to John and Ann Flanagan and Charlie Rayl, and then headed out to see the sights of Philadelphia.

In the late afternoon, we returned to the hotel; and as we passed through the lobby on the way to our room, I noticed the lobby was packed, and the bar was about two deep. We made it to our room, took a shower and a nap, and headed back downstairs. The cash-register tape was cascading down behind the bar again, and it was apparent that this hotel was making a ton of money just on the volume of drinks sold in the lobby. The staff was having a very hard time keeping enough liquor and beer on hand. It was early evening; we had a snack in the lobby, surrounded ourselves with these comrades, and picked up where we had left off last night (actually this morning). We moved back upstairs into one of the ballrooms and spent the rest of the night and early-morning hours singing all those great songs from the sixties and dancing the night away. A couple of times that evening, we did the "shag" and the "stroll," which amazed some of the children who thought it was their generation who invented line dancing. I was flying and having a great time! I hadn't felt like dancing like this in years, and soon Eileen handed me off to Ann Rochat, who then handed me off to Carol Brown who handed me off to Sandy Ellis, and then they started playing "We've Got to Get Out of This Place." We stopped dancing and started singing. And so it went through the night and into the early hours of the morning.

Waking up, it was the Fourth of July, and we went downtown to observe the parade and visit some military displays around the city. That evening, as is the custom at every VHPA reunion, we donned coat and tie for the banquet. Carol Brown had to damn near threaten bodily harm to get Larry out of his jumpsuit. We had arranged to have Bravo and Echo troops seated at adjacent tables, and we were having a great time. The president of the association called us to order and went through the normal "thank you" to the people who put all of these together. He then called our attention to the vacant table adjacent to the head table. This table had a complete place setting, with no one sitting at it. He went on to explain the symbolism of a plate of food that will never be eaten, a glass of wine that will never be drunk, and that this table represented all of those who gave their life in Vietnam. He then proposed a toast to our fallen comrades. We stood, raised our glasses, and said, "To our fallen comrades." As I drank the glass of wine, tears welled in my eyes as I saw the smiling face of Lou Porrazzo, and I silently said, "*Here's to you, Lou.*"

We had dinner; the guest speaker was the mayor of Philadelphia who welcomed us to the city; and within an hour and a half, dinner was finished, and most of us wandered out to watch the fireworks. We returned, changed clothes, and went back upstairs to continue the party. We had a live band that played all the great songs, and several of our heroes made it on stage to help the band sing some of the songs. As we got lubricated, we were soon back to our best party mode, and Larry was wandering around in his jump suit, with a chemical light on his head, shining through the bullet hole in his Cav hat. On one rendition of "We've Got to Get Out of This Place," Carol was on Larry's shoulders, in the middle of the dance floor, as we all sang it one more time! Eileen and I were leaving in the morning, and not knowing if we would see everyone in the morning, we said goodbye to all before we turned in.

The next day, as our Lufthansa plane was flying back to Germany, I sat in my seat with my eyes closed and thought of all those middle-age men who had made such a difference in my life.

Those warriors, those magnificent men, were absolutely beyond belief, and every one of them was larger than life it self. I was content, satisfied, and at peace. Although we didn't have the American public support while we were in Vietnam, we had one another, and in the final analysis, that's all that matters. While history recorded Vietnam as a defeat for America, we who fought together in Vietnam had a flame of shared danger that was as *white hot* as the flame of an acetylene torch, and each firefight was the welding rod that melded us together.

A smile crossed my face as I dozed off to sleep, and I thought, "*If you ain't cav, you ain't shit!*"

AFTERWORD

The task of defending this country and serving our nation is unending and thank God for the patriots who step forward to do what most are unwilling to do. There are some families who particularly understand what sacrifices are necessary to preserve our freedom and liberty.

Colonels Larry and Carol Brown and Lieutenant Larry Brown Jr., you have kept this circle of brotherhood going and as a Cavalryman of Bravo Troop, First Squadron, 9th Cavalry I salute you.

B/1-9 Cav. Warrant Officer Larry Brown,
(White One Four) next to his H-13, Vietnam 1967

B/1-9 Cav. First Lieutenant Larry Brown Jr.,
(Red One One), next to his HMMWV, Iraq, 2004

GLOSSARY OF TERMS

ADC—Assistant Division Commander.

AFN—Armed Forces Network (Radio or Television Station).

AGL—Above Ground Level—altitude notation when flying as opposed to altitude above sea level.

AK-47—Standard NVA assault rifle.

ALPHA—The letter A in the Army's phonetic alphabet. The phonetic alphabet was used to spell out letters in radio conversations. Thus A Company would also be called Alpha Company.

AO—Area of Operations.

ARA—Aerial rocket artillery.

Arc Light—B-52 bomb strike.

ARP—Aero Rifle Platoon.

ARVN—Army of the Republic of Vietnam (pronounced Arvin).

Arty—Abbreviation for Artillery.

BDA—Bomb damage assessment.

Battery—The basic building block unit in the artillery, i.e., firing battery; also is the smallest unit in the artillery in which the commissioned leader is considered a commander.

Blues—Aero Rifle infantry platoon of the 1st Squadron, 9th Cavalry—the Blue Platoon.

Blue Lift—Helicopters assigned to carry the Blues.

Blue Max—The call sign for the Aerial Field Artillery (AFA), also called the Aerial Rocket Artillery (ARA).

BRAVO—The letter B in the Army phonetic alphabet, as in Bravo Troop.

C-130—Air Force Hercules transport aircraft.

Caribou—Army twin-engine transport aircraft.

Cav Hat—The black, wide-brimmed Stetson hat with crossed sabers device, reminiscent of the old horse cavalry hat, originally worn by members of the 1st Squadron, 9th (Air) Cavalry. Reintroduced by LTC John B. Stockton, the hat was non-regulation headgear, highly resented and disapproved of by many and considered sacred by the troopers who wore it.

C and C—Aircraft in which a troop or unit commander circles a battle area to direct the conduct of the fight. The letters mean command and control.

CG—Commanding General

Charlie—The letter C in the Army phonetic alphabet. Charlie was also slang for the Vietcong.

Chicken Plate—Ballistic armor chest plate worn by aerial crew members.

CHICOM—Chinese Communist.

Chopper—Slang for helicopter.

Chinook—Name of the CH-47 tandem rotor helicopter, often called a "Hook" by soldiers.

Claymore—Antipersonnel mine that spews out 700 steel balls in a 60-degree arc, lethal up to 50 meters.

Company—The smallest unit in which the commissioned leader is a commander; it is the basic building block unit for all non-artillery and non-cavalry units in the Army.

CP—Command Post.

CS Grenade—Tear gas grenade.

Delta—The letter D in the Army phonetic alphabet; also Delta Troop, the ground cavalry troop in the Air Cavalry Squadron.

Divarty—Division Artillery; the term usually means the headquarters but could also refer to all the artillery in the division.

Division—The Army's major maneuver element; ranging in strength from 18,000 to 24,000 men, depending on the type; usually commanded by a two-star general.

DMZ—Demilitarized Zone, created by Geneva Convention along the 17th parallel.

DOD—Department of Defense

Dustoff—Medical evacuation helicopter; a term used in non-1st Cavalry units.

DZ—Drop Zone

Eagle Flight—A reaction force circling in aircraft while awaiting a target.

Echo—The letter E in the Army phonetic alphabet.

EM—Enlisted man (men).

F-4C—Air Force fighter-bomber; also known as a Phantom.

F-105—Air Force fighter-bomber.

FAC—Forward Air Controller; an officer of the air control team, directing air strikes from either the ground or the air.

FDC—Fire Direction center; at battery level in the artillery; mortar platoon level in the infantry.

Flare—It is an illumination device (noun). It is also the landing attitude of an aircraft (verb).

FLIR—Forward Looking Infrared.

FM—Frequency modulation, also known as Fox Mike; used in most ground tactical radios.

FO—Forward Observer, usually provided by the supporting artillery batteries or mortar platoons to the rifle companies to adjust indirect fire.

FOB—Forward Operating Base.

Frag.—Fragmentation grenade; also used to denote a fragmentary order for a unit action or movement.

Free fire zone—A geographic area that has had the civilian population removed; any personnel moving in such an area are considered enemy combatants and may be preemptively engaged and killed or captured.

G-1—Personnel officer at division level or higher.

G-2—Intelligence officer at division level.

G-3—Operations and training officer at division level.

G-4—Logistics officer at division level.

GI—Term for American soldier, carried over from World War II.

Green Berets—The popular name for the Special Forces, taken from the color of their distinctive headgear.

Guard—Emergency radio frequency, 243.0 UHF and 121.5 VHF.

H-13—The Army's light observation helicopter, notorious for being underpowered.

HE—High explosive ammunition.

H & I—Harassing and Interdiction fires.

Hog—The armed Huey B/C-model helicopter with a square rocket container on either side that carried 48 rockets.

Hot LZ—A landing zone under fire from the enemy.

HQ—Headquarters.

Huey—UH-1, the utility helicopter that was the workhorse of Vietnam. The name arose from the original designation of the aircraft—UH-1 (Utility Helicopter). The Army's official name, Iroquois, never caught on. The distinctive, Whop, Whop, Whop, sound of the Huey's rotor blades is the sound most associated with the Vietnam War by almost all veterans.

KIA—Killed in action.

Kit Carson Scout—Former VC or NVA who has defected to the ARVN and scouted for U.S. troops.

Klick—Slang for kilometer.

Line One—Code for Killed In Action.

LNO—Liaison Officer.

Loach—Hughes OH-6A light observation helicopter (LOH) with one pilot and one or two gunner-observers.

LP—Listening post.

LRRP—Long range reconnaissance patrol unit (pronounced Lurp).

LZ—Landing zone.

M-16—U.S. caliber 5.56mm, the basic rifle of the infantryman.

M-60—U.S. caliber 7.62mm platoon and company machine gun.

M-72—Light anti-tank weapon, called a LAW. Fired a 66mm projectile from a disposable launcher. Sometimes used as a bunker buster in Vietnam.

M-79—The 40mm grenade launcher that looked like a stubby, sawed-off shotgun.

MACV—Military Assistance Command Vietnam, the highest U.S. command authority in the Republic of Vietnam.

Medevac—Term used in the 1ˢᵗ Cavalry for aerial medical evacuation. *See also* Dustoff.

Medic—Medical aid man.

Minigun—A Gatling gun with 9 barrels that rotate when fired, mounted on a helicopter.

MOH—Medal of Honor, the highest award for valor in the U.S.

MR—Military Region.

M-102—The 105mm howitzer used by 1st Cavalry artillery units.

MTI—Moving Target Indicator.

Napalm—Jellied gasoline used in air strikes.

NCO—Noncommissioned officer, a sergeant, sometimes referred to as noncoms.

Net—Short for radio network, all tactical radios operated within a defined network on a designated frequency.

NVA—North Vietnamese Army, this was the term for any soldier or group of soldiers from the North.

OCS—Officer Candidate School.

Old Man—Military slang for commander.

Order of Battle—A listing of units committed to a theater of operations. Obtaining a correct OB on the enemy was a major intelligence effort to collect.

OP—Observation post.

OPCON—Operational Control.

Organic—Military term for hardware items—vehicles, aircraft, weapons—that belong to a specific unit. All other materiel comes to units on a mission basis and the commander sometimes has limitations in its employment.

Phantom—F-4 fighter plane.

Pink Team—A White bird (scout helicopter) and a Red bird (weapons helicopter) flying together as a team.

PIO—Public Information Officer.

PF—Popular Forces, native military forces locally recruited and employed within their home districts by district chiefs.

POL—Petroleum, Oil and Lubricants.

Police—Military term for the clean up of an area. Implies a clean thorough search of the battlefield.

POW—Prisoner of war.

Prep—Short term for preparatory fires on a landing zone.

PZ—Pick-up zone.

QRF—Quick Reaction Force.

Recon—Reconnaissance.

Red Platoon—The weapons platoon of an Air Cavalry Troop.

RRF—Ready Reaction Force.

RF—Regional Forces. Native military forces recruited and employed by provincial chief within a province.

RPG—Soviet rocket-propelled grenade that fired a 82mm warhead, basically an antitank weapon, the NVA also used it as an antipersonnel weapon.

RTO—Radio Telephone Operator.

RVN—Republic of Vietnam.

S-1—Personnel officer at brigade or battalion.

S-2—Intelligence officer at brigade or battalion.

S-3—Operations and training officer at brigade or battalion.

S-4—Supply officer at brigade or battalion.

Satchel Charge—Explosive package fitted with a handle for ease of handling or throwing.

Short-timer—Not much time left on a tour of duty—also referred to as "Getting Short"

Sitrep—Situation report.

SKS—Soviet carbine.

Slick—Term for the Huey troop transport helicopter, so named because it lacked the outboard weapons mounts that the gunships had.

SOP—Standard Operating Procedures.

Squadron—Calvary unit containing four Troops.

Strip Alert—State of readiness for a reaction force that generally meant they were either next to the aircraft or actually sitting in the aircraft that parked along an airstrip.

TACAIR—Tactical Air.

TAOR—Tactical Area of Operational Responsibility.

TOC—Tactical Operations Center.

TROOP—Basic component of a Cavalry Squadron. A Squadron consisted of 3 Air Cavalry Troops and 1 Ground Cavalry Troop (with Jeeps). Each Air Cav Troop consisted of 27-29 helicopters and 130-150 men.

20 Mike-Mike—The 20mm Gatling gun carried in fighter aircraft that fired up to 4,000 rounds per minute.

Tube artillery—Artillery that fires projectiles from a gun barrel or tube, as opposed to rocket artillery.

USAF—United States Air Force.

USARV—U. S. Army Vietnam; the Army component headquarters that controlled logistics.

VC—Vietcong, also known as Victor Charlie.

White Platoon—The scout platoon of a Troop.

WIA—Wounded In Action.

WOC—Warrant Officer Candidate.

WP—White phosphorus; also known as Willie Pete, a hold over term from WWII and Korea.

XO—Executive officer—the assistant to the commander of units below division level.

CPSIA information can be obtained
at www.ICGtesting.com
Printed in the USA
BVHW071202101019
560718BV00002B/4/P